TODAY IN THE PAST

OCTOBER 21
2008, NEW YORK CITY: This book is officially published.

"MORE"

COMPANION TITLES

ALSO IN THIS SAME SERIES:
THE AREAS OF MY EXPERTISE

THE BOOK YOU ARE READING NOW:
MORE INFORMATION THAN YOU REQUIRE

FORTHCOMING, IMMINENTLY:
THAT IS ALL

FORTHCOMING, POSSIBLY:
HODGMINA: AMERICAN BABY, AMERICAN LIFE

HODGMANILLO, THE FORGOTTEN YOUNGER CHILD:
A LIFE IN THE SHADOWS

HODGMAN'S GUIDE TO BOARDING SCHOOLS FOR INFANTS

LE PÉTOMAINE: MYTH? OR ACTUAL FARTING,
FRENCH MONSTER?

CHICKEN NUGGET!: A CULTURAL HISTORY OF THE FOOD
THAT CHANGED EVERTYHING IN THE WORLD,
INCLUDING POETRY. YES, POETRY!

MY STUNT MEMOIR YEAR: THE TRUE STORY OF A MAN
WHO SPENT 365 DAYS WRITING A MEMOIR TO SEE
WHAT WOULD HAPPEN (IT MADE HIM FAT AND RICH!)

A DISCLAIMER

As I learned since publishing my last book, many of my readers are under the age of thirty-seven. For this reason, I have made an effort to curtail references to sexual situations and masturbation unless they are absolutely necessary or sexy. And in all situations when I would normally use the word BULLSHIT, I have substituted instead the word BULLROAR. I am a father myself, after all.

FOR YOUR CONSIDERATION, THE FIRMS OF DUTTON & RIVERHEAD BOOKS OF NEW YORK CITY, PUBLISHERS OF KEN FOLLETT, DARIN STRAUSS, DAVID REES, AND THE RZA

PRESENT IN THE ENGLISH LANGUAGE:
A FURTHER COMPENDIUM OF COMPLETE WORLD KNOWLEDGE
IN "THE AREAS OF MY EXPERTISE."
ASSEMBLED AND ILLUMINED BY ME,

JOHN HODGMAN

A FAMOUS MINOR TELEVISION PERSONALITY*

* * * * * * * * * * OFFERING * * * * * * * * * *

MORE INFORMATION THAN YOU REQUIRE

ON SUBJECTS AS DIVERSE AS:

THE PAST (AS THERE IS ALWAYS MORE OF IT),
THE FUTURE (AS THERE IS STILL SOME LEFT),
ALL OF THE PRESIDENTS OF THE UNITED STATES,
THE SECRETS OF HOLLYWOOD,
GAMBLING, THE SPORT OF
THE ASTHMATIC MAN
(INCLUDING: HERMIT-CRAB RACING),
STRANGE ENCOUNTERS
WITH ALIENS,
HOW TO BUY A COMPUTER,
HOW TO COOK AN OWL,
AND MOST OTHER SUBJECTS
PLUS: ANSWERS TO YOUR QUESTIONS POSED VIA ELECTRONIC MAIL, AND: 700 MOLE-MAN NAMES, INCLUDING THEIR OCCUPATIONS

WRITTEN IN BROOKLYN, 2008

OCTOBER 23

1978, CBS: *2001: A Space Odyssey—A Television Program* premieres. One of several science fiction shows to be rushed into production following the success of *Star Wars,* including *Buck Rogers in the 25th Century, Battlestar Galactica* (a "reimagining" of the classic *Battlestar Galactica* radio program from the '20s), and *Taxi.* It was one of the most expensive television shows to produce, and it attracted enormous ratings at first. But the audience dropped off after a few episodes when it was revealed that the only cast members were apes and floating fetuses, and all of the dialogue was telepathic.

*Formerly a Former Professional Literary Agent and Professional Writer, AKA "The Deranged Millionaire"

DUTTON

Published by Penguin Group (USA) Inc.
375 Hudson Street
New York, New York 10014
U.S.A.

Penguin Group (Canada),
90 EGLINTON AVENUE EAST, SUITE 700,
TORONTO, ONTARIO M4P 2Y3, CANADA
(A DIVISION OF PEARSON PENGUIN CANADA INC.);

Penguin Books Ltd,
80 STRAND, LONDON WC2R 0RL, ENGLAND;

Penguin Ireland,
25 ST STEPHEN'S GREEN, DUBLIN 2, IRELAND
(A DIVISION OF PENGUIN BOOKS LTD);

Penguin Group (Australia),
250 CAMBERWELL ROAD,
CAMBERWELL, VICTORIA 3124, AUSTRALIA
(A DIVISION OF PEARSON AUSTRALIA GROUP
PTY LTD);

Penguin Books India Pvt Ltd,
11 COMMUNITY CENTRE, PANCHSHEEL PARK,
NEW DELHI-110 017, INDIA;

Penguin Group (NZ),
67 APOLLO DRIVE, ROSEDALE,
NORTH SHORE 0632, NEW ZEALAND
(A DIVISION OF PEARSON NEW ZEALAND LTD);

Penguin Books (South Africa) (Pty) Ltd,
24 STURDEE AVENUE, ROSEBANK,
JOHANNESBURG 2196, SOUTH AFRICA;

Great Auk Ltd, a division of
Penguin Group (USA),
22 WEEPING CAVES,
MOLEMANSYLVANIA, THE LANDS BELOW.

Penguin Books Ltd, Registered Offices:
80 STRAND, LONDON WC2R 0RL, ENGLAND

**PUBLISHED BY DUTTON, A MEMBER OF
PENGUIN GROUP (USA) INC.**

OCTOBER 24
1976, BERMUDA: The Bermuda Triangle is finally captured.

FIRST PRINTING, OCTOBER 2008

1 3 5 7 9 10 8 6 4 2

COPYRIGHT © 2008 BY
JOHN HODGMAN
ALL RIGHTS RESERVED

— REGISTERED TRADEMARK —
MARCA REGISTRADA

LIBRARY OF CONGRESS
CATALOGING-IN-PUBLICATION DATA
HAS BEEN APPLIED FOR.

ISBN 978-0-525-95034-9

PRINTED IN THE UNITED STATES
OF AMERICA

DESIGNED BY SAM POTTS
SET IN THE USUAL MANNER
WITH HOPE > 10%

CONTINUED ON PAGE 234

OCTOBER 25

1986, BOSTON: The final, unpublished prophecy of Sarah Woodhope comes true.[a]

a. Please see page 96 of *The Areas of My Expertise* (HC) under the heading "Some Prophets Who Were Not Actuaries."

AS PROMISED,

THIS BOOK

IS FOR

LEH

Portions of this work previously appeared in a somewhat different, often substantially shorter and less indulgent form, in the following publications, radio programs, and daily shows:

THE SELECTION ENTITLED ...
"How to Be a Famous Minor Television Personality"
PREVIOUSLY APPEARED IN A SOMEWHAT DIFFERENT FORM ...
On the radio program *This American Life*
UNDER THE TITLE ...
"I'm Not a TV Star, But I Play One on TV"

THE SELECTION ENTITLED ...
"The Best Mas Ever"
PREVIOUSLY APPEARED IN A SOMEWHAT DIFFERENT FORM ...
On the radio program *This American Life*
UNDER THE TITLE ...
"No Tenenbaum, No Tenenbaum"

THE SELECTION ENTITLED ...
"Some Questions That Were Actually Asked on the Internet, If Not Exactly 'Frequently,' Then at Least Once"
PREVIOUSLY APPEARED IN A SOMEWHAT DIFFERENT FORM ...
In *The Believer* (formerly *The Journal of American Credulity*)
UNDER THE TITLE ...
"Ask a Former Former Professional Literary Agent"

OCTOBER 26
1958, NEW YORK: Pan Am's *Clipper America* inaugurates transatlantic jet service from New York to Paris. Early commercial air travel was luxurious and comparatively formal compared to today's. Women often wore their finest jewelry, relaxed in full-sized powder rooms, and enjoyed France's finest Valiums, while men were required to wear jackets and ties and to have sex with stewardesses. BUT COMPARED TO TODAY'S FIRST CLASS, IT IS NOTHING. Take it from me: A FIRST-CLASS PERSON.[a]

Figure 30: Women on Pan Am's *Clipper America* Enjoying Their Valiums

a. Please see page 428 under the heading "The Perks of Fame."

THE SELECTION ENTITLED ...	PREVIOUSLY APPEARED IN A SOMEWHAT DIFFERENT FORM ...	UNDER THE TITLE ...
"Speaking of Parasites, How Do I Protect My Child From the Scourge of Head Lice?"	On *The Daily Show with Jon Stewart*	"Expert-Teaser"
"Possible Contacts with Alien Life"	In *Wired* magazine (which I believe is the trade journal of the National Steel Wire and Wire Products Association).	"What We Don't Know Yet"
"700 Mole-man Names"	In *THE AREAS OF MY EXPERTISE*	"700 Hobo Names"

ADDITIONALLY
Portions of this work were written at the Chateau Marmont writers' retreat, Room 33.

*If perchance thou shouldst come to know him, tell him from
me that I do not hold myself aggrieved; for I know well what
the temptations of the devil are, and that one of the greatest is
putting it into a man's head that he can write and print a
book by which he will get as much fame as money, and as
much money as fame; and to prove it I will beg of you, in your
own sprightly, pleasant way, to tell him this story.*
                    —*The Ingenious Gentleman Don Quixote of
                    La Mancha, Part II,* by Pierre Menard

*Every man should be capable of all ideas, and I believe that
in the future, he will be.*
                    —*The Argentine National Poultry
                    and Rabbit Inspector's Little Book
                    of Shitty Aphorisms*

OCTOBER 28

1947, NEW YORK: *You Bet Your Life,* starring Groucho Marx, debuts on radio. Though Groucho had never actually worn a mustache in real life (in the movies he used an extra eyebrow), he is forced to grow one when listeners complain that they "cannot hear the whiskers."

OCTOBER 29
1999: Blasting off in the "space shuttle"
Discovery, John Glenn becomes the oldest person to be hired by the government
to fake a space flight. "It was amazing,"
he was quoted as saying in *The Redacted*
(newsletter of the Secret World Government). "It was just like I remembered it
from my first fake space flight. I'm an old
man, but the scale and the majesty of the
phony pictures they put outside the space
shuttle window make you realize just how
young you actually are, in fake-space-
time."

TABLE OF CONTENTS

AN INTRODUCTION

THE PRESIDENTS OF THE UNITED STATES: ARE THEY THE NEW HOBOES?

CONTENTS CONTINUES

THE FUTURE AND OTHER SUPERSTITIONS

OCTOBER 30
1938, NEW YORK CITY: Orson Welles broadcasts *The War of the Worlds,* sending the nation into panic over a supposed alien invasion. Amazed by its success, Welles planned an ambitious follow-up: an innovative radio adaptation of Walt Whitman's *Leaves of Grass,* in which the famed poem is expressed in a series of fake news bulletins and incredible sound effects (the majestic "yawp" is accomplished using a glass bottle and a balloon). Listeners fall for it again: Across America, hysterical citizens run through the streets singing the body electric, and falling in love with teenage boys.

ADVICE, HOW-TO, AND MISCELLANEOUS

CONTENTS CONTINUES

GAMBLING: THE SPORT OF THE ASTHMATIC MAN

HOW TO BE FAMOUS

CONTENTS CONTINUES

NOVEMBER 1

1800, WASHINGTON, DC: John Adams moves into the recently completed "White House." At first he could not believe his good fortune, as he could never have afforded an executive mansion on his own poor salary. But only four months later, he fled the house in the dead of night, leaving all his possessions behind, vowing never to return. To this day, no one knows exactly what happened.

THE HIDDEN WORLD (NOT INCLUDING MOLE-MEN)

EVEN MORE MORE INFORMATION THAN YOU REQUIRE, WITH A SPECIAL EMPHASIS ON FOOD AND ANIMALS (A KIND OF FOOD)

CONTENTS CONTINUES

THE MOLE-MEN: ARE THEY THE NEW HOBOES?

SOME LISTS I CONFESS TO COMPILING

CONTENTS CONTINUES

NOVEMBER 3

1957, BAIKONUR COSMODROME, RUS-
SIA: The Soviet Union launches *Sputnik
II* into orbit, bearing a sole passenger: the
doomed space dog, Laika. Controversy
eventually arose over the decision to send
a stray puppy into a spacecraft that was
designed to never be retrieved. But what
may seem like cruelty overlooks the pure
scientific fact that Laika was a very, very
bad dog that deserved to die.

ALL OF YOUR QUESTIONS ANSWERED, OR AT LEAST FIVE MORE

AN OUTRODUCTION

TABLE OF TABLES

CONTENTS CONTINUES

NOVEMBER 4

2008: According to the annual telepathic decree from the Electoral College, NY, today shall be this year's ELECTION DAY.

TABLE OF FIGURES

CONTENTS CONTINUES

NOVEMBER 5

1605, LONDON: Guy Fawkes is captured in the catacombs beneath the House of Lords and accused of being a mole-manic spy. Though it is true he was wearing a suspicious mask, he was in fact merely a Catholic revolutionary hoping to blow up Parliament and assassinate the king. Nevertheless, the legend persists, and English children today still commemorate Guy Fawkes Day by burning a mole-man alive, if they can find one.

Figure 31: Fawkes's "Human" Mask

CONTENTS CONTINUES

CONTENTS CONTINUES

NOVEMBER 7

1917, ST. PETERSBURG: Revolutionary forces in Russia are victorious when the Bolsheviks use their secret, silent "Caterpillar Drive" to storm the Winter Palace.

1951, MANHATTAN: In his ongoing effort to make New York City more car-friendly, parks commissioner and highway czar Robert Moses drains the canal along Canal Street and fills all of the city subways with cement.

MORE
INFORMATION
THAN YOU
REQUIRE

NOVEMBER 9

1828: Noah Webster publishes his *American Dictionary of the English Language.* Born in West Hartford (previously spelled Weste Heartefourdeslkjhlfg), Connecticut (previously spelled Cocnnecticcuct), Webster desired to simplify English word spellings and codify a new American lexicon that was simple, direct, and included the word "skunk." Not surprisingly, if you look up "dictionary" in the dictionary, you will see Webster's picture there. He is portrayed looking up "dictionary" in the dictionary, and seeing his own picture there, looking up "dictionary" in the dictionary. If you look in that little dictionary, you will see Webster again, looking up "dictionary" in the dictionary, and so on. Yes, this may seem like fun, but when Webster himself did this, he disappeared in a cloud of oily smoke, so I don't advise it.

NOVEMBER 10
1969: *Sesame Street* debuts on PBS.
Viewers who grew up on the series may be
surprised to learn that in early episodes,
Oscar "the Grouch" was orange, Gordon
was played by nine different men, the body
of Mr. Hooper was not yet embalmed and
on display behind a glass panel outside his
store, and most of the story lines revolved
around the subject of when Elmo would
arrive and save them all.

AN INTRODUCTION

Good evening.

I trust we need no introduction, you and I.

If you are familiar with my previous book of COMPLETE
WORLD KNOWLEDGE, and if you also have successfully completed my popular seminar in EXPERT MEMORY TRAINING,[48]
then you likely recall this simple fact:

My name is John Hodgman.

But I do not wish to be presumptuous. Perhaps you do not know
who I am. Perhaps you were dealt some terrible blow to the head
and are now suffering amnesia, and so do not recall my previous
bestselling work, *THE AREAS OF MY EXPERTISE.*

If that is the case, allow me to explain. My name is John Hodgman; you live on the planet Earth; and everything is going to be
fine.

Why? Because the item you are holding in your hand is called a
"BOOK." Specifically, it is called *MORE INFORMATION THAN*

---

48. If no, please see "How to Remember Any Name, Especially the Name 'John Hodgman,'
page 349.

YOU REQUIRE, and, like its predecessor, it contains within it all sorts of useful information on ridding your house of annoying pests, hints for winning at the gambling table, famous animal acts, useful recipes, the molemen and their hideous steeds, the U.S. presidents and *their* hideous steeds, everything that happened before today, and SUNDRY MORE FACTS OF SCIENTIFIC, SOCIAL, AND HISTORICAL MERIT, ALL OF WHICH ARE MADE UP BY ME.

(For, also like its predecessor, this book is unique in the desk reference game insofar as the amazing true facts within it are almost entirely false. The precise reason for this is well established in my earlier writings. Suffice it to paraphrase the great detective and repeat that REALITY, while generally PROBABLE, is not always INTERESTING.)

In short, here is a volume that contains all that you wish to know—truly MORE INFORMATION THAN YOU REQUIRE— as you seek to recover from your amnesia, learn the secret of your forgotten identity, and find out how you got that terrible scar.[49]

Good luck, my amnesiac friend.

But now, I wish to return my attention to those readers who have not lost their memories and who are scarred only on the inside. That is to say: those who have read *THE AREAS OF MY EXPERTISE.*

First of all, let me say that I am glad we got rid of the amnesiacs.

NOVEMBER 11

1922, THE UPPER WEST SIDE OF MANHATTAN: Grant's tomb is discovered in Morningside Heights, New York. The first four humans to enter the tomb (Lord Carnarvon, Professor Firecracker, Dick Smotheringwell, and little Cheepy, the Exotic Child of the East) were initially treated as celebrities, touring the country with the amazing relics they found there (cigars, old sabers, 1,000 mummified cats). But then, mysteriously, they all contracted strange ailments: cottonmouth, headaches, and severe dehydration. Doctors, eager to dismiss rumors of "Grant's Curse," claimed that they were only suffering common hangovers; but only the child, Cheepy, was known to take a drink. And curiously, he was the only one to survive. After three days of torment, the rest of the adventurers died in their sleep on the same stormy night. Some blamed Cheepy, who later would climb to the top of a rope and disappear. Others blame the vengeful ghost of U. S. Grant, noting that each of the corpses was discovered with remnants of cigar ash on its nightshirt. Either way, the secret of *who* is actually buried in the tomb died with them.

---

49. Please see "The Secret of Your Identity and How You Got That Terrible Scar," page 587.

NOVEMBER 12
1943: HAPPY BIRTHDAY, WALLACE SHAWN! Insofar as he pioneered the role of the highly educated-writer-turned-nebbishy-character-actor, one could argue that I would have no career were it not for Wallace Shawn. It's also true that he would have been cast as the PC had I not poisoned him with iocane powder.

What a tiresome bunch of whiners.

Now I expect you are wondering . . .

"If your last book contained COMPLETE WORLD KNOWLEDGE, why, then, the need for this second volume?"

Don't ask me how I know you are wondering this.[50] I JUST KNOW.

But though I appreciate your skepticism, if you just read on, I think you will see that the need is pressing, not just for ONE further volume, but indeed FOR TWO.

But I get ahead of myself.

As you may know, since our most recent communication,[51] several THINGS HAVE OCCURRED.

1. Like all humans, I have aged, and grown wiser and more mature. I have, if you can believe it, *learned more than I knew before.* ESPECIALLY ABOUT THE OKAPI.

2. Perhaps more notably, I have added to my list of bona fides and duties the title of "FAMOUS MINOR TELEVISION PERSONALITY."[52]

3. Largely because of the responsibilities associated with this new title (being photographed wearing tuxedoes, riding in jets with heiresses, meeting Emo Philips IN

---

50. (Hint: I am inside your house.)

51. Please see my introduction to the paperback edition of *The Areas of My Expertise.*

52. Please see "Where You May Have Seen Me on Television," page 401.

PERSON, etc.), I accidentally forgot to write the book I promised you on the subject of my daughter, whom, for reasons of privacy, I refer to solely as HODGMINA.

NOVEMBER 13
1789: Benjamin Franklin coins the famous phrase "In this world nothing can be said to be certain, except death, taxes, and the enduring popularity of the glass harmonica, the musical instrument I invented. Mark my words: They will be playing our national anthem on it for years to come! (PS: our national anthem, which I wrote, is called 'Turkey in the Straw')."

4. Indeed, while I find all references to my personal life loathsome (except for the part above about meeting Emo Philips, which you can appreciate is a fabulous fantasy come true), you might have nonetheless heard that there is an addition to my family. He is a human male who is roughly three years of age, based on a standard counting of his bodily growth rings. For easy reference I shall refer to him solely as HODGMANILLO. While he is as yet too young to handle a pen or plume, I hope that, in the future, he will take after his father and become a PRO-FESSIONAL WRITER and, ideally, write that book about HODGMINA I promised. My hope is that he will get started as soon as this Christmas, when we send him to boarding school, where he should not have any distractions.[53]

5. And yet, in the midst of all of this dizzying and bizarre good fortune, I began to feel an extraordinary measure of melancholy.

6. Also, as has been reported: one of my cats died, proba-

---

53. Except for the calisthenics!

NOVEMBER 14

1765: HAPPY BIRTHDAY, ROBERT FULTON! Fulton would gain fame and fortune designing the first commercially viable steamships, and later, he would be commissioned by Napoléon to build the first practical spacecraft, the *Nautilus*. But he would meet a gruesome end in 1815. Only fifty and still at the peak of his powers, Fulton was demonstrating his new steam-powered military exoskeleton at the Storm King Exoskeleton Proving Grounds in Cold Spring, New York. While the flying and man-crushing demonstrations had gone smoothly, the amphibious-mode demonstration ended tragically when Fulton, piloting his own creation, realized too late that metal is heavier than water.

bly due to neglect by Jonathan Coulton,[54] who cannot prove otherwise.

But let us leave that matter for the moment and turn back to the subject of melancholy.

As a FORMER PROFESSIONAL LITERARY AGENT, I had often observed the sadness that sometimes grips an author after he has published his first book. Writing a book is a long, intimate affair. Many feel that seeing their first book published is like giving birth to a child.

Or, more accurately, it is like giving birth to a child and then sending that child to be raised in a chain bookstore, far away. Maybe even in Michigan. And there, that child would have to fend for himself, feeding at night on stale muffins from the coffee bar and hiding by day in the humor section, secure in the knowledge that he will never, ever be found there. NOT IN ONE MILLION YEARS.

For many authors, this is depressing to consider.

BUT NOT ME. Once my book was done, I felt TERRIFIC.

I felt a profound sense of wholeness and relief. I had caught within the pages of a single book COMPLETE WORLD KNOWLEDGE . . . a book that now has traveled the world[55] and been welcomed in every home. It has become, I venture to say: THE ABSOLUTE STANDARD IN ALMANACS OF ASSORTED FAKE FACTS in the United States, and I was proud of that, and ready to direct my

---

54. Please see page 443 for further details pertaining to COULTON.

55. Well, not the *whole* world. But a bona-fide offer was made to publish the book in the Portuguese language for the Portuguese (no mention of the Brazilians), and I am proud to report that that offer is PENDING.

attention to my compelling new
hobby: ASTONISHING WEALTH.

NOVEMBER 15
1979, WASHINGTON, DC: Congress is
accidentally photographed wearing their
blood-red robes of state. All negatives are
destroyed.

Yes, it is true: When last we
spoke, I was but a poor, loathsome
writer who, like many, was forced to
live off credit cards and the pity lunches of his editors and agents,
and to rent his own pants.

But now, between my work for television, my lucrative publishing advances, and my side businesses in RING TONES and DECO-
RATIVE PLATES, I now am in a position to buy BEAUTIFUL
NEW PANTS every day, often made of whalebone and silver. And
quickly—so quickly—this fabulous lifestyle became as normal to me
as breathing underwater.[56]

Yes. I was perfectly satisfied with my life. I had a happy family,
and at least one cat that Jonathan Coulton had not yet killed. Not to
mention a beautiful, new nine-hundred-foot speed zeppelin that I
had bought from Emo Philips.

And so for a time I floated with great speed, high above the earth,
and rarely did I look down to see you, dear reader. And when I did,
you looked so small. You looked like ants to me, with your strangely
segmented bodies and horrid mandibles. I would see you and think,
*Why don't those little people get their mandibles removed? Surely there is
surgery for that sort of thing by now.*[57]

But then I would turn back to the skies and forget about you once
more.

My speed zeppelin, as you probably know by now, was named
Hubris.

Why Emo Philips chose that name for the zeppelin is still a mystery to me. But it was apt, my friends. It was apt.

---

56. What? You have not received the gill operation yet? That is because YOU ARE POOR.

57. It turns out, there isn't.

NOVEMBER 16

1952. HAPPY BIRTHDAY, RANDY "MACHO MAN" SAVAGE! The famous wrestler, noted for his husky voice and trademark sunglasses, was a spokesperson for Slim Jim meat sticks. The rumor that they used his skin to make them is true.

Figure 32: The Good Ship *Hubris*
(Known in the Press as *Emo's Folly*)
Being Menaced by the Ant-Men

FOR IT WAS NOT LONG BEFORE MY BALLOON WAS LITERALLY[58] POPPED AND I WAS LITERALLY[59] BROUGHT BACK DOWN TO EARTH.

It began when I was asked to appear in a MAJOR MOTION PICTURE. Specifically, I appeared in the comedy *Baby Mama* as the "Tweedy Former Professional Literary Agent Turned Fertility Specialist": a small but pivotal role in which I hilariously explain to Tina Fey that she is barren and can never bear children. Now, this is a classic routine from old Vaudeville, but I like to think I brought my own unique take to it (a double spit-take, followed by wheezing laughter). Even so, it's hardly worth mentioning, except for this:

You may recall from my previous book a list of movies in which I had made cameo appearances, including *The Muppet Movie, Just*

58. Not literally. A zeppelin is not a balloon.

59. Literally, but only if you presume I am telling you the truth about the zeppelin.

Cause, and *Mimic.* But of course, I had never appeared in any of those movies. It was all lies. But now here I was, sitting in front of the lights and the cameras (I guess Tina Fey was there as well, but who can really know for sure, with all the special effects they use these days?), making an ACTUAL CAMEO APPEARANCE in an ACTUAL FILM.

NOVEMBER 17
1982, CBS: *Bring 'Em Back Alive* debuts. A rollicking adventure series set in the 1930s, "B'EBA" (as it's known to fans) was presumed by many critics as yet another attempt to cash in on the popularity of the film *Raiders of the Lost Ark.* But in fact, it was a long-planned spin-off featuring the telepathic ape named "Frank Buck"—the only character to have resonated with viewers from the quickly canceled *2001: A Space Odyssey—A Television Program.*

And that is when the melancholy set in. *THE AREAS OF MY EXPERTISE* was founded on a simple maxim: TRUTH MAY BE STRANGER THAN FICTION, but never as strange as lies.[60] But now truth seemed to be catching up. Now that my own reality was outpacing my ability to make jokes, what would be left for me to do? A low, existential dread infected me in that moment. (You can see it in frame 17,326.) And it took some time for me to shake it. Indeed, all the way until the end of the scene. Then I am glad to say that, after a long martini bath and money-counting session, I had forgotten all about it.

But then I had another startling revelation—one that could not be so easily washed off with vermouth. . . .

As you may recall, my previous book conveyed a certain amount of information on the history and habits of the wandering men of the '30s known as HOBOES.

This sparked a measure of HOBOMANIA among a certain segment of the reading population. I was grateful to receive factual information you had uncovered about HOBOES, and especially news of HOBO-THEMED PRODUCTS AND SERVICES that hoped to seduce customers with the timeless, romantic allure of being a drunk,

---

60. Or as true.

NOVEMBER 18

1928, CALIFORNIA: Disney releases one of the first sound cartoons, *Steamboat Willie*. It features Mickey Mouse, but in an earlier, darker incarnation of the character—a steamboat-driving, hard-drinking "Willie" with pitch-black eyes and a habit of torturing small animals and enslaving dogs. His maniacal laughter was provided by Walt Disney himself.

penniless vagrant during the Great Depression.

Examples included:

- "HOBO" BRAND HOBO SOUP
- THE HOBO DELI OF KINGS-TON, NY
- HOBO HALLOWEEN COS-TUMES FOR CHILDREN
- And CLIPS OF THE CANADIAN CHILDREN'S PROGRAM *THE LITTLEST HOBO*

Figure 33: "The Best Oiled Ham in Kingston"

(Which, it turns out, is not about a miniature, doll-sized hobo at all, but instead follows the adventures of an unemployed dog that hops trains, eats garbage, and drinks wood alcohol until it dies.)

But the fun stopped when news came to me via the Internet[61] re-

---

61. COURTESY: one HOBO-MAD individual who goes by the Internet handle "Adam Koford"

garding an actual product: DICK VAN PATTEN'S "HOBO CHILI" FOR DOGS.

At first blush, it all seemed perfectly innocent: a hobo-themed dog

NOVEMBER 19

1990: Pop duo Milli Vanilli are stripped of their Grammy when it is revealed that they had lip-synched all of their top pop-dance hits, and as well that all of their top pop-dance hits were actually "Edelweiss" as performed by Christopher Plummer.

Figure 34: Nourriture Pour Chiens Hoboes

food created and sold by the actor DICK VAN PATTEN (though he was now going by the sobriquet "CHEF WOOFGANG").

But upon further investigation, I learned that CHEF WOOFGANG was not only making hobo chili for dogs. He was also offering THREE OTHER ETHNIC-THEMED dog foods, including "IRISH STEW" for dogs and "CHINESE TAKE-OUT" for dogs,[62] each

---

62. As of this writing, Dick Van Patten's "Italian Spaghetti with Beef in Meat Sauce" is not yet available, though I look forward to its MEATY REDUNDANCY.

NOVEMBER 20

1975: George C. Scott turns down the role of Obi-Wan Kenobi when George Lucas refuses Scott's demand to perform the role in the nude.

featuring an illustration of Dick Van Patten in an ETHNICALLY APPROPRIATE COSTUME, accompanied by an ETHNICALLY APPROPRIATE DOG.

Figure 35: Astonishingly, NOT MADE UP

Now, normally I would cheer such a sublimely unlikely product. Except for the fact that it is FACT. Absolutely none of this was made up. And since you and I are friends, I trust you can appreciate how, for someone in my line of work, the HIDEOUS VERACITY AND NON-JOKENESS of this product would be distressing, to say the least.

You might even say that Dick Van Patten was literally[63] stealing

---

63. Not literally.

food from the mouths of my children
AND FEEDING IT TO ETHNIC
DOGS.

THAT, my nonamnesiac friends,
CANNOT STAND.

And so I realized the time had
come to bring *Hubris* to ground and
restock the pond of fact with fiction,
as it were, with MORE INFORMA-
TION THAN YOU REQUIRE.

You will see from the page num-
bering that this book is not a sequel, but a direct continuation of the
work that was begun in my last volume. And, further, I announce
here that this work will not be complete until the third and final
volume emerges, sometime IN THE FUTURE.

For if I have ever had a mission in this endeavor (beyond IN-
CREASING MY ALREADY ENORMOUS WEALTH), it would
be that the lies collected here remind us of the actual balm of the
uncanny: the odd coincidences, curious synchronicities, strange
truths, and stranger dog foods that make wretched reality FEEL
like fiction, and rescue our lives from grim, relentless plausibility.[64]

But as I learned that day on set with Tina Fey, if the uncanny is
to become commonplace, indeed, LITERALLY UNCANNED,[65] and
served up daily as just so much more Hobo Chili for Dogs, then we
might cease to notice it altogether. And *that* is why I return to you
now. That is why I must work triply hard to re-strange the world
with lies, lest we neglect, as I nearly did, to savor every beautiful,
Van-Patteny bite.

And when this project is finished, and all three volumes stand

---

NOVEMBER 21

1783, PARIS: The Montgolfier brothers succeed in sending the first human aloft in an untethered hot-air balloon. For the first time in human history, man had left the earth. Upon hearing the news some weeks later, Sgt. Ezra Lee, who had gone mad while manning the first U.S. submersible, the *Turtle*,[a] vowed death to all "cowards who would escape the sea by taking to the air," thus beginning one of the longest and most pointless feuds in American history: submariners vs. zeppeliners.

a. Please see page 146 of *The Areas of My Expertise.*

---

64. YOUR lives, at least. Tina Fey and I are safe, because we are MOVIE STARS.

65. Quasi-literally.

NOVEMBER 22

1963, DALLAS: Lee Harvey Oswald aims the rifle that kills President Kennedy, but he did not act alone. Historians now agree that there were at least four other men with Oswald in the Texas Book Depository: one to open the window, one to give Oswald a boost, one to fire a "distraction arrow," and one to pull the trigger.[a]

a. This, of course, does not include the many dozens of conspirators on the ground, in the air, and buried under various knolls and backup knolls.

together as one great, massive book of COMPLETE WORLD KNOWL-EDGE, finally complete, then it will be very handy indeed. You could use it to press down pâtés or keep children from blowing away, just to name two examples.

And then, and only then, will I write:

THAT IS ALL.

NOVEMBER 23
1865, AMSTERDAM: Gregor Mendel wins *High Times* magazine's inaugural Cannabis Cup.

ONE OF MY GREAT REGRETS

As you know, my last book, *THE AREAS OF MY EXPERTISE*, did not just appear in HARDCOVER, but also in several other editions, including:

A "SOFTCOVER" EDITION, for people who dislike things that are hard.

AN AUDIO RECORDING, for the illiterate or merely lazy.

A DIRECT COMPUTER DOWNLOAD EDITION, for computers to read.

A LIVE BOOK TOUR, for people who don't feel like buying things.

A PAPERBACK BOOK CLUB EDITION. Sorry: only for members of A SECRET CLUB.

A TELEPATHIC EDITION, for sensitives, telepaths, and other "step-ups."

A KLAXON EDITION, which sounded a Klaxon whenever it was opened. This prevented people from reading the book in their sleep.

And now, I have just been told, my publisher is offering a very special, rare "REMAINDERED" edition. Look for them in great big "point-of-purchase" piles near the front of the store: They cost only thirty cents, or you get one for free if you agree to buy an "ITTY BITTY BOOK INCINERATOR" as well.

This is naturally very gratifying, but as has been proven sadly true again and again, "riches do not cease our wanting," or as Shakespeare put it: WHY HAS MY PLAY *HAMLET* NOT BEEN RELEASED AS A PAGE-A-DAY CALENDAR?

The bard asks a fair question.

NOVEMBER 25

2008: HAPPY BIRTHDAY, JULIUS ROBERT VON MAYER! The German physicist turns 194 years old today. Famous for observing that "Energy can neither be created nor destroyed," he then went on to invent immortality. He would later live to regret it, and then unregret it, and then regret it again, and then reconsider his regret once again, and then really regret it, and then forget that it happened, and then remember. He currently lives in a hospital in his hometown of Heilbronn, where he keeps active by pushing pieces of crumpled-up pieces of paper around on a tray and thinking about his children, whom he has outlived, and his many failed suicide attempts.

For despite everything, I confess I always hoped that some enterprising page-a-day-smith would offer to purchase the calendar rights to my book. And yet, to date, THIS HAS NOT OCCURRED.

And so this time I am taking matters into my own hands and taking preemptive action. For as you may already have discovered, this volume serves not just as a book, but also something useful: a calendar.

Did you miss it? Look back to page 229 and you will see that, beginning with the publication date of this book, each page is marked with the successive date, accompanied by an interesting historical fact that did not occur on that date, because I made it up.

If you cannot look back to the beginning of this book, perhaps because you are the sort of person who reads books by tearing out the pages as you go, well then, friend, I APPLAUD YOU, for you ALREADY KNOW HOW TO READ A PAGE-A-DAY CALENDAR.

It brings me pleasure to offer you these enhanced reading features and little hidden bonuses in the margins, and my only wish is that they distract you from the lack of meaningful content on the pages they surround.

NOVEMBER 26

SOMETIMES THIS IS THANKSGIV-
ING. While this most "American" of
North American, non-Canadian national
holidays recalls the grateful feast of eels
and smallpox the Pilgrims shared with the
Wampanoags in 1621, it did not actually
become a national holiday until Abraham
Lincoln sought reconciliation with the eels
who had so long been demonized in American society.[a] To this end, he ceremonially
"pardoned" an eel named Darla in a Rose
Garden ceremony in 1863. Thereafter, we
ate turkey.

a. Please see page 203 of *The Areas of
My Expertise* under the heading "Colonial
Jobs Involving Eels."

NOW: READ ON . . . FOR MORE INFORMATION THAN YOU REQUIRE.

NOVEMBER 27
1929, LONDON: Sir Alexander Fleming
first breeds contempt in a petri dish from
a culture of simple agar and purified fa-
miliarity.

1892, NEW HAVEN, CT: Walter Camp is ordered by the Secret World Government at Yale University to come up with "some kind of sporting diversion that will distract the public mind from our almost total influence over all world affairs and especially our role in the planned World Wars 1, 2, 3, and 3.5, aka `The Battle Beyond the Stars.'" Accordingly, Camp designed a new sport called American football, in which he modified traditional British rugby by adding a scrimmage, a safety, and machetes (later replaced with thin leather helmets).

THE PRESIDENTS OF THE UNITED STATES: ARE THEY THE NEW HOBOES?

NOVEMBER 29

1877, NEW JERSEY: Thomas Edison demonstrates the first phonograph, earning him the title "The Wizard of Menlo Park." The previous Wizard of Menlo Park was then forced to leave town in shame, dying many years later in Cherry Hill. History neither recalls his name nor the purpose of the invention that had initially earned him the title: a mysterious substance called CHEESEQUAKE.

NOVEMBER 30

1993, HOLLYWOOD: David Hyde Pierce undergoes secret plastic surgery to make himself resemble Kelsey Grammer in order to better play the role of Grammer's brother on the TV show *Frasier*. The patented process, called "Grammerizing," becomes a brief fad in the Philippines.

SOME NOTES ON THE UPCOMING PRESIDENTIAL ELECTION

Last May, I was enjoying a plate of oysters with my Publisher at a fancy restaurant in Manhattan. (I think my Publisher was eating some sort of salad, but who cares?)

Now, I know what you are thinking. I know you are not supposed to eat oysters in May, or any month that does not contain the letter "R," because oysters spawn during these months, and thus tend to beg for their lives when you eat them.[66] Some people find this unpleasant (not to mention embarrassing to the oyster), but I don't subscribe to such hypocrisies. When you are eating a creature alive, you ought to expect some screaming. Such is the carnivore's burden.

I was explaining all this to my Publisher when suddenly, for some reason, he decided to say something.

"Did you know," he asked, "that when we publish your next book, it will be a presidential election year?"

Needless to say, I jumped from the table, overturning it as I did so, and ran out of the restaurant at top speed.[67]

Once home, I consulted my globe and discovered that my Publisher was correct. This is indeed one of those years in which we engage in one of the great privileges of citizenship: pretending to vote for president.[68]

---

66. Please see page 485 on the subject of when to eat oysters.

67. I did not do this because I was startled. This is how I conclude every lunch with my Publisher, and when you become a published author, I advise you to do the same. After all, the Publisher is picking up the check. You may as well give him or her some entertainment.

68. I am referring to the year 2008. If you are reading this book in a different year, please use a time machine and get with the damn program.

But wait, you say. Why do you say "pretend"? Do we not vote for our president? Is this not a democracy?

Well, that is a very confusing way to ask those questions, but the answers, respectively, are I WILL EXPLAIN, OF COURSE NOT, and YES: this is not a democracy.

A DEMOCRACY is a form of government first developed by the ancient Athenians. Meaning alternately "rule by the governed" or "rule by demons," Athenian democracy was perhaps the purest form of participatory government: Each and every Athenian cast a vote on each and every matter facing his society. (Minus slaves, of course, and women. But curiously, white marble sta-

DECEMBER 1

1903: Edwin Porter's *The Great Train Robbery* debuts. The plot: a wisecracking former cop fights train-jackers at 15 mph. Thrilling audiences with its pioneering realism and papier-mâché trains, the final scene—in which the villain turns and fires his gun directly at the camera—was said to have so terrified audiences that they would often shriek in terror, screaming out, "YIPPIE KY YAY, MOTHERFUCKER!" as one.

Figure 36: A Sad Woman Brings Her Water Pitcher So That It May Vote in an Athenian Election. Note the Statues, Taunting Her.

DECEMBER 2

1942, "CHICAGO": In undisclosed location, code-named "Chicago," Enrico Fermi produces the first self-sustaining artificial nuclear chain reaction. It is the dawn of the atomic age, and many of Fermi's colleagues would later report that it would not have happened had Fermi not first touched the atomic pile with a strange, glowing crystal of unknown origin that he always carried around his neck.[a]

a. Please see page 461 under the heading "Possible Contacts with Alien Life."

tues *were* given the vote, even if they were statues of women. Also: urns.)

This is a noble idea, but you can imagine how, when EVERYONE had a say, even the most simple matters of everyday governance became endlessly complicated. Why, to this day, the Greeks cannot agree on how to pronounce "GYRO!"[69]

For this reason, our government is not, in fact, a PURE DEMOCRACY, but a REPUBLIC. In this system, borrowed from ancient Rome, the day-to-day tasks of statecraft are delegated to a SENATE . . . that is, until such time as an all-powerful EMPEROR arises, forces the SENATE to heap upon him endless honors and untold powers, and finally returns the Republic to decadent, unchecked monarchy.

That is where our president comes in, and our strange way of electing him.

A CURIOUS INSTITUTION

When Jefferson and Hissfurther drafted the Declaration of Independence,[70] their mission was merely to reject the British king and, if possible, put a deadly curse on him.[71] It was hardly clear at the time what form of government the new nation would adopt, or who would lead it.

---

69. The correct pronunciation is "JY-roh."

70. Please see page 505 under the heading "The Seven Portals to the Hollow Earth."

71. Please see page 558 under the heading "An Urban Legend Regarding the Declaration of Independence."

Would there be a single president or, as some suggested, a committee of three executives, representing the southern, northern, and middle

DECEMBER 3
1978, WISCONSIN: The *Milwaukee Sentinel* reports a brisk rain of human teeth.

states respectively—your classic presidential three-way?[72] What sort of powers would the president have? Could he turn things invisible? These were the questions that were hotly debated at the Constitutional Convention of 1787.

Advocates of strong central government, such as Alexander Hamilton, believed the president should serve for life and wear golden robes and live in a bank.[73] Others, such as Edmund Randolph, considered the very idea of the president to be "the fetus of monarchy," which is disgusting. Plus, you would agree, a fetus would not be very effective at leading a very young nation.

I have always said: BABIES SHOULDN'T BE HAVING BABIES.

Still, Randolph and his ilk had a reasonable point. They feared that a single head of state was too similar to the royalty they had worked so hard to overthrow. And they worried that a strong personality might quickly overshadow Congress and replace it with tyranny.

But the Hamiltonians made a powerful counterargument, which was: THAT WOULD NEVER, EVER HAPPEN, BECAUSE THE SUPERPRESIDENT WOULD BE TOO BEAUTIFUL AND GOOD TO ALLOW IT. And so the Convention turned around and gave the presidency to George Washington, a man so revered and celebrated for his leadership in the war that one effort had already been mounted to crown him king of America.

But Washington would not be king. He was at once a Virginian

---

72. Only Benjamin Franklin suggested that the country should be ruled by lightning, but since he was the colonies' sole lightningmonger, he had something of a conflict of interest. He was always peddling his own inventions in this sort of unseemly way.

73. Please see page 277 under the heading "Our American Full-Sultan."

DECEMBER 4
1998, NEW YORK: I complete my controversial shot-by-shot remake of the film
Pierre Menard, Author of Don Quixote.

aristocrat and a toothless farmer, and so the nation would find in him the compromise they sought: a be-wigged half-sultan whose powers would be carefully checked and balanced by those of Congress and the Supreme Court, but who would all the same wear white pancake makeup and have hemophilia. The Fetus of Monarchy would be re-tained, but would serve instead as vice president,[74] where its duties were largely ceremonial. And everyone agreed: The president should be able to make things invisible.

THE ELECTORAL COLLEGE

The great Washington would serve us well as president, but one fear remained: WHAT IF HE WERE NOT IMMORTAL? Thus, it was ordered that a system be established by which a SECOND president would be chosen, should such a ridiculous need arise.

Though the framers of the Constitution had rejected monarchy, that did not mean that they liked actual *people*, or trusted them to choose their leaders. Indeed, the initial plan was for the president to be elected by the Senate, which in turn would be elected by the House of Representatives, which in turn was chosen by the Cottage of Proxies, which in turn was selected by the Chamber of Landown-ing Gentlemen and Their Beautiful Dogs. Ordinary citizens would have almost no sway over the choice of president at all, though they were welcome to write persuasive letters to the dogs.

But by the end of the Constitutional Convention, a simpler method of insulating the presidency from the people was suggested: THE ELECTORAL COLLEGE.

---

74. Please see page 314 under the heading "A Curiouser Institution."

You have probably heard of the Electoral College. Some of you may even have visited it. Located in Upstate New York, it has a truly beautiful campus. But let's face it: The town of Electoral is pretty much a shit-hole.

You might have reasoned that when you cast your vote in November of each "election" year, your little colored rock goes into a giant bucket

DECEMBER 5
1791, VIENNA: Italian-born composer Antonio Salieri finally succeeds in murdering his young rival Wolfgang Amadeus Mozart by stabbing him with a knife dipped in rheumatic fever. Most of Salieri's peers agreed it was a well-planned, respectably executed crime of envy. But honestly, it wasn't the best murder in the history of eighteenth-century composing. It certainly wasn't as good as the time Mozart himself killed a minor Austrian noble at a costume party with his famous high-pitched "sonic scream." Now *that* was a beautiful murder!

at the White House, where it is counted equally among every other citizen's little rock. NOT SO. Nor are votes then tallied up, as you may expect, by a man wearing purple robes and a bald-eagle mask. Nor is the candidate who has earned the greatest number of ballots necessarily awarded the burning crown of the presidency, and then

Figure 37: The Electoral College's Beautiful Sense-Dep Hall

DECEMBER 6
1801, VIRGINIA: While Thomas Jefferson
did not technically invent the "french fry,"
he did write down the first recipe for same
on this day in his journal, under the heading "pommes de terres, frites à la hommes-
môlemaniques."

required to kill a goat dressed as the Imp of Tyranny with nothing but his hands and his cornstalk scepter. You may think this is true, but you are wrong. First of all, we do not even use the rocks anymore. Now we use little wooden tiles, and after they are collected they are shipped to the Electoral College and put into a warehouse deep underground and never looked at again. Then it is time for the actual Presidential Electors to go to work.

Who are these Electors? No one really knows for sure. All we really know is that they are very special men and women chosen by their respective state legislatures because they know better than you. They are sent to the College every four years in proportion to the population of each state. Then they are shaved all over and put into a sensory deprivation tank full of a kind of nutrient slime— often orange flavored, sometimes banana. There, held in slimy darkness for weeks on end, they go into a kind of trance and predict who the next president will be. And here is the great genius of our American system: They are almost always correct.

To be fair, there are some people who think that this process is unfair and undemocratic. And indeed, there have been cases when the Electors have rejected the candidate who won the most votes and instead gave the presidency to Rutherford B. Hayes.[75] This has happened at least twice. For some reason they just have a thing for Hayes.

But others argue that this so-called Hayes Attraction does not mean we should abandon the Electoral College system. For one thing, the system ensures balance among the large and small states, ensuring that even meaningless states like Massachusetts and Upper and

---

75. In cases where Rutherford B. Hayes is dead, the Constitution stipulates that the presidency should go to whichever candidate's father or grandfather was also a president. You have to admit, that's only fair.

Lower Dakota have some representation in the electoral process. Second, if we shut down the Electoral College, what would we do with the Electors? The last thing we need is a bunch of naked, shaved Electors wandering the countryside, nutrient slime[76] dripping off them, looking for handouts.

DECEMBER 7

2007, THE MEATPACKING DISTRICT: I honor the memory of the soldiers who died at Pearl Harbor by having my picture taken with Brooke Shields at the new Apple Store in Manhattan's Meatpacking District.

No. While the Electoral College may have its flaws, it is, at the very least, needlessly complex, and thus worth preserving.

ON THE MATTER OF NUTRIENT SLIME

While the exact composition of the "nutrient slime" the Presidential Electors eat and bathe in is a state secret, we may get some idea of what the basic components are by examining the recipe of a "MUCH IMPROVED LIFE-PASTE" offered by Hayes to the Electors, supposedly as a bribe to make him president.

Take a large portion of filtered water and mix within it . . .
— 35 POUNDS OF GROUND OATS
— 30 POUNDS OF COW HOOF JELLY
— 18 POUNDS OF LIQUEFIED CARROTS AND PEAS
— 18 POUNDS OF GROUND MARROW
— 9 POUNDS OF GIANT BLOODWORM CASTINGS[77]
— 1 POUND OF BEAR BILE
— 1,000 GRAHAM CRACKERS
— SALT

76. Please see the following section under the heading "On the Matter of Nutrient Slime."

77. Please see page 505 under the heading "Seven Portals to the Hollow Earth."

DECEMBER 8

2006, NEW YORK CITY: NBC's Matt Lauer asks legendary fitness pioneer Jack LaLanne, then ninety-two, if he ever slipped human growth hormone into his morning "power juice." Though Lauer later claimed he was just making a joke, LaLanne became immediately incensed, lifting Lauer out of his chair and throwing him through a plateglass window into Rockefeller Plaza. LaLanne then went on a rampage through New York City that lasted twenty-seven hours, only managing to calm himself down after swimming around the island of Manhattan nine times.

— MACERATED ORANGE (OR BANANA) FOR FLAVOR

— XANTHAN GUM AS A STABILIZER

— AN OUNCE OF GROUND UNICORN HORN

Agitate well until it is a slime, and serve by pouring into a tank.

Nutrifies one human in a tank for up to nine months.

Most scholars agree that Hayes's only innovation was the addition of the Graham crackers, which were considered to be a health food and cure-all at the time, though are now known to be as fictitious as xanthan gum.

WERE YOU AWARE OF IT?
"OUR AMERICAN FULL-SULTAN"

Were you aware that Hamilton actually went so far as to ask Prince Henry of Prussia to become our American monarch in 1786?

THIS IS ABSOLUTELY TRUE. Please. You must believe me.

In his secret letter to the Prussian prince, Hamilton wrote . . .

"I would wish that you consider my invitation to become our Ameri-Sultan seriously, but I must also be frank. Yours shall be a strange and new kind of monarchy. For you will be a king of the New World, and as such, your vestments shall not be of ermine but of American beaver, your scepter of corn, your crown of tomatoes. And, if Your Highness agrees, I would ask that he walk around with a wild

CONTINUED

turkey upon his shoulders, for they are wise and practical birds, and also I have lost a small bet with Franklin."

When Prince Henry proved unresponsive, Hamilton sent out a form letter to more than 100 minor royals, all across Europe, begging them to come rule the new nation and save it from the dirty farmers and illiterate toilers who populated the country and still do.

DECEMBER 9
1998: Ford unveils the Lincoln Navigator, a glossy, gigantic vehicle for wealthy people that represents a series of automotive firsts: the first "luxury" SUV; the first automobile to come with a dumbwaiter and secret "butler's compartment"; and the first automobile designed exclusively to drive on top of other cars.

This letter, widely considered history's first "SPAM," still circulates in a modified form today on the Internet. And while it had been widely discredited on Web sites such as SNOPES.com, it still entraps a few dozen minor nobles each year who, having wired considerable money to Hamilton's long-defunct First National Bank, show up in New York City penniless and confused, looking to collect their tomato crown.

NOT ONLY IS THIS TRUE, IT IS ALSO A GOOD IDEA FOR A COMEDY MOVIE! [78]

HOW TO VOTE

As the election approaches, you may be wondering, how do I vote?

First you must ask, are you even allowed to vote? It used to be

---

78. Those of you who recall page 46 of *The Areas of My Expertise* will recall my suggestion for a BLOCKBUSTER ACTION MOVIE in which all animals attack all humans. As you may know if you read *Variety,* another writer named Mike Sobel has recently sold a screenplay that explores a very similar premise, one in which all animals attack all humans. Some of you have presumed that I would be angry about this, but it is not so. Ideas are not property, they are infections. And anyone who reads everything will know that ideas have no allegiance to their host body: They pass from brain to brain untraceably, or simply break out spontaneously, separated by continents or even centuries, without explanation. Mike Sobel will not be the last to write about all animals attacking all humans any more than I am the first to write about the mole-men, and we are all entitled to our take on these classic story lines. All I ask is that I get a cameo in the movie as "The Man Who Gets Venomous-Foot-Spurred to Death by the Platypus." IT'S ONLY FAIR.

DECEMBER 10
1936, LONDON: King Edward VIII abdi-
cates the British throne in order to have
sex with an American woman. This is
where we get the crude term "abdication
fever."

that only those white male Free-
masons over the age of twenty who
owned property were eligible to vote.
Later, the vote would be extended to
women and blacks and other minori-
ties as long as they could answer a simple quiz on yachting terms and
the rules of polo, and/or they weren't black or female.

Nowadays, however, if you are eighteen years old, a citizen of the
United States, and the owner of a plantation or a mill, you are allowed to vote for president.

That's where those little wooden tiles come in (NOT ROCKS!). If
you are a registered voter, you probably got one in the mail several
months ago.[79] This is your BALLOT, and you must keep it secret,
for that is one of the cornerstones of our democracy. No one is allowed to see your wooden tile or even know that you have it. I'm not
suggesting you actually hurt anybody. But if a friend or family member sees your ballot, knock them unconscious with a club. Or use the
AMNESIA SPRAY I am developing.

Voting procedures differ from county to county.[80] You may ask
why we do not create one consistent way of voting for the entire
country. But this would be chaos, for if voting procedures were clear
and easily understandable, then probably *everyone* would want to
vote. This would create a glut of voters, and as we have seen when
there is large voter turnout, the system is simply not built to handle
it. It is better to leave the voting to the few specialists (some of them
paid) who have no other distractions or jobs to go to when voting
day actually arrives.

In some counties, the procedure is as simple as going into a little

---

79. If you are not yet a registered voter, it's too late. You don't count.

80. Quick quiz! What county are you in? Write it down here _____. Guess what! You
are wrong.

booth, carving the name of your chosen candidate into your tile, and then
dropping it into a box. Other counties
may require you burn your candidate's
initial into the tile with a small iron,
or whittle his likeness in bas-relief.

In Florida, they once used the controversial "Butterfly Ballots" that
caused so much trouble in the year
2000. If you see such a ballot, you
have to be very careful to mark the
wings properly, or else you may end
up voting for the wrong person. Don't

DECEMBER 11
1799, OXFORD: Zoologist George Shaw
synthesizes the first duck-billed platypus.
Initially horrified by his creation, he referred to it as a "horrid patchwork beaver" and angrily cast it out to fend for
itself. It befriended a blind priest, and for
a time was happy, until it accidentally poisoned him with its weird, venomous foot-
spur. Chased from the college town with
torches, it was eventually caught and sentenced to live out its strange, egg-laying-
yet-mammalian life in the penal colony
of Australia. (Some historians suspect
that the hope was it would foot-spur the
Australians to death as well.) But in fact,
it thrived, and does so to this day, though
it still feels most comfortable around the
blind.

worry: It is appropriate for the butterfly to die during this process.

Many of you, however, may discover that your county has
switched over to an ELECTRONIC VOTING SYSTEM. These are
machines that take your wooden tile and immediately destroy it. But
don't worry: What you have marked on the tile is carefully remembered by a computer.

It's true that these machines are controversial, and there is still a
lot of suspicion surrounding them. This is entirely natural. As we
have seen throughout history, it is entirely natural for people to be
frightened of new technology that is good for everyone and should
not be questioned. Some people are even afraid that "hackers" might
tamper with the computer and the results. But before you let your
imagination run away with you, think about it reasonably: Have
computer systems ever been hacked before? Maybe, but not more
frequently than old-fashioned elections *were rigged*. So what are you
complaining about?

That said, I am somewhat more sympathetic to those people who
are afraid the machines will give them an electric shock. That is going

DECEMBER 12

1970, NEW YORK CITY: Signet Books publishes *The Deconstructor #1*. Though credited to "Dixon Hand," the first twenty-five novels in this popular series were actually ghost-written by renowned avant-garde short-story writer Donald Barthelme. *The Deconstructor* novels all followed the exploits of Dick "The Deconstructor" McKitt, a retired Army sniper with one arm who is recruited by the Secret World Government to fight the Mafia using literary theory and a bazooka. The Dick McKitt books were similar to other men's adventure series of the time, in that they were violent, juvenile, and peppered with sexual innuendo (McKitt was described as being a "Level 9 Telepathic Lovemaker"); but they were distinct in that they were all exactly twelve sentences long.

to happen. It is simply a necessary precaution to prove to the computer that you are human and not a "robot voter" deployed to fix the election. But the simple fact that YOU are not trustworthy does not mean you should not trust the machines.

Think of the alternative: In past elections, it might take hours to tabulate the results of a single polling place. With the MACHINES, it will take mini-hours. Moreover, they are less confusing to the average voter. Indeed, they are as simple to use as

Figure 38: A Typical Voting Machine

an ATM or a Colecovision or a mechanical Turkish man playing chess.
(These are the three main kinds of
voting machines.)

And if you should have any problems at all, just follow this simple
troubleshooting guide.

DECEMBER 13
1833, OFF THE COAST OF ARGENTINA:
The British and the Argentines build the
Falkland Islands. In a dedication ceremony,
officials from both countries read a joint
declaration: "Let us thank the God we both
adore for the gift of these barren, pointless islands, and let them be a source of
arbitrary, violent conflict between our two
great nations for generations to come."

TABLE 20: A TROUBLESHOOTING GUIDE
TO THE NEW VOTING MACHINES

TROUBLE	SHOOT
The machine does not seem to be working.	Is it plugged in?
The machine is plugged in but does not seem to be working.	Is the touch screen smashed in?
No. The touch screen is not smashed in.	Then it really should be working. Is it turned on?
I see what happened now: The touch screen was smashed in. I am now ready to cast my vote, but I don't see my choice for president listed among the candidates.	Are you sure you've made the correct choice? The computer is designed to correct your errors as you make them. So check again, and try picking someone else.
I found a candidate I like, but when I touch the screen, nothing happens.	Is your finger very cold? Try warming it up by rubbing it on your jeans.
I have rubbed my finger on my jeans, but it still is not registering my vote.	Are you using your own finger? If you are using a mechanical pointer or a finger you found on the street, your vote cannot be counted.
	CONTINUED

DECEMBER 14

1978, ON THE AIR: *Masterpiece Theatre* begins broadcasting the BBC's ambitious twenty-part adaptation of *The Call of Cthulhu,* filmed entirely on video on a single small set. A little TV trivia for you: Cthulhu is actually played by future *Star Trek* star Patrick Stewart with a live octopus strapped to his head.

TABLE 20: *continued*	
TROUBLE	**SHOOT**
Why can't I use my mechanical pointer?	Because we need your fingerprints.
The mechanical chess player just stares at me and does not move the chess pieces. (Applicable to the mechanical-chess-player voting machine only)	Is there a little man inside the machine controlling the mechanical chess player? If the little man is taking a break, then the machine will not work.
I have used my own finger to cast my vote. How do I know for sure that the vote has been counted?	Your vote has been counted. YOU DO NOT NEED TO ASK ANY MORE QUESTIONS.

WHO IS GOING TO WIN THE PRESIDENTIAL ELECTION?

As of this writing (1809) there are now three major candidates running for the presidency. By the time this book has been published, that number will have most likely dwindled to two. This makes it very tempting to attempt to predict WHO is going to win the election, since it's essentially a fifty-fifty shot.

But even so, it would be foolish. In presidential politics, even a mere few weeks are an eternity. (Hours are roughly ninety-three minutes long.) And in politics, you never can tell what will happen next. Indeed, because of my Hollywood connections, I've actually had a chance to read the final few scripts of the campaign, and let me say that YOU ARE IN FOR SOME REAL SURPRISES. I don't want to be a spoiler, but just to give a hint of some of the plot twists to come . . .

DECEMBER 15

1963, NEW HAVEN: In a series of experiments, the controversial Yale Feline Studies Lab proves that a cat will willingly administer painful electric shocks to a second, unseen cat in another room in return for little pieces of lunch meat.

1. One of the candidates is going to become "unstuck in time."

2. At one of the upcoming debates, one of the candidates will reveal a hook for a hand—IN THE MOST DRA-MATIC WAY POSSIBLE.

3. Remember: YOU CAN NEVER COUNT A CLIN-TON OUT, not even if all electoral math, logic, and common sense demands it . . . and indeed, NOT EVEN IF THEY HAVE LOST THE ELECTION. Because it turns out they have some kind of magic amulet.

4. It will be revealed that the winner of the election is ac-tually a woman.

NOW, I DON'T WANT TO SPOIL IT FOR YOU BY TELL-ING YOU HER NAME. But if you look back at all the historical precedents, you'll see a number of clues and repeating patterns that might give you some idea of what we have to look forward to.

Please see Table 2: "The Precedents of the United States," on the following page.

TABLE 21: THE PRECEDENTS OF THE UNITED STATES

NAME OF PRESIDENT

Geo. WASHINGTON 1789–1797

"NICKNAME" OF PRESIDENT

"The Bewigged Half-Sultan of Democracy"

HUMANIZING DETAIL

Please see *The Areas of My Expertise*, page 202.

HOOK FOR A HAND?	WAS HE A WOMAN?	WAS HE BLACK?
No	No	No

DECEMBER 16

1936, PARIS: Walter Benjamin writes his seminal essay, "The Work of Art in the Age of Mechanical Reproduction," in which he argues that ancient works of art, such as sculpture and pottery, have an "aura" that cinema and books, which exist only as copies, do not. Benjamin went on to claim that only he could see this magical aura, and when the time was right, he would tap its energy to fuel the massive PSYCHIC RESONATOR he was developing to halt the rise of the Nazis. IT WOULD HAVE WORKED, TOO, had the Nazis not destroyed his enormous cache of urns.

NAME OF PRESIDENT

J'hn ADAMS 1797–1801

"NICKNAME" OF PRESIDENT

"OBNOXIO"

HUMANIZING DETAIL

Born in Braintree, Massachusetts, Adams was a lawyer and simple brain-tree farmer who was drawn to the cause of revolution by his high intellect and his bad temper. Even among his friends, he was known for being outspoken, cantankerous, and spitty. He intellect was matched—and his manners overshadowed—by his wife, the formidable Abigail Adams, who frequently counseled her husband to stop grabbing his political enemies by the neck and scrotum and who devised simple mouth exercises to cut down on the spit.

HOOK FOR A HAND?	WAS HE A WOMAN?	WAS HE BLACK?
No	No	No

CONTINUED

TABLE 21: *continued*	
NAME OF PRESIDENT Thos. JEFFERSON 1801–1809	**DECEMBER 17** 1977, THE NETHERLANDS: Wil Huygen and Rien Poortvliet publish the book *Gnomes*.
"NICKNAME" OF PRESIDENT "Long Tom," "Lazy Susan"	

HUMANIZING DETAIL		
Please see page 505, under the heading "The Seven Portals to the Hollow Earth."		
HOOK FOR A HAND?	**WAS HE A WOMAN?**	**WAS HE BLACK?**
Yes	No	No

NAME OF PRESIDENT		
Jas. MADISON 1809–1817		
"NICKNAME" OF PRESIDENT		
"Little Jemmy"		
HUMANIZING DETAIL		
They called him Little Jemmy because, at 5' 4", he was our shortest president, and also because humans didn't yet know that the actual nickname for James is "Jimmy." Jemmy means nothing.		
HOOK FOR A HAND?	**WAS HE A WOMAN?**	**WAS HE BLACK?**
No	No	No

CONTINUED

TABLE 21: *continued*

NAME OF PRESIDENT

Jas. MONROE 1817–1825

"NICKNAME" OF PRESIDENT

"Old Doctriney"

DECEMBER 18
1990, NEW YORK CITY: Stephen Sondheim's musical *Assassins* debuts off-Broadway. To this day, he claims that the music and lyrics were the work of a single man.

HUMANIZING DETAIL

Like Madison, Monroe was a protégé of Jefferson's. His famous "Doctrine" establishing U.S. hegemony over the Western Hemisphere and the entire Under-sphere was actually written by John Quincy Adams.

HOOK FOR A HAND?	WAS HE A WOMAN?	WAS HE BLACK?
No	No	No

Figure 39: Make No "Bones" About It: J. Q. Adams Looked Like a Freaky Living Corpse. HEEE-HEEE HA-HA-HA-HA!

NAME OF PRESIDENT

J'hn Qu'cy ADAMS 1825–1829

"NICKNAME" OF PRESIDENT

"The Cryptkeeper"

HUMANIZING DETAIL

Cerebral, arrogant, and skeletal, most children were afraid that "Old JQ" would take them in the night and impress them into work gangs, forced to build his long-planned National Observatory.

HOOK FOR A HAND?	No
WAS HE A WOMAN?	No
WAS HE BLACK?	No

CONTINUED

TABLE 21: *continued*

NAME OF PRESIDENT

A'drew JACKSON 1829–1837

"NICKNAME" OF PRESIDENT

"Old Hickory," "Folksy Lunatic"

HUMANIZING DETAIL

After the aristocratic presidencies of the founding fathers (and one founding son) who preceded him, Jackson, a populist, would forever redefine the mythos of the presidency as a common, folksy lunatic, Indian killer, and log cabineer. He was the first president to wear a necklace of shrunken heads at his inauguration.

DECEMBER 19

1988, NEW YORK CITY: Billy Crystal and Meg Ryan film the famous "fake orgasm" scene at Katz's Deli in NYC. According to Hollywood legend, Crystal himself suggested the scene, having grown up listening to family stories about the deli and all the orgasms his mother used to have there.

HOOK FOR A HAND?	WAS HE A WOMAN?	WAS HE BLACK?
No	No	No

Figure 40:
The Sixth Martin Van Buren

NAME OF PRESIDENT

M'rtin VAN BUREN 1837–1841

"NICKNAME" OF PRESIDENT

"Old Kinderhook," "Little Van," "Martin Van Ruin," "Bureny Van Economic Crisis," "Fancy Van Ascot, the Little Magician," "Old Many Nicknames"

HUMANIZING DETAIL

Jackson's former VP,[81] Van Buren vowed to "walk in my predecessor's

81. Please see page 314 under the heading "A Curiouser Institution."

CONTINUED

TABLE 21: *continued*

DECEMBER 20
1978, VIRGINIA: After hearing of Milwaukee's tooth shower, Richmond reports
a heavy rain of frogs *and* toads.

footsteps, even though it will not be exactly comfortable, because they are filled with Indian blood." But Van Buren's shrunken-head necklace was imported from France, and in all respects he was known as something of a free-spending dandy, favoring brightly colored vests and ascots and strange, luminous waistcoats. Only later did we find out that this was because he was a Time Lord.

HOOK FOR A HAND?	WAS HE A WOMAN?	WAS HE BLACK?
Yes	No	No

NAME OF PRESIDENT
Wm. H'ry HARRISON 1841–1841

"NICKNAME" OF PRESIDENT
"Tippecanoe," "Old Quick-to-Die"

HUMANIZING DETAIL

Though it was raining on his inauguration day, WHH insisted upon giving his full three-day oration without a hat. He also insisted upon standing in a bucket of ice while naked and while handling the feces of a goat. Many scholars believe this is how he got so terribly sick, causing his death after just a month in office. But that is ridiculous. Here is the truth: Just before the inauguration, he received a mysterious note revealing that he had been poisoned with slow-acting pneumonia. The note further explained that he had thirty-one days to solve his own murder. (He didn't. Harrison was a great Indian-killer, but not much of a sleuth.)

HOOK FOR A HAND?	WAS HE A WOMAN?	WAS HE BLACK?
No	No	No

CONTINUED

TABLE 21: *continued*

NAME OF PRESIDENT

J'hn TYLER 1841–1845

"NICKNAME" OF PRESIDENT

"Tyler Too"

HUMANIZING DETAIL

Tyler was the first VP to assume the office upon the death of his predecessor, and it haunted him. Harrison's ghost would regularly visit Tyler in the middle of the night and sit at the end of his bed, glowering, his necklace of Indian heads of which he had always been so proud now drawn tightly, like chains, around him. When Charles Dickens visited the White House in 1842, Tyler told him of these terrible visions. Then the president threw open the window and screamed at a passing child, ordering him to buy a goose. As you might guess, this later inspired Dickens to write his Christmas masterpiece *Fatal Vision*, in which the novelist accused Tyler of being Harrison's killer. He didn't get it right either. (It was Tecumseh.)

DECEMBER 21

1970, WASHINGTON, DC: Elvis Presley meets Richard Nixon. At their meeting, Presley asked the president to name him a Special Federal Agent in charge of swearing at hippies and shooting at things. Mainly to get rid of him, Nixon instead offered to make Presley the first Federal Marshal for the Preservation of the Nixonian Timeline, or, more colloquially, a "Time Cop."

Figure 41. Elvis Models the "Old-Timey Uniform" He Proposed to Wear as the Nation's First "Time Cop."

HOOK FOR A HAND?	No
WAS HE A WOMAN?	No
WAS HE BLACK?	No

CONTINUED

TABLE 21: *continued*
NAME OF PRESIDENT
Jas. K. POLK 1845–1848
"NICKNAME" OF PRESIDENT
"Young Hickory"
HUMANIZING DETAIL

Polk appointed his own wife to every cabinet position. They locked themselves in the Oval Office and frequently worked throughout the day, barking out strange slogans through the door[82] and refusing to eat until Texas had been annexed. Polk only emerged briefly when Henry David Thoreau refused to pay his taxes for Polk's war with Mexico. Polk went to Thoreau's jail cell, smacked him around, and rifled through his pockets, turning up a dime and three nickels, while his wife stood by and laughed. You may think this cruel, but it was warranted: It was these thirty-five cents that won the war.

DECEMBER 22

1992, NEW YORK: Anthony Robbins publishes the bestselling success manual *Awaken the Giant Within,* in which he encourages personal and spiritual growth via guided meditation, deep-breathing techniques, firewalking and, most controversially, the ritualistic "molting" of one's human skin to reveal the gigantic Anthony Robbins clone that lives inside all of us. To date, according to the book, only Robbins himself has been able to achieve this final step.

HOOK FOR A HAND?	WAS HE A WOMAN?	WAS HE BLACK?
No	No	No

82. Please see page 185 in *The Areas of My Expertise,* under the heading "Oregon."

CONTINUED

TABLE 21: *continued*

NAME OF PRESIDENT

Zach'y TAYLOR 1849–1850

DECEMBER 23
1977, OREM, UT: *The Donny & Marie Show* hires an innovative young bandleader named "Philip Glass."

"NICKNAME" OF PRESIDENT

"Young Quick-to-Die"

HUMANIZING DETAIL

A hero in Polk's Mexican War, Taylor was drafted into the presidency against his will by the Whig Party.[83] He hated the job so much that, on July 4, 1850, he killed himself by gorging on cold milk and cherries. It was not a pleasant way to go, not least because milk and cherries are not normally poisonous. It took Taylor five days and an intense amount of concentration to convince his spiteful body to die of delicious, wholesome things. Imagine if he had turned such will to the issue of slavery! (Answer: There probably would have been slavery, but slightly less.)

HOOK FOR A HAND?	WAS HE A WOMAN?	WAS HE BLACK?
No	No	No

NAME OF PRESIDENT

Mill'rd FILLMORE 1850–1853

"NICKNAME" OF PRESIDENT

"Milard"

HUMANIZING DETAIL

No one bothered to give him a nickname, so he made up his own, by removing the second "L" from his first name. It is a terrible nickname, especially when you consider that "The Great Guano-Compromiser" was still available. Look it up.

HOOK FOR A HAND?	WAS HE A WOMAN?	WAS HE BLACK?
No	No	No

83. So named for their fondness for wigs and the letter "H."

CONTINUED

TABLE 21: *continued*		

NAME OF PRESIDENT

Frnkl'n PIERCE 1853–1857

"NICKNAME" OF PRESIDENT

"Hawkeye"

HUMANIZING DETAIL

Hawkeye Pierce liked nothing more than to retire to his tent—nicknamed "New Hampshire"—and there enjoy a martini from his illicit still. He was known for trading quips and barbs with Jefferson "BJ" Davis, his secretary of war, often at the expense of Caleb Cushing, the stuffy Bostonian attorney general. But although he appeared lighthearted and drunk, his easygoing nature concealed a dark streak. When he couldn't save the life of William R. King, his young, tubercular vice president, Pierce went into a deep depression and refused to name a successor. "Goddamn this war," he muttered, pulling off his presidential surgical gloves. But there was no war: YET.

DECEMBER 24

IT IS CHRISTMAS EVE. Some families traditionally open one present on Christmas Eve. These families are dead to me.

HOOK FOR A HAND?	WAS HE A WOMAN?	WAS HE BLACK?
No	No	No

NAME OF PRESIDENT

J'mes BUCHANAN 1857–1861

"NICKNAME" OF PRESIDENT

"Old AfterPIERCE," "Worsty"

HUMANIZING DETAIL

James Buchanan did not feel it was legal to go to war to keep the country together, but he did send an army out to kill Brigham Young for being a Mormon. Historians now believe that this was Buchanan's idea of a joke.

HOOK FOR A HAND?	WAS HE A WOMAN?	WAS HE BLACK?
No	No	No

CONTINUED

TABLE 21: *continued*

NAME OF PRESIDENT

Ab'ham LINCOLN 1861–1865

"NICKNAME" OF PRESIDENT

Antebellum: "The Railsplitter"; Postbellum: "The Railuniter"

HUMANIZING DETAIL

Lincoln was not who you think he was.[84]

HOOK FOR A HAND?	WAS HE A WOMAN?	WAS HE BLACK?
No	No	No

NAME OF PRESIDENT

A'drew JOHNSON 1865–1869

"NICKNAME" OF PRESIDENT

"Old Impeachable"

HUMANIZING DETAIL

Johnson's notoriously combative relationship with the Republican congress culminated with his impeachment (the first in history). Ostensibly the charge against him was opposing universal suffrage among the freed slaves and violating the Tenure of Office Act, but we all know what it was really about.[85]

> **DECEMBER 25**
> And now comes December 25, also known as CHRISTMAS, also known as CHRIST'S MASS to the very religious, or, to pornographers, as "XMAS." For some history on this holiday, please see page 566, under the heading "The Best Mas Ever."

HOOK FOR A HAND?	WAS HE A WOMAN?	WAS HE BLACK?
No	No	No

84. Please see page 322 under the heading "Were You Aware of It? President Booth."

85. Please see page 356 under the heading "February 24."

CONTINUED

TABLE 21: *continued*
NAME OF PRESIDENT
U. S. GRANT 1869–1877
"NICKNAME" OF PRESIDENT
"Drunky," "Beardy," "Debty," "Ulysseysy"
HUMANIZING DETAIL

Financial scandals plagued the Grant administration, though historians debate how much Grant knew about it due to his fondness for whiskey and for not knowing things. We do know that when the robber baron Jay Gould proposed to take all of the nation's gold and hide it in his private mountain, he invited Grant to join his heist as a grappling-hook man.[86] But Grant declined. His skill with the grappling hook may have won the Civil War, but he was not corrupt. He saw the White House as a brief chance at drunken peace and an opportunity to work on his many hobbies, such as throat cancer.

HOOK FOR A HAND?	No
WAS HE A WOMAN?	No
WAS HE BLACK?	No

86. He had already lined up VP Schuyler Colfax to work surveillance and drive the getaway buggy.

CONTINUED

DECEMBER 26

Today the English observe BOXING DAY. The name dates back to a medieval custom in which the English people would spend the day after Christmas looking for a wren. When they captured one, they would put it in a box and ceremoniously ask it for a prosperous new year. Like most of the old superstitions, it doesn't make a lot of sense. Why would a wren grant someone a prosperous and healthy new year directly after it had been captured and put in a box? If I were a wren in the same situation, I would probably suggest that the English person remove me from the box so I could stick my beak in his throat (in case you don't know, wrens have very sharp beaks, and also speak English).

TABLE 21: *continued*

NAME OF PRESIDENT

Ruth'f'd B. HAYES 1877–1881

"NICKNAME" OF PRESIDENT

"His Illegitimacy," "Rutherfraud B. Hayes," "Frauderfraud Bogus Hayes," "His Excellency, Fakey Votethief," "El Stealo"

HUMANIZING DETAIL

While he lost the popular election by a quarter million votes, he none-theless won the Electoral College, largely by promising the Electors more and better nutrient slime. This caused many in the press to cease-lessly question his legitimacy as president, which is how they did it in the olden days. Truth to tell, it really was very good nutrient slime.[87]

HOOK FOR A HAND?	WAS HE A WOMAN?	WAS HE BLACK?
No	No	No

NAME OF PRESIDENT

J'mes GARFIELD 1881–1881

"NICKNAME" OF PRESIDENT

"Garfield"

HUMANIZING DETAIL

He was our nation's first left-hooked president. Historians agree that, had he had an actual left hand, he proba-bly could have caught the bullet that killed him.

> **DECEMBER 27**
> 1831, PLYMOUTH, ENGLAND: Charles Darwin sets sail in the *Beagle* for a tour of the Galápagos Islands, accompanied by his faithful talking chimpanzee, named Man-Ape. "Soon, my friend," Darwin is reported as saying, "when I complete my work, they will HAVE to let us marry."

HOOK FOR A HAND?	WAS HE A WOMAN?	WAS HE BLACK?
Yes	No	No

87. Please see page 276 under the heading "On the Matter of Nutrient Slime."

CONTINUED

TABLE 21: *continued*

NAME OF PRESIDENT

Ch'ter A. ARTHUR 1881–1885

"NICKNAME" OF PRESIDENT

"Odie"

DECEMBER 28

1978, WISCONSIN: Milwaukee reports a blizzard of human teeth. The city informs Richmond that many Milwaukeeans are trapped at home because the roads are blocked with shoulder-height incisor banks.

HUMANIZING DETAIL

Nicknamed "Odie" due to his "odious" reputation as a pawn of New York political fixture Roscoe Conkling, and also due to his constant slobbering, he nonetheless instituted important patronage reforms. The price of obtaining a prime cabinet position, for example, went up to $129. Only the very wealthy could afford it.

HOOK FOR A HAND?	WAS HE A WOMAN?	WAS HE BLACK?
No	No	No

NAME OF PRESIDENT

G'ver CLEVELAND 1885–1889

"NICKNAME" OF PRESIDENT

"The Beast from Buffalo," "Old Cryonic"

HUMANIZING DETAIL

Our only president to serve two nonconsecutive terms. Most historians want you to believe that he simply lost the election to Harrison, and then after Harrison bearded it all up, he got reelected. They do not want you to know about the secret zinc chamber in which he was kept, frozen in suspended animation, until they found a cure for the cancer invading his upper palate.

HOOK FOR A HAND?	WAS HE A WOMAN?	WAS HE BLACK?
No	No	No

CONTINUED

TABLE 21: *continued*

NAME OF PRESIDENT

Benj. HARRISON 1889–1893

"NICKNAME" OF PRESIDENT

"The Human Iceberg"

HUMANIZING DETAIL

Ironically, though he was never frozen in a zinc chamber hidden beneath the Rose Garden, it was HARRISON they called "The Human Iceberg." This was because of his notorious standoffishness and his ability to freeze the moisture in the air and create ice-bridges.

> **DECEMBER 29**
> 1964, NEW HAVEN: The controversial Yale Feline Studies Lab reports that cats can be conditioned to not purr simply by strapping them into a chair and forcing them to watch countless hours of film containing disconnected scenes of violent purring.

HOOK FOR A HAND?	WAS HE A WOMAN?	WAS HE BLACK?
No	No	No

NAME OF PRESIDENT

G'ver CLEVELAND 1893–1897

"NICKNAME" OF PRESIDENT

"Half-Face"

HUMANIZING DETAIL

Eventually, scientists found a cure for Cleveland's cancer: surgery. So as not to panic the country, doctors prepared to remove the president's tumor in absolute secrecy while aboard his yacht *Oneida*, drifting in Long Island Sound. The tumor was successfully excised, but because they were performing surgery ON A BOAT, they also cut half his face off. In a panic, they built for him a prosthetic half-face of hard rubber and celluloid.

HOOK FOR A HAND?	WAS HE A WOMAN?	WAS HE BLACK?
No	No	No

CONTINUED

TABLE 21: *continued*

NAME OF PRESIDENT

Wm. MCKINLEY 1893–1901

"NICKNAME" OF PRESIDENT

"Anarchist-bane"

HUMANIZING DETAIL

Figure 42: The Face That Launched at Least One Presidential Assassination

While visiting the Pan-American Exposition in Buffalo, New York, McKinley was assassinated by the anarchist Leon Czolgosz (pronounced "Leon Cholshlolsohdnshioadhoih"). Accordingly, Czolgosz was instantly named Emperor of the Anarchist States of America. As he was being crowned, Czolgosz reportedly cried out, "No, no. You have it all wrong. I just wanted to have sex with Emma Goldman." Well, you cannot blame him. Who wouldn't?

HOOK FOR A HAND?	WAS HE A WOMAN?	WAS HE BLACK?
No	No	No

DECEMBER 30

1863, SOUTH CAROLINA: Despite what you may have read on the Internet about a machine called "Boilerplate," the first actual military robot goes into service on this date aboard the Confederate submarine *Hunley*. While the device is not much to look at—little more than a small, wheeled perspiration drone designed to collect the sweat of the crewmen and convert it to breathable water—it nonetheless was far more valuable than the *Hunley* itself, and to this day is considered the ultimate prize by collectors of pre-twentieth-century robots.

NAME OF PRESIDENT

Theo. ROOSEVELT 1901–1909

"NICKNAME" OF PRESIDENT

"The Terrible, Terrible Bear"

HUMANIZING DETAIL

Please see page 318 under the heading "Fast Facts About Teddy Roosevelt."

HOOK FOR A HAND?	Yes
WAS HE A WOMAN?	No
WAS HE BLACK?	No

CONTINUED

TABLE 21: *continued*

NAME OF PRESIDENT

Wm. H'w'd TAFT 1909–1913

"NICKNAME" OF PRESIDENT

"William Howard Obese Man"

HUMANIZING DETAIL

Look, we all know Taft was a large man. We all know that he got stuck in the White House bathtub because of his fatness. We all know that they had to install a new, much larger bathtub, and that Taft filled it with cream cheese and ate his way out (until he got stuck again). We all know he kept a cow on the lawn for fresh milk and that he would occasionally drink blood from its neck like a Masai warrior. And then the cow mysteriously disappeared, and no one knew what had happened to it until Taft accidentally farted it out. We all know he kept a bowl of live frogs by his resting slab in the Oval Office that he would snack on during meetings. We all know the Oval Office was originally *round*. The bloggers of the day would never let him forget it. So why dwell on it? Especially when you consider that, for all his faults

DECEMBER 31

1912, DIMENSION 29: The great winged serpent Quetzalcoatl decides to give humanity exactly one hundred years more in which to prove itself worthy of him. Otherwise, he will come for us in 2012, covering our earth forever in the black shadow of his gigantic snakey wings. HOW CAN WE PROVE OURSELVES TO QUETZAL-COATL? That is a matter of some debate. But buying The Hodgman Literary Tone Detector is probably a good start.[a]

a. Please see page 523 under the heading "The Hodgman Literary Tone Detector and Why You Should Buy It."

(again, we are talking primarily of his fatness), he was, after all, the LAST PRESIDENT TO WEAR A MUSTACHE. So give old lard-stache a break.

HOOK FOR A HAND?	WAS HE A WOMAN?	WAS HE BLACK?
No	Yes	Yes

CONTINUED

TABLE 21: *continued*

JANUARY 1
45 BC, ROME: Julius Caesar makes this day the FIRST DAY of the New Year, which under the old Roman calendar had traditionally been observed on March 1. As Julius Caesar was due to be assassinated on March 15, he bought himself an extra sixty days of life this way. These two months would forever be known as his "salad days," after the salad he invented on February 15, now known as "The Ides of Romaine."

Figure 43:
An Incredible Likeness
of a Human Being

NAME OF PRESIDENT

W'd'w WILSON 1913–1921

"NICKNAME" OF PRESIDENT

"Edith"

HUMANIZING DETAIL

In 1919, Wilson suffered a severe stroke, largely incapacitating him and making him seem even more stiff and wooden than before. Unable to carry out his duties, he was confined to a special container called a "stroke box." His wife, Edith, allowed no one near him, instead issuing orders on his behalf and earning herself the nickname "The Secret President Who Is a Lady." Edith always denied that she had usurped her husband's power and sought to prove it by wheeling out the stroke box from time to time so that Wilson could tell his cabinet to leave her alone. Some speculated that this was just a Woodrow Wilson ventriloquist dummy—a popular novelty of the age. And they were right, except for one thing: It was a Woodrow Wilson ventriloquist dummy MADE ENTIRELY OUT OF WOODROW WILSON!

HOOK FOR A HAND?	WAS HE A WOMAN?	WAS HE BLACK?
No	No	No

CONTINUED

TABLE 21: *continued*

NAME OF PRESIDENT

W'ren G. HARDING 1921–1923

"NICKNAME" OF PRESIDENT

"Ole' Teapot Domey"

HUMANIZING DETAIL

Here's what you need to know about Teapot Dome: Teapot Dome was neither a teapot, nor a dome, nor a crude nickname for Harding's penis. It was a mountain in Wyoming full of oil that Harding gave to his friends in big business for nothing. "Ole' Teapot Domey," on the other hand, was a nickname for Harding's penis—because it was the most corrupt penis in presidential history.

HOOK FOR A HAND?	No
WAS HE A WOMAN?	No
WAS HE BLACK?	No

JANUARY 2

1920: HAPPY BIRTHDAY, ISAAC ASIMOV! Contrary to legend, Asimov was not born with a bolo tie, just sideburns. The bolo tie was a robot he added later. It was named Dr. Theopolis and could solve complex math and sideburn problems.

Figure 44: Asimov and Theopolis

Figure 45: It Wasn't Just His Penis: Also, His Eyebrows Were Corrupt

CONTINUED

TABLE 21: *continued*

NAME OF PRESIDENT
C'vin COOLIDGE 1923–1929

"NICKNAME" OF PRESIDENT
"Silent Cal"

HUMANIZING DETAIL

Calvin Coolidge was called "Silent Cal" because he never spoke. In fact, he rarely even moved. For a long time people worried they had gotten another Woodrow-Wilson-in-a-Box type of president, but it was merely that Calvin Coolidge was a quiet, introspective man who had accidentally cut his own tongue out while shaving. All the same, it did not stop the '20s from "roaring" or Coolidge from occasionally grunting hollowly when he required food.

HOOK FOR A HAND?	No
WAS HE A WOMAN?	No
WAS HE BLACK?	No

CONTINUED

JANUARY 3

1980, ON THE RADIO DIAL: "Celebration" by Kool & the Gang burns up the charts. Contrary to popular belief, Kool & the Gang were not the first pop-funk band to be openly sponsored by a cigarette company (that distinction belongs to Parliament), but they were arguably the most successful.

Many have forgotten the original lyrics of the song after it was changed for reasons of "political correctness" and "because it caused cancer":

> "There's a party goin' on right
> here
> A celebration to last throughout
> the years
> So bring your good times, and
> your laughter too
> We gonna mentholate your party
> with you."

TABLE 21: *continued*

NAME OF PRESIDENT

H'bert HOOVER 1929–1933

"NICKNAME" OF PRESIDENT

"Tesla Hater"

HUMANIZING DETAIL

Though he failed to foresee or stop the Great Depression; though he sent the army to attack its own destitute veterans encamped on U.S. soil; though he stole Tesla's dreams and, some say, a sizeable chunk of Tesla's brain that he had lacquered into a watch fob; though his name became synonymous with the "Hoovervilles" (special metal boxes for the storage of extremely poor people), still do not forget his humanizing detail: An autopsy suggested he may actually have been at least half human.

JANUARY 4

1903, CONEY ISLAND: Thomas Edison uses the alternating current (AC) technology of his rival, Tesla, to electrocute "Topsy," a circus elephant, before a large crowd. Using his own proprietary cameras, Edison filmed Topsy's gruesome death and displayed the short movie around the country in order to show the world a) that Tesla's AC was as dangerous as Edison claimed, and b) that Edison would keep on killing elephants until the nation surrendered to his own direct current (DC).

HOOK FOR A HAND?	WAS HE A WOMAN?	WAS HE BLACK?
No	No	No

NAME OF PRESIDENT

F. D'lano ROOSEVELT 1933–1945

"NICKNAME" OF PRESIDENT

"Chairy"

HUMANIZING DETAIL

Roosevelt was perhaps our last president to openly embrace smoking. Everyone will recall the iconic image of Roosevelt, chin pitched optimistically skyward, his aristocratic jaw clamped down upon a hookah

CONTINUED

TABLE 21: *continued*

Figure 46: FDR Shows Off His Batman Cape to Churchill, Stalin, Other Men

JANUARY 5

1998, SAN DIEGO: Jammy and Bindle, the famous chess-playing brain sharks of Sea World, escape their tanks by hypnotizing their keepers and briefly reversing time. They are still at large.

hose. Roosevelt loved his hookah, which had been a gift from Lucy Mercer. Mercer was with him on his last day in Warm Springs, when Roosevelt suffered a cerebral hemorrhage while sitting for a painting. But historians rarely mention what that painting depicted: the surprisingly frail president at the beginning of his third term, his face sunken and wearied, yet still princely in his trademark Batman cape, and enjoying a smoke while sitting on top of a giant toadstool.

HOOK FOR A HAND?	WAS HE A WOMAN?	WAS HE BLACK?
Yes	No	No

CONTINUED

TABLE 21: *continued*

NAME OF PRESIDENT

Har. S. TRUMAN 1945–1953

"NICKNAME" OF PRESIDENT

"Hell Giver"

HUMANIZING DETAIL

A small, energetic man, he was known for taking brisk daily walks around the White House on his own, occasionally scraping out a little burrow for a nap when he got tired. While he had a reputation for being a man of the people, he routinely paid up to a nickel for a haircut. He loved to play the piano, but no one had the heart to tell him that it involved more than just slamming his hands up and down on the keys with his palms. Cute, right? Also: He dropped the bomb(s).

HOOK FOR A HAND?	WAS HE A WOMAN?	WAS HE BLACK?
No	No	No

NAME OF PRESIDENT

"DD" EISENHOWER 1953–1961

"NICKNAME" OF PRESIDENT

"Ike"

JANUARY 6

1979, VIRGINIA: Richmond reports not only regular rains of frogs and toads, but also several human spit showers and brandy squalls. Richmond names itself the STRANGE RAIN CAPITAL OF THE UNITED STATES.

HUMANIZING DETAIL

Eisenhower was called "Ike" because he loved Mike and Ike candies and he was not named Mike. Among his other hobbies were golf, being bald, and wacky conspiracy theories. He believed in something called "the military-industrial complex," which was somehow going to "influence" our government. In his farewell address, he hinted that we needed an interstate highway system in order to escape the military industrialists and their "shadow warriors." Then Vice President Nixon put him in the basement. The *New York Times* headline: GOOD RIDDANCE, KOOK!

HOOK FOR A HAND?	WAS HE A WOMAN?	WAS HE BLACK?
No	No	No

CONTINUED

TABLE 21: *continued*	

| JANUARY 7 | NAME OF PRESIDENT |
| 1970, WASHINGTON, DC: President Nixon unwittingly causes an international incident when, at a state dinner for the visiting Queen Elizabeth II, he calls for his favorite meal: roast corgi and ketchup. | J'hn Fitz'g'ld KENNEDY 1961–1963 |

NAME OF PRESIDENT

J'hn Fitz'g'ld KENNEDY 1961–1963

"NICKNAME" OF PRESIDENT

"Jack Catholic, the Camelot Kid"

HUMANIZING DETAIL

When you consider the novelistic details of Kennedy's administration that have so invaded our cultural imagination—his youthful glamour and the beautiful family he hid under his desk . . . the inspiring call to idealism and the mysterious orders from the pope . . . and finally his tragic assassination by at least 100 men—it is somewhat hard to believe that Kennedy's brief presidency actually happened. Indeed, some historians now speculate that it was either a mass hallucination, a dream, or the vague recollections of a TV movie we all watched.

HOOK FOR A HAND?	WAS HE A WOMAN?	WAS HE BLACK?
No	No	No

NAME OF PRESIDENT

L'don Baines JOHNSON 1963–1969

"NICKNAME" OF PRESIDENT

"Scarbelly," "Your Number One Giant Sardine Man"

HUMANIZING DETAIL

Lyndon Baines Johnson was a great big Texan who wanted to create a "Gigantic Society" in which there would be no poverty or social injustice and everyone would drink Fresca all the time.[88] When it all came crashing down, however, Johnson lost his will not just to govern, but to live. He blamed the Republicans, the press, his own handling of Vietnam. But the real problem was the Fresca. Let's face it: No one ever follows a Fresca man.

HOOK FOR A HAND?	WAS HE A WOMAN?	WAS HE BLACK?
No	No	No

88. It is true: It was his favorite drink (he called it "the Treatment").

CONTINUED

TABLE 21: *continued*		
NAME OF PRESIDENT		
Rich. NIXON 1969–1974		
"NICKNAME" OF PRESIDENT		
"Milhous," "Tricky Dick," "Trichard Richard"		
HUMANIZING DETAIL		
Nixon was the first to install air-conditioning in the White House in order to maintain the incredibly low temperatures his body needed to survive. But he loved a fire, and he would often build a roaring blaze in the Oval Office fireplace while writing to the many children of America who had signed up to join Uncle Dick's Secret Swear-Words Club. You see, he was not a complete monster. And many an American child learned the word "kike" by his hand.		
HOOK FOR A HAND?	**WAS HE A WOMAN?**	**WAS HE BLACK?**
Yes	No	No

NAME OF PRESIDENT	**JANUARY 8**
G'ld FORD 1974–1977	Today is the technical anniversary of January 8.
"NICKNAME" OF PRESIDENT	
See "humanizing detail"	

HUMANIZING DETAIL
Ford was a cat fancier, as you will recall from page 89 of *THE AREAS OF MY EXPERTISE*. He was originally named Leslie Lynch-King after his father, but his mother soon left his biological father and changed her son's name before he was three years old. Later she would confess the reason for the change: She worried that people would conclude that little Leslie was (a) a woman, (b) someone who likes to lynch people, or (c) a "king"-like figure who was never elected to either the presidency or the vice presidency but nonetheless held

CONTINUED

TABLE 21: *continued*

both offices. After a long string of trial names, including Bobby Duly-elected, Howard Nolynchpeople, and "Thing," she finally settled on Gerald Rudolph Ford. However, he was never able to escape the nickname "Leslie Lynch-King."

HOOK FOR A HAND?	WAS HE A WOMAN?	WAS HE BLACK?
No	No	No

NAME OF PRESIDENT

J'mes CARTER 1977–1981

"NICKNAME" OF PRESIDENT

"Jimmy Teeth," "Nutsy McMalaise"

HUMANIZING DETAIL

Carter served on a nuclear submarine when he was in the Navy. But in his heart, he lusted for peace. He was always tolerant of the zeppeliners, and his search for an end to the bloody feud led to the Camp David Air and Underwater Accords: the first time a submarine and zeppelin commander shook hands without poisoining one another. But the truce would not last (after shaking hands, they strangled each other), and Carter would later be accused of idealism, naïveté, and a lack of loathsome, ruthless assholism. Alas, it was true: He was our nation's first non-jock president— EVIDENCE OF WHICH CAN BE FOUND THROUGHOUT HISTORY.[89]

JANUARY 9
January 8 is observed.

HOOK FOR A HAND?	WAS HE A WOMAN?	WAS HE BLACK?
No	No	No

89. Please see TODAY IN THE PAST under the headings February 2, March 3, March 8, June 4, June 7, and August 20.

CONTINUED

TABLE 21: *continued*

NAME OF PRESIDENT
Ron'd REAGAN 1981–1989

"NICKNAME" OF PRESIDENT
"The Great Communicator," "The Reager," "Nancy Boy"

HUMANIZING DETAIL

After a failed assassination attempt on Reagan's life, Nancy Reagan reportedly slept with one of his shirts to be comforted by his familiar aroma. Presumably it was not the shirt he was wearing when he was shot, because the president rarely smelled like blood. Rather, one historian described Reagan's scent to be "a kind of folksy, doddering man-musk, the round, reassuring nose lingering somewhere between pancakes, saddle oil, and grandfather fart, with just a hint of crushed air traffic controller." After his death in 2004, some entrepreneurs briefly marketed a "Reagan" brand cologne and body spray based on the scent, but it was discontinued when it was discovered that wearing it caused Nancy Reagan to show up at their house, wanting to cuddle with you.

JANUARY 10
1729, LONDON: Jonathan Swift publishes his famous essay "A Modest Proposal." Little-known fact: HE WASN'T JOKING.

Figure 47: A Promotional Image for "Reagan Cologne"

HOOK FOR A HAND?	**WAS HE A WOMAN?**	**WAS HE BLACK?**
No	No	No

CONTINUED

TABLE 21: *continued*

NAME OF PRESIDENT

Geo. H. W. BUSH 1989–1993

"NICKNAME" OF PRESIDENT

"The Spit-Comet"

HUMANIZING DETAIL

When the Japanese prime minister tried to feed him broccoli, an ancient Japanese delicacy, Bush responded the only way he knew how: He vomited all over himself and others. You can't blame a man for his upbringing. That is how they eat in Kennebunkport.

HOOK FOR A HAND?	Yes
WAS HE A WOMAN?	No
WAS HE BLACK? [s]	No

JANUARY 11
1978, LOS ANGELES: After *Star Wars* made him a household name, Mark Hamill suffers a terrible landspeeder accident. He is severely injured, requiring extensive facial plastic surgery. When he returns to the *Star Wars* franchise with *The Empire Strikes Back,* they explained the difference in his appearance by writing in a scene in which a jealous Han Solo throws hot bacta in Mark Hamill's face in a spat over Princess Leia. This scene, of course, ended up on the cutting-room floor . . . but not the scene in which Mark Hamill tongue kisses his own twin sister, Carrie Fisher.

NAME OF PRESIDENT

Wm. Jeff'son CLINTON 1993–2001

"NICKNAME" OF PRESIDENT

"BossHogg," "Bubba," "Slick Penis Euphemism"

HUMANIZING DETAIL

Here's a little fact you might not have known: Bill Clinton liked getting blowjobs. This was very unusual for any man, never mind a sitting president. All the same, he was devoted to this hobby. Long after everyone would go home, Clinton would often stay in the office late at night for the sole purpose of getting blowjobs. None of his male friends could understand it. That's just the way he was. But what you hear about him playing the saxophone—that's just disgusting.

HOOK FOR A HAND?	WAS HE A WOMAN?	WAS HE BLACK?
No	No	Yes. He was our first black president!

CONTINUED

TABLE 21: *continued*

NAME OF PRESIDENT

Geo. W'lker BUSH 2001–2009

"NICKNAME" OF PRESIDENT

"W'lker"

HUMANIZING DETAIL

George W. Bush is the only president to have invented his own humanizing details. Discovered among his papers at Yale is an old D&D character sheet outlining in detail the tough-drawling, non-Yalie, God-loving, former-drunk he would portray throughout his political life.[90] He also included a little sketch of himself, and in fact, it wasn't a terrible likeness. What more qualifications do you want?

HOOK FOR A HAND?	WAS HE A WOMAN?	WAS HE BLACK?
Yes	No	No

NAME OF PRESIDENT

?????!!!!

"NICKNAME" OF PRESIDENT

"Old Interrobang"

HUMANIZING DETAIL

Please see the paperback edition of this book, SOMETIME IN THE FUTURE!

HOOK FOR A HAND?	WAS HE A WOMAN?	WAS HE BLACK?
?	?	?

JANUARY 12

1973, NEW YORK: Finding no publisher willing to take the risk, Harold Bloom self-publishes his page-a-day calendar version of *The Anxiety of Influence*. A perennial favorite, it has sold some ten million copies, and frankly, that drives me crazy.

90. While his Strength, Wisdom, and Constitution stats are about what you'd expect, his Dexterity roll clocked in at a SURPRISING 16!

JANUARY 13
1898, PARIS: Emile Zola pens his famous open letter "J'accuse," condemning the French government over the Dreyfus Affair. The text of the letter would later be transformed into a top-ten dance hit by Soft Cell in 1981.

AN EERIE SIMILARITY BETWEEN KENNEDY AND LINCOLN

YES: They were born in different centuries. BUT WERE YOU AWARE THAT THEY BOTH HAD OFF-BRAND FRIED CHICKEN RESTAURANTS NAMED AFTER THEM?

Figure 48: Exhibit One

Figure 49: Exhibit Two

IT IS SO. Other than that, THERE WERE ABSOLUTELY NO SIMILARITIES BETWEEN THEM.

WERE YOU AWARE OF IT? "WILLIAM JENNINGS BRYAN'S CROSS OF MONKEY CORPSES"

After failing three times in his effort to become president, famed orator and agrarian populist William Jennings Bryan finally gave up politics and returned to the quiet life of persecuting public school teachers. The Scopes Monkey Trial famously pitted Bryan against Clarence Darrow in a courtroom battle of words that came to symbolize the fight between biblical creationism and the theory of evolution that still rages on today.

While Bryan's arguments that all the dinosaurs were actually

CONTINUED

Christians was impassioned, the depth of his animus toward Darwin was not discovered until 1963. That year, a local construction crew hired to dig a pool uncovered a gruesome secret: the skeletons of nearly 1,000 monkeys and apes buried in what had once been Bryan's backyard.

JANUARY 14
1979, WISCONSIN: Milwaukee reports an angry hail of sharp stones, tiny coffins, and shells from mollusks that don't exist, followed by strong gusts of opium smoke. The *Milwaukee Sentinel* publishes an editorial: "Maybe we don't have a lot of frogs and toads like some other cities we could name, but we do have tiny coffins lying all over our city, and that frankly seems A LITTLE MORE STRANGE to us."

Forensic analysis of their skulls revealed that Bryan did not let the sun set without shooting at least one monkey in the head, usually after dinner.

DID YOU KNOW THIS GRUESOME FACT?

AND DID YOU KNOW THAT WHEN THE CONSTRUCTION CREW DUG EVEN DEEPER, THEY DISCOVERED THE BONES OF A TRICERATOPS KNEELING IN PRAYER?

I suspect you did not.

A CURIOUSER INSTITUTION

John Adams famously called the vice presidency "the most insignificant office ever the invention of man contrived or his imagination conceived."

Adams was, as you know, one of the premier architects of our independence, a ruthlessly intelligent yet unsubtle man with little patience for debate. It was not uncommon at the Second Continental Congress for him to smash chairs apart when he did not get his way. Later, when he was sent to join Franklin as an envoy to France, Adams could not tolerate Franklin's extremely indirect style of diplomacy, which mostly involved receiving erotic massages. And he

JANUARY 15
1965, NEW HAVEN: In a secret report, the controversial Yale Feline Studies Lab suggests that, given the correct doses of psychedelic drugs, a black cat will eventually consider *itself* bad luck, and then will eventually drive itself insane as it constantly attempts to avoid crossing its own path.

was eventually recalled from the mission after head-butting the French foreign minister. ("I was merely trying to get the contents of my brain into his own as quickly as possible," he wrote in his diary. "But I am a Massachusetts man: plain, direct, and virtuous. I was not about to give the minister an erotic massage, no matter how much Dr. Franklin urged it.")

So you may appreciate how difficult it was for Adams to bear the ceremonial stillness of the vice presidency, whose duties mostly amount to sitting around waiting for someone to die. But he had no choice. Once the Fetus of Monarchy resigned the vice presidency early in Washington's administration,[91] Adams was the only one who could fit in the jar.

Adams stewed there angrily for eight long years, occasionally breaking ties in the Senate or cutting ribbons at a public events. (In one twist of particularly cruel fate, he was once asked to cut the ribbon at a new mill charged with producing mechanical ribbon-cutters, after which the crowd cheered in unison: "You are no longer needed!") But mostly he spent his time turning his imagination (and incredibly strong, bony forehead) toward the design of a NEW, more meaningful vice presidency.

His best-known scheme was to suggest the vice president act as a kind of evil version of the president. "Perhaps," he wrote from his jar, "we might take a cue from the infernal office itself, and emphasize less the president, and more the vice." In this conception, it was expected that the vice president would dress similarly to the president, but in an evil way (i.e., with a great, black cape). This way, the president would always have access to competing points of view, in-

---

91. In disgrace.

cluding evil ones, and in need, a
cape.[92]

But he also made several more
propositions . . . that the vice president should sit next to the president

JANUARY 16
1745, GREAT BRITAIN: Under a new
law, barbers are told that they can no longer perform surgery, unless the patient's
hair is made of flesh.

at all times, and that they should devise a secret language so that he
could tell the president exactly what to do. That maybe the vice
president should *pretend* to be the president from time to time, just
to give the president a rest (because after all, they looked so much
alike).[93] That the vice president should at least be allowed to run
Rhode Island.

In his effort to prove his usefulness, Adams even went so far as to
invent the Internet. But still Washington politely rebuffed his pro-
posals, time and again, and he turned back to his hobby of tossing
silver dollars across the Potomac. He still had it.

In 1796, however, Adams himself was finally elected president,
and suddenly his views on the vice presidency changed. At that time,
as you know, the office of vice president went automatically to the
runner-up in the general election. That was how Thomas Jefferson
became Adams's VP, even though their early friendship had with-
ered now into personal and political rivalry,[94] and even though
Adams threw Jefferson into a secret prison under the Alien and Se-
dition Acts.[95]

(That is why we refer to the office as "The Secret Prison." And
that is why, even though the vice president no longer lives in a cell

92. Adams had a lot of capes.

93. They didn't.

94. Jefferson had become a "Republican," which ironically enough meant that he believed the
federal government should not be allowed to do whatever it wanted and imprison people who
criticized it. And by ironically, here, I mean "ironically."

95. See page 488 under the heading "July 4."

JANUARY 17

1973, WASHINGTON, DC: Congress passes the Human Genetic Dignity Act, banning carnival sideshows from breeding snake-women, goat-men, and other monsters. The law also bans human cloning except for legitimate scientific experimentation and/or millionaires seeking immortality. This marked the end of the once-powerful Carny lobby in Washington and the birth of the newly powerful Deranged Millionaire lobby.

but in a beautiful miniature White House of his own, he still has to drink out of an open toilet.)

Given this new arrangement, Adams lost interest completely in empowering the vice presidency. And so it remained the ceremonial deathwatch it was designed to be, with very few major changes over the years. In 1804, the 12th Amendment did away with the runner-up scheme. And of course we have now fully abandoned the use of the Fetus Jar.[96] Since 1950, most vice presidents have been encased in Lucite until they were needed, which is much more comfortable and hygienic.

The exception, of course, is Dick Cheney, vice president to George W. Bush. While Bush is largely forgotten now, Cheney in his time was considered to have been the most powerful vice president in history. He not only exercised unprecedented influence upon Bush's policies, but also added to Adams's suggestions (and cape) a bold initiative of his own: The vice president should be draped with cobras.

But whether this bodes a lasting change in the vice presidency or not remains to be seen. As an office with few formal obligations, its purpose is written and rewritten by each who holds it. But it is almost certain Cheney will take the cobras with him when he goes. They are the only creatures he loves.

---

96. As is tradition, it is currently kept in the home of Al Gore.

WERE YOU AWARE OF IT? "PRESIDENT MONDALE"

JANUARY 18

1979, VIRGINIA: Richmond admits that, since the last strange rain, all of Richmond's precipitation has been traditional and water-based.

As you know, the vice president is but a "heartbeat away from the presidency." But were you aware that because Jimmy Carter suffered a mild cardiac arrhythmia, Walter Mondale was technically president, OFTEN FORTY TIMES A DAY?

THEY KEEP SUCH SECRETS IN ORDER TO PROTECT YOU!

FAST FACTS ABOUT TEDDY ROOSEVELT THAT HAVE BEEN CIRCULATED ON THE INTERNET

We've all gotten those e-mails that have been circulating about Teddy Roosevelt, retelling the strange feats and amazing physical prowess of our 26th president.[97] But how many of these astonishing tales are true? Here is the answer: ALL OF THEM.

— Caught up in the spiritualism craze of the early twentieth century, Roosevelt participated in more than thirty séances—AS THE TABLE.

— Roosevelt began every day by wrestling his entire cabinet and throwing them out the window. He accidentally killed Secretary of War Elihu Root this way.

---

97. Some say our most 26ieth.

JANUARY 19

1953, HOLLYWOOD: Lucy and Ricky Ricardo's son, "Little Ricky," is born on *I Love Lucy*. The program had incorporated Lucille Ball's actual pregnancy into its story line, and the decision to depict her condition with relative candor was provocative at the time, as many Americans in the 1950s did not know what sex or pregnancy was. Moreover, because they had always seen Lucy and Ricky retiring to separate beds in incredibly intricate three-piece pajamas, a large portion of the audience presumed that Lucy and Ricky were merely friends, and that Lucy was getting grotesquely fat.

© Bettmann/Corbis

Figure 50: Lucy Goes into Labor

All was revealed, however, during the historic "Home Birth" episode, in which Ball actually gave birth live on television without medication. She was coached by Fred and Ethel Mertz while Ricky uttered the immortal line, "Lucy! You got some pushin' to do!"

— When offered the "Presidential Option" to cover up any murder in the White House,[98] he GUFFAWED MIGHTILY and insisted that he could easily bring Root back to life VIA STRENUOUS EXERCISE AND BLACK MAGIC.

— HE WAS RIGHT!

— When rejected by the mainstream Republican Party, Roosevelt created the "BULL MOOSE" Party. Initially, only moose were allowed to join, as Roosevelt admired their solid, stubborn nature, their hatred of trusts, and their ability to LEGALLY HAVE SEX WITH FEMALE MOOSE.

— LATER, PARTY MEMBERSHIP WOULD BE OPEN TO ANYONE WHO COULD GROW ANTLERS.

— Only JANE ADDAMS could manage it!

---

98. Please see the film by my friend Wesley Snipes, *Murder at 1600*.

Figure 51: Jane Addams,
Pre-Antlers

JANUARY 20
TODAY IS INAUGURATION DAY, though
it was not always so.

Prior to 1936, presidents were inau-
gurated in a private ritual in the Capitol
rotunda. The president-elect would be
blindfolded and stripped to his waist. The
chief justice would then tattoo the text of
the Constitution onto his chest, so that he
might never forget it. While this process
would begin on January 20, it typically did
not end until March or April, factoring in
blood loss and occasional comas, at which
point the president would give a two-day
speech.[a]

As he approached his second inauguration in 1920, Franklin Roosevelt decided
to toss out this old tradition. "I ask you,"
he said to the Inaugural Committee, "how
many times must a man be tattooed with
the entire Constitution in his life?"

If he had bothered to read the writing
below his own left nipple, Roosevelt would
have known the answer was "only twice."
But all the same, he condensed the pro-
ceedings to a simple oath on a single cold,
miserable, January day, and he thought-
fully moved the ceremony outside, so that
everyone could hate it as much as he did.

a. Except in the case of William Henry Harrison. Please see page 289 in Table 21.

— TR's daughter, the spirited
Alice Roosevelt, would regu-
larly STRANGLE PONIES
for the delight of the White
House press corps. WHO DO
YOU THINK TAUGHT
HER *THAT* TRICK?

— The "Teddy Bear" was named
after Teddy Roosevelt because of his LOVE OF BEAR
MEAT and the fact that he was covered in fur.

— Teddy Roosevelt had a HOOK FOR A HAND. But
then, you already knew this.

— Teddy Roosevelt originally built the American Museum
of Natural History as a kind of lepidopterist's "killing
jar." But instead of butterflies, he put dinosaurs inside
and starved them UNTIL THEY WERE SKELETONS.

JANUARY 21
2003, ON COMPUTERS: Microsoft spell check begins automatically capitalizing the word "Internet." This unprompted development is considered to be the first documented evidence of computer self-awareness and self-importance.

— He did the same thing with lepidopterists. THEIR BLEACHED SKULLS AND PATHETIC LITTLE NETS WERE KEPT AS TROPHIES IN HIS OFFICE.

— Roosevelt installed a nine-person, gold-plated hot tub in the Oval Office and filled it with scalding hot oil. HE CALLED IT A "BULLY BATH" and claimed it cured him forever of SHINGLES.

— Roosevelt was originally from New York, but HE SHAT PENNSYLVANIA.

— Roosevelt once had a presidential aide who was suffering from the dread disease tuberculosis. TR organized a staring contest and STARED THE TB RIGHT OUT OF HIM.

— Together, TR and his son, Kermit, explored Brazil's River of Doubt. When they were done with it, it was renamed THE RIVER OF UNQUESTIONABLE CERTAINTY.

— TR named his son Kermit. THAT SHOWED HIM!

— Roosevelt died fighting an old lion and was buried in Mount Rushmore, WHERE HIS GIGANTIC, FOSSIL-IZED FACE STILL STARES OUT OVER THE COUN-TRY HE BEAT INTO SHAPE TO THIS VERY DAY.

WERE YOU AWARE OF IT? "PRESIDENT BOOTH"

Only due to a recent Freedom of Information Act request do we now know that, from 1861 to 1863, ABRAHAM LINCOLN WAS ANOTHER PERSON.

Specifically, during these years, Lincoln was portrayed by the famed actor Edwin Booth, who was supposedly touring England at the time.

Just after the beginning of the CIVIL WAR, Lincoln's faith in his generals was shaken, and so he made an unusual choice: to command the Union armies from BEHIND ENEMY LINES. In order to spy on the enemy unnoticed, he shaved his beard and acquired a stoop, lowering his height to a mere seven-foot-nine so that he would not be perceived as a monster. Thus he traveled from slave state to slave state, observing the movements of the Confederate armies, always presenting himself as a simple traveling homosexual by the name of John F. Kennedy.

The beard, meanwhile, was preserved at the White House to be worn by Booth as his own disguise. It also contained within it a primitive, beard-mounted radio transmitter, thus allowing Lincoln to direct

JANUARY 22

1979, WISCONSIN: As Richmond's skies remain clear and unstrange, Milwaukee reports a beautiful summer shower of schadenfreude. It makes a kind of music as it falls, like the sound of a faraway oboe. It covers the whole town, twinkling on car windshields, tapping out messages on tin roofs, and collecting in wells and rain barrels. Some of this collected schadenfreude will later be used as the signature ingredient in the beer known as "Milwaukee's Best."[a]

a. Short for: "Milwaukee Is Best."

Figure 52: Edwin Booth Performs His Uncanny Abraham Lincoln Impersonation

CONTINUED

JANUARY 23

1910, VIENNA: Sigmund Freud first treats the Russian aristocrat known as the "Wolf Man." Over many years of analysis, Freud makes several key discoveries about wolf-men, including their sensitivity to silver and *Aconitum vulparia* (wolfsbane), and the fact that they cannot have bowel movements without the aid of an enema. Treatment ended in 1919 after the mauling incident.

affairs of state from the field. The Emancipation Proclamation was dictated to Booth from Lincoln in this way, and it is accepted that the depth and beauty of the Gettysburg Address came from Lincoln's having seen war and slavery firsthand (as opposed to Booth, who had drafted his own version of the address that mainly dwelt on the Gettysburg area's reputation for fine furniture manufacture and some lines from *As You Like It*).

It is unclear why Booth bothered to write a draft at all. It was the only instance of him actually performing any presidential duties, and perhaps lends credence to the controversial claim that, by the end of his fraudulent tenure, he had gone mad and had come to believe he *was* Lincoln. According to this theory, Booth refused to give up the charade until Lincoln himself came to Gettysburg and won back his own name in a rail-splitting contest. But this is only

Figure 53: The President's Cabinet Listens to "The Beard"

CONTINUED

widely propounded by lumber-jacks and other rail-splitting enthusiasts.

Booth later would flee to England, largely in order to avoid the wrath of his brother, John Wilkes Booth, who had vowed to kill him. Sadly, as it is well known, it was Abraham Lincoln—the true Lincoln—who died in Booth's stead at Ford's Theater during a production of *Our American Cousin*, starring Tony Curtis.

COULD YOU HAVE EVER GUESSED?

JANUARY 24

41 BC, ROME: The mad emperor Caligula is assassinated by his own horse. He was hoof-stabbed—the classic method of equine assassination. Incitatus, the stallion that Caligula had named for a senator, began to plot against his master when Caligula would not make him co-emperor. But the horse's mad plans for power were then foiled by Caligula's own Praetorian Guard, who could not understand Incitatus's whinnying, and so they killed and ate him.

JANUARY 25

852, ROME: Pope John VIII is revealed to be a woman when, while mounting a horse, he accidentally bears a child. "Pope Joan" was not the only non-white non-male to hold the title: It is largely believed that Pope Screech was a mole-man, and Pope Peter, Paul, and Mary was a hermaphrodite. But if I say any more, the Church will hunt us down.

THE FUTURE
AND OTHER
SUPERSTITIONS

JANUARY 26
1979, VIRGINIA: Still suffering a strange rain drought, Richmond hires Champ Stanley, occult meteorologist.

JANUARY 27

1888, WASHINGTON, DC: The National Geographic Society is founded with the purpose of making Americans more comfortable with nakedness.

HOW TO TELL THE FUTURE: MORE OMENS AND PORTENTS FOR THE COMING YEAR

In my previous book, I advised you that, when it comes to the future, it is best to rely on the dispassionate, scientific calculations of the actuaries, for they have many complex tables and charts of omens and portents, and what do you have? Maybe one chart? FORGET IT.

Yet though I am a man of science, that doesn't mean that the witches didn't know what they were doing. After all, they conjured the whole city of Salem out of a cornstarch slurry, a cat's paw, and the bones of 1,000 Puritans, and that's pretty impressive. Not surprisingly, the witches were accused of sorcery and dealt with harshly at the time.[99] But now that we look back, we realize that Puritan bones are actually an incredibly durable building material (we call it "rebar").

Indeed, much of what we now deride as "superstition," "folk wisdom," and "fairy-tale bullroar" was actually a kind of proto-science. It was through careful observation over countless fall slaughters that the old Scandinavian farmers learned that the size and shape of a fresh-killed pig's spleen can predict the weather.[100] It was through repeated experimentation that the seventeenth-century housewife determined that a paste of goose grease, nutmeg, and black pepper will easily blind a cat.[101] And say what you will about the practice, it was only through drowning witches in the increasingly icy New

---

99. Please see page 496 under the heading "What to Expect While Serving as a Juror."

100. For they know what the ancients did: The entrails of an animal tell a story of how that animal lived, from which we may extrapolate what is yet to come. (Also, animals know the future and psychically transmit that information to their organs.)

101. Which in turn would cause it to rain.

England lakes and rivers that those same strong-boned Puritans accidentally discovered the early principles of cryonics that would make them so wealthy later on.

JANUARY 28

1878, NEW HAVEN: The *Yale Daily News,* the nation's oldest college daily newspaper, releases its first English-language edition. Prior to that, it had been published only in the ancient, universal language of God, known only to members of the Secret World Government and their personal newspaper-readers.

Of course, this intuitive, semimagical approach was uneven in its results, and many of the old folkways are simply ridiculous.[102]

Figure 54: The "House of the Seven Freeze Tubes," Salem, MA

But still, there is a germ of truth behind much of the folk magic of our ancestors that we would be unwise to ignore today. "Don't toss out the baby with the bathwater," goes the old saying. And it is true that soaking in baby-steeped bathwater is really the only way to chase out the eczema demons.

So if you are stuck in the wild without an actuary, you can still predict future events the way the old Yankee farmers did: by smoking a big corncob pipe of "homegrown" marijuana and just staring, staring at the world around you.

---

102. Leeches, for example, do not actually suck blood, but SPIT IT BACK INTO YOU.

JANUARY 29
1845, PHILADELPHIA: Edgar Allan Poe
publishes "The Raven," an ode to a stuffed
bird that would later be adapted to television screens as *That's So Raven.*

SOME LESS SCIENTIFIC METHODS OF TELLING THE FUTURE THAT ACTUALLY WORK

— IF YOU WERE TO SEE A WOOLY BEAR CATER-
PILLAR, for example, and you did not observe a corresponding PORTENT with which to make a valid,
scientific prediction of the future,[103] what would you do?
Probably you would just crush it out of spite, right?

NOT IF YOU WERE AN OLD YANKEE
FARMER. Because in that case you would have
learned on your pappy's bony knee that the size of the
orange band on a wooly bear caterpillar serves as an
astoundingly accurate indicator of the coming winter:
The larger the band, the longer the winter.

— ALTERNATELY, you could just ask the caterpillar
about the future. For the old Yankee farmer knows, if
you smoke enough "homegrown" marijuana, the caterpillar WILL TALK TO YOU. And then you can go
ahead and crush it.

— IF YOU HEAR THE FROGS CROAKING EARLY
IN THE MORNING, it is going to rain.

— BUT IF YOU HEAR *TOADS* CROAKING, it is
going to rain frogs.

---

103. Please see the table of omens and portents on page 32 of *The Areas of My Expertise.*

— IF YOU SEE TWO SNAKES
ON THE SAME MORNING,
there's going to be a snake
fight.

— IF THE COWS ARE LYING
DOWN, then it is going to
rain heavily.

— UNLESS: there is someone
going around drugging cows. In which case: FAIR TO
PARTLY CLOUDY.

JANUARY 30
HAPPY BIRTHDAY, PHIL COLLINS!
He was born in 1951, though his coming
was foreseen. Ten years earlier, the Oracle
of London[a] had publicly predicted the
birth of a singer who was also a drummer
(an insane proposition), saying she could
"feel it coming in the air tonight." Collins would later forge the prophecy of his
own birth into a hit song, because he is an
egomaniac.

a. The Oracle of London, as you know, was
a half-blind, autistic young woman named
Sussudio.

— HERE'S an old folk saying:
   "IF THE OAK FLOWERS BEFORE THE ASH,
      we shall have a splash
   IF THE ASH FLOWERS BEFORE THE OAK,
      we shall have a soak
   IF THEY FLOWER SIMULTANEOUSLY,
      your children are all going to die!"

— IF THE MONTH OF MARCH COMES IN "LIKE A
LION," it will go out "LIKE A LAMB." That is to say, the
month will be slaughtered early, while "the meat is sweet."

— HOWEVER, IF MARCH COMES IN "LIKE A
LAMB," then a lion will appear on your property before
the end of the month and terrorize you and your family.

— IF A GROUNDHOG SEES ITS SHADOW, it means
the sun is unusually low in the sky. Thus we will either

JANUARY 31
1949, ON THE AIR: *These Are My Children,* the first soap opera, is broadcast. Set in the fictional city of Chicago, the first episodes were rudimentary, largely consisting of an Irish-American widow introducing her children to various people. But things get interesting by episode 19, when it is revealed that the woman's nineteenth child is actually the evil twin of her eighteenth. Both children were played by a young Robert Culp.

have a longer winter, or else the sun is about to crash into the earth. There is no way of knowing which. Don't ask the groundhog. Even if you do manage to capture him, he won't tell you, no matter how high you are.

HOW TO TELL THE FUTURE
USING A PIG'S SPLEEN

First, get a pig's spleen. They are often just lying around. Please note to only use spleens from pigs killed in fall or winter. Spleens from spring-slaughtered pigs tend to be bitter in taste and deceitful in manner and WILL ATTEMPT TO CONFUSE YOU WITH THEIR LIES. Lay out the spleen and mark it into six equal sections. The comparative thickness, color, and texture of each section will

Figure 55: A Good Spleen   Figure 56: An Evil Spleen

forecast the weather for the coming six months. But a really good pig-splenologist will be able to glean other hints of what the future holds. If you see a black mark on the spleen, for example, it means you will soon be visited by a stranger. If you find a

FEBRUARY 1
1913, NEW YORK: Grand Central Terminal is completed. Few New Yorkers know that the illuminated constellations in the ceiling of the main concourse are actually arranged backwards, as if viewed from space. As well, the vast marble floor was originally designed to be a giant Ouija board. And the Oyster Bar is a secret tunnel to hell.

gold coin embedded in the spleen, you will soon come into wealth. If you eat the spleen without cooking it or refrigerating it properly, you are probably going to get very sick and die.

Thanks to Pino's Meats of Greenwich Village, New York, I was able to acquire a pig spleen, which I reproduce for you here, with the proper interpretations attached.

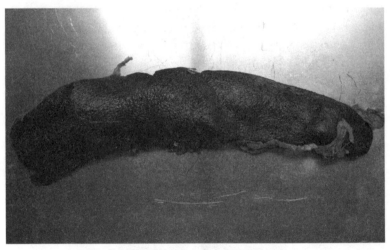

Figure 57: The Pig's Spleen: Beautiful Organ of Truth

Normally this would be in color, but my publisher balked once again. Perhaps in the special CD-ROM you will get to see the spleen in color. Or look at your own spleen as a guide. Or color it in with red marker.

FEBRUARY 2

1977, ON THE AIR: President Jimmy Carter addresses the nation while wearing a cardigan. His message—that Americans should turn down the thermostat to conserve energy—prompts the accusation that he was never able to shake: that he was in the pocket of Big Cardigan.

TODAY IS GROUNDHOG DAY. If the groundhog predicts that the sun is going to crash into earth,[a] please see your local government Sun Crisis Office for instructions on where to find the nearest suicide center.

a. Please see page 329 under the heading "Some Less Scientific Methods of Telling the Future That Actually Work."

TABLE 22: YOUR TWELVE-MONTH SPLEENCAST	
DESCRIPTION	**PREPARE FOR . . .**
SPLEEN REGION: JANUARY / FEBRUARY	
thin, smooth, pink	Light rain, persistent damp.
SPLEEN REGION: MARCH / APRIL	
thicker, smooth, mottled	Wind and rain and melting ice caps.
SPLEEN REGION: MAY / JUNE	
thin, rough, red	Cloudy, hazy, all crops fail. Humans, trapped between rising oceans and massive dust storms, make Columbus, Ohio, the capital of the Remaining Inhabitable Regions of America (RIRA).
SPLEEN REGION: JULY / AUGUST	
moderately thick, smooth, red	Bleary sun. The waterfront of Columbus is fortified against the polar bears (displaced and hungry) and the Pennsylvanians (deformed and hungry). Construction of the Dome commences.
SPLEEN REGION: SEPTEMBER / OCTOBER	
very thick, very rough	Showers, foot riots. Those who are impure are cast out of the Dome. You will hear their horrible screams. And then: nothing.
SPLEEN REGION: NOVEMBER / DECEMBER	
fiery red	Cold, so cold. We cannot hold out much longer. They are coming . . . They are comnasndmz kvjagu;u jnm. . . .

HERE THE PIG SPLEEN ENDS. Unless you find another pig spleen, I think we can presume that the future is over.

MORE WISDOM OF THE
HIGH OLD FARMER

"A RULE OF THUMB"

IF YOU ARE WALKING IN MAS-
SACHUSETTS and you suddenly
realize you are no longer married to
your same-sex partner, you can be
sure you have crossed over into
NEW HAMPSHIRE.

FEBRUARY 3

1979, VIRGINIA: After a long period
of meditation, secret rituals, and nightly
"strangecasts" on Channel 6 Eyewitness
News, Champ Stanley, occult meteorologist,
finally succeeds in summoning a thunder-
storm of fairies. As thunder rumbled high
above, hidden in weird yellow clouds, the
tiny creatures fell and fluttered throughout the town. They flew into cars and open
windows, laughing in people's ears and
whispering secrets to children. And even
after they all flew down into the sewer
and were gone, all the manholes and
drainage grates in town glowed for weeks
after. Champ Stanley became Richmond's
favorite local TV personality—even more
popular than consumer advocate Al "The
Shamer" Starnes.

TABLE 23: SOME LUCK SIGNS	
GOOD LUCK	**BAD LUCK**
An owl defecates on you. A dove defecates on you. Anything pees on you.	A grown man defecates on you.

SOME FOLK REMEDIES

Hey: They're worth a try![104]

IF YOU HAVE A TOOTHACHE, place some tobacco between the affected tooth and the gum to numb the pain.
Continue treatment until addicted. Seek no further
treatment.

---

104. NOTE: They are *not* worth a try. DO NOT TRY THEM. Please see a doctor.

FEBRUARY 4
1789, ELECTORAL, NY: The first Electors correctly predict that George Washington will become president of the United
States. They psychically ask if they can
attend his inauguration in Manhattan, but
they are told to stay hidden in their vats.

IF YOU HAVE BOILS, make a poultice of goose grease, cornmeal, hot water, and vinegar. Rub this all over your face. Seek no further treatment.

IF YOU HAVE A CHEST COLD, rub a black cat on your chest for about twenty-five minutes. Seek no further treatment.

IF YOU HAVE ARTHRITIS, rub a black cat with an old bootlace. Tie the bootlace around the affected joint. Tie a nutmeg seed to the end of the string. Seek no further treatment.

IF YOU ARE HORRIBLY SCRATCHED BY A CAT, maybe stop rubbing the cat for a while. Cover yourself with goose grease. Seek no further treatment.

IF YOU HAVE WARTS, paste a toad to the affected area. Make a lard-fly poultice and feed it to the toad. If the wart has not disappeared by the time the toad has died, start again with a better toad. Seek no further treatment.

IF YOU HAVE ECZEMA AND YOU DO NOT HAVE A BABY TO PUT IN YOUR BATH, make a salve of cat fur, candle wax, goose grease, boiled carrots, and cornmeal. Eat this, and then vomit into a sack. If you can get someone to open the sack, then theoretically they should catch your eczema and you should be cured.

THEORETICALLY. In any case, seek no further treatment.

IF YOU HAVE LOST A FINGER, numb the pain with a poultice of goose grease and pine needles. Leave the poultice on the finger stump until it becomes sticky. Now find another finger. Stick it on there and seek no further treatment.

IF YOU ARE BLEEDING FREELY FROM A DEEP WOUND, steep some nutmeg in hot rosewater and add honey. Drink this tea slowly. Take your time. Enjoy it. Relax. Seek no further treatment.

IF YOU HAVE CANCER, make a chemo-poultice of goose grease and anti-cancer medicines. Rub it all over the affected area nine times a day. Chew on a pinecone. Boil an onion and put it in a sock and wear it around your neck, changing the onion nine times a day. Chew on a twig of sarsaparilla. Keep changing the onion. Keep applying the poultice. Think positive. Only drink hot water. Eat the tongue of a black cat. Think positive. Together we're going to beat this. Continue until end of life.

FEBRUARY 5

1938, ON THE AIR: Abbott and Costello perform "Who's on First?" on *The Kate Smith Radio Hour*. While the famous "confusion-over-baseball" routine would become their trademark, "Who's on First?" had actually been a vaudeville staple for decades, and in fact traces its roots to an ancient Mesopotamian comedy hit called "Backgammon."

SOME HANGOVER CURES
INVOLVING GIN

If you have drunk too much the night before, I have found the fruit of the juniper bush, combined with other natural botanicals, to be a helpful medicine, especially when they are dissolved in alcohol.

Here are some of my favorite hangover remedies using only natural ingredients and a simple working knowledge of the healing plants that surround us.

1. Pour one part "Juniper in Alcohol Solution" into a tall glass of ice. Add 6 parts tonic water. Stir and drink.

   Ancient wisdom of the herbalist: It is said among the Quechua of Peru that the quinine in the tonic water is a natural muscle relaxant and will also cure your malaria!

2. Combine one part "Juniper Solution" and one part sweet vermouth and one part Campari in a tumbler of ice. Stir and strain into a glass.

   Ancient wisdom of the herbalist: The aromatic cascarilla bark in the Campari is also said to aid digestion, relieve flatulence, and stimulate the mucous membranes!

3. Pour 3–4 oz of "Juniper Solution" into a glass. Add several strong dashes of Angostura Bitters.

   Ancient wisdom of the herbalist: The herbal medicinal compound known as "Angostura Bitters" was first concocted by Dr. Johann Sigert, Surgeon General to Simón Bolívar, to help cure his army of gout. To this day, the army of Bolivia is largely goutless!

4. Combine 6 parts "Juniper Solution" with 1 part dry vermouth and plenty of ice. Stir
and strain into a glass. Gar-
nish with a Percocet tablet.

FEBRUARY 7
1978, BURBANK, CA: On *The Gong
Show,* the Unknown Comic introduces his
son, the Unknown Comic Jr., who is portrayed by a young Spike Jonze with a bag
over his head.

Ancient wisdom of the herbalist: "Percocet" is a powerful narcotic!

THINGS TO KNOW ABOUT BABIES

Before we had books to tell us how to raise our babies, we were
afraid of them, and understandably so. Babies are bizarre creatures
with gigantic heads who feed on our very bodies and poop utter
chaos . . . whose screams and rattling chains[105] haunt our nights like
ghosts, reminding us of the horrible frailty that bookends our short
lives. It's no surprise that we would attempt to swaddle them safely
in a blanket of folklore and familiar superstitions such as these.

— A baby who is born with teeth will be a financial success . . . EVEN WHILE HE IS STILL A BABY.

— A baby who is made to wear false teeth will be a financial failure . . . SO DON'T BOTHER. Trust me: It
doesn't work.

— A baby born with a fever will become a blacksmith.

— A baby who smiles at himself in the mirror will become an actor. If he was also born with teeth, you can

---

105. Babies love chains.

FEBRUARY 8

1978, LAKE WINNIPESAUKEE, NH: SPACE INVADERS game console arrives in the United States. A defining classic of early arcade gaming, few know that the game was originally designed as a training simulation for the Army's new "Rolling Back and Forth Missile Launcher" (RB-FML). However, the game's tactical purpose was scrapped when it was determined that, when they invade, the Space Invaders would probably not just slowly drop down to Earth in a two-dimensional plane, and the RBFML was eventually phased out in favor the GALAGA defense system.

go ahead and retire. BUT I WARN YOU: You have a scary baby.

— A baby who frowns at himself in the mirror will become a writer.

— A baby who hates himself in the mirror will become a writer of short stories.

— A baby born with clothes on will be no trouble at all.

— A baby born with a tiger's eyes will either become either a famous boxer or the Antichrist.

REMEMBER: A baby only cries when another baby, somewhere in the world, is silent.

AND: A mother who keeps her baby's caul with her will have good luck . . . UNTIL THE BABY GROWS UP AND DISCOVERS IT IN HER PURSE. Then they will both realize it's just creepy.

WERE YOU AWARE OF IT?
"A SWEEP IS AS LUCKY AS LUCKY CAN BE"

As you may know from the movie *Mary Poppins,* if you shake hands with a chimney sweep, then you will have good luck for the rest of the day, and your father will finally love you.

But were you aware that in Poland, the women of the house

CONTINUED

traditionally PINCH chimney sweeps in order to squeeze the luck out of them? It is so. Other traditions include kissing a chimney sweep, shaving him, stealing all his clothes, licking him, and drinking a bottle of his sweat.

FEBRUARY 9
2003, NEW YORK: No matter what you may have read on the Internet, I did not sell marijuana to Ben "The Dell Dude" Curtis on this day. I WAS OUT OF THE COUNTRY AT THE TIME.

However, I would not advise kidnapping the chimney sweep and imprisoning him in your chimney. YES, you will have good luck for at least as long as the chimney sweep lives. However, you won't be able to use your fireplace again without considerable screaming.

BEAR IT IN MIND, GUV'NOR!

ADVICE, HOW-TO, AND MISCELLANEOUS

FEBRUARY 11

1980, VIRGINIA: For the first time since arriving in Richmond, Champ Stanley does not appear on the Channel 6 Eyewitness News broadcast. It is explained that he is out of town on "an errand." Al Starnes reads the Richmond forecast in his stead. According to the radar: butterflies by noon.

FEBRUARY 12
1980, WISCONSIN: In a terrible, unexpected tragedy, Milwaukee is destroyed by a violent downpour of skulls. It is later determined by a group of FEMA experts that the skulls (and some decomposing heads) somehow came from cemeteries throughout the Milwaukee region. What's more, the vast majority of people's homes were destroyed by the heads of their own family members: waves and waves of successive generations, from ancient ancestors to recently deceased parents and siblings, falling from the sky relentlessly for twenty-one hours. Richmond sends no aid.

HOW TO DEAL WITH SOME COMMON INFESTATIONS

Whether you live in the country or live in the city, probably you have woken up in the middle of the night and discovered that all of the feathers in your pillow have been replaced with horrible, biting red ants.

As much as we want to believe we have conquered nature, the triumph of civilization is an illusion that is shattered every time we see a cockroach in our kitchen, find a raccoon in our attic, or discover that our walls are full of beavers. Perversely, there are those who even invite nature INTO their homes, in the form of houseplants, such as the dreaded oxalis.[106] Fighting such pests is a losing war typically left to the professional exterminator and his arsenal of complex chemicals and killing fogs.

But over time, these approaches breed a resistance to pesticides among the very creatures you are trying to destroy. And occasionally, the exterminators themselves "go native" and start living in your crawl spaces.[107]

---

106. Personally, I never could understand the appeal of this practice. My only guess is that, due to some mental problem, some people just enjoy being silently mocked by that which will soon enough use our brain and bone and muscle for food. For nature is patient, and as hard as we may fight to exterminate the ants, for example, we spend just as much time exterminating ourselves. And when that deed is finally done, then nature will return, as if we never existed. The plants will not remember us, and the ants will finally get back to their simple business of ruling the earth by lifting things they really shouldn't be able to lift.

107. It is said that there are now several generations of exterminators living within the walls and attics of the famed Dakota building on Manhattan's Upper West Side. Residents of the posh address report that they will often go into the kitchen at night for a snack only to find two or three exterminators pawing through their refrigerator, stealing cakes and beer. As soon as the light hits their pale skin, they scatter back into the walls. The strange thing is, they never go into Yoko Ono's apartment. Indeed, her neighbors have discovered they get some relief from the exterminators by putting a fake Yoko Ono in their kitchen, or plugging a device into the wall that replicates Yoko Ono's voice. There is no question that it helps. But they still have to deal with the droppings.

But why not fight nature *with* nature? Indeed, there is much you can
do on your own to keep your home

FEBRUARY 13
1980, VIRGINIA: Champ Stanley is back
on the air.

pest-free using just what you have around the house, plus a little
diligence and, surprisingly often, fire.

MICE

No creature better evokes our ambivalence about the natural world
than the common mouse. Mice are cute when they are hanging around
amusement parks in tuxedoes or being fed to snakes. They are not
cute, however, when they are defecating in your silverware drawer or
swarming all over you while you are trying to watch television. Does
that make humans hypocrites? Or mice? Only the philosophers can
answer that one. Meanwhile, here is how you exterminate them (mice,
not philosophers).

First, you will have to lay traps. DO NOT get the wire-spring
traps you remember from old cartoons. They are very dangerous,

Figure 58: Cute!

FEBRUARY 14

1898, CALIFORNIA: Newspaper mag-
nate William Randolph Hearst holds a re-
hearsal of the Spanish-American War on
the grounds of his San Simeon estate.

Teddy Roosevelt, who had stopped by the
Hearst Private Zoo in order to bludgeon
some zebras to death, observed the mock
battles and phony charges up a papier-
mâché San Juan Hill, and called Hearst's
spectacle a "bully little fake war." He
urged Hearst to make it a reality.

Hearst, who knew that war with Spain
would send his newspaper sales soaring,
simply smiled knowingly. "Rosebud," he
said (for that was Hearst's nickname for
Roosevelt), "you furnish the bludgeoned
zebras, and I'll furnish the war."

especially to children. Instead, use glue traps. These are essentially fly-paper for mice, and in case of an accident they can safely be removed from a child's foot using surgery.

When baiting your traps, do not fall prey to the old stereotype about cheese. Mice actually hate cheese, and if they see a trap baited with it, they will laugh at your expense. Try peanut butter instead. But not crunchy. I REPEAT: NOT CRUNCHY.

Another popular option is the humane trap, which is an intricate contraption involving a bathtub and a marble which, after forty-five minutes, slowly lowers a cage onto the mouse. These have the benefit of trapping the mice alive. Then you can let them go in a meadow or feed them to your snake or just toss the whole contraption into the fire.

Finally, a little prevention goes a long way: Make sure your doors and windows are well sealed and your kitchen is clean, and try not to smear yourself all over with peanut butter. (Unless it is crunchy peanut butter, of course. But then what would be the point?)

RATS

Unlike mice, rats are never cute. Do not listen to the Goth kid at the pet store: They are not nurturing parents or devoted companions. They are disgusting wingless pigeons that sleep in your toilet and give you the plague. You must kill them all. Do it with fire.

SILVERFISH

You are crazy. There are no fish living in your walls. There are, however, axolotls living your pipes.

FEBRUARY 15
1898, OFF THE COAST OF HAVANA:
The actual Spanish-American War begins
when U.S. dreadnought *Maine* mysteriously
explodes—in precisely the same manner
that a three-quarter-sized *Maine* exploded
and sank in William Randolph Hearst's
indoor pool not twenty-four hours before.
COINCIDENCE?

Figure 59:
Do Not Look at This Image.

AXOLOTLS[108]

Do you know what an axolotl is? It is a kind of prehistoric half-salamander, half-puppy that is kept in some countries as a disgusting pet.

If you manage to get axolotls into your pipes, you will have real trouble, as their fat, hairless bodies will cause blockages and their bizarre, external frill-like gills will make your water taste uncanny. Also, if you look at one too long, you become one. So if you see one peering up at you from the drain in your bathroom sink, DON'T LOOK AT IT. Just stab at it blindly with your bathroom knife.

TERMITES

Monkeys with long sticks always work for me.

SCOTTIE DOGS

The dogs themselves are not so much the problem. It's their flaky dander, and their tunnels. I recommend fire.

---

108. Please see page 347, under the heading "Were You Aware of It? The Literary Axolotl."

FEBRUARY 16

2007, NEW YORK CITY: As is becoming increasingly common in my life, I hang out with some celebrities. Tonight, I partied with Food Network personality Sandra Lee and famous beard model Zach Galifianakis at the Jose Cuervo "Early Spring" party celebrating their new margarita mix. Don't believe me? Check it out:

Figure 60: Note as Well the Famous Book-Jacket Designer Elizabeth Connor.

TIDES

Tides cannot be completely eliminated, but they can be beaten back. Your local hardware store should carry a tide stick or paddle. Plan to beat back the tide twice each day, for about five hours at a time. If that doesn't work, fire.

REPLICANTS

There are all sorts of folk remedies for a replicant infestation, including the Voigt-Kampff test, or spreading replicant powder around. But this is one of those rare situations where you really do need a professional. There's nothing for it but to call in a Blade Runner.

WERE YOU AWARE OF IT?
"THE LITERARY AXOLOTL"

On the subject of axolotls, were you aware the Argentine novelist Julio Cortázar wrote a famous poem about these disgusting creatures?

It goes like this:

"Tap, tap the ketchup bottle
None will come, then axolotl."

THIS POEM ALSO CAN BE READ BACKWARDS!

HOW TO COOK OWLS

It's simple.

1. Look into its eyes.
2. Kill it.
3. Remove the thing that makes it purr.
4. Remove its clockwork innards.
5. Rub it all over with myrtle and salt.
6. Sacrifice 100 goats to Athena.
7. Don't discard the little bolus of mouse bones you find in its tummy—that's a delicacy!

Then cook as you would crows.

FEBRUARY 17

1864, SOUTH CAROLINA: The Union sloop *Housatonic* is sunk in Charleston Harbor by the Confederate submarine *Hunley*. Soon after, the *Hunley* itself is sunk, air-torpedoed by the French mercenary zeppelin *Pilâtre de Rozier,* which had been hired by the Union. Some historians believe that the *Pilâtre de Rozier* could

---

WERE YOU AWARE OF IT?
"THE DREADED OXALIS"

The oxalis, or wood sorrel, plant is photosensitive. Not only does it dislike being photographed, but when night comes, its broad, cloverlike leaves slowly close in on themselves, like little leafy claws. It will stay that way for the duration of the night. No one knows exactly what it is doing, but most experts agree it is either seething or plotting. When sunlight returns, the leaves will slowly unclench again and wait for its prey.

Figure 61: The Oxalis, Mid-Scheme

CONTINUED

easily have saved the men of the *Housatonic* had the zeppelin not spent so much time letting the guiding-bats get a sonar lock on the *Hunley*'s position. But the French captain was unapologetic: "I did not come here to save the lives of seamen. I came to kill subs."

> THIS IS ABSOLUTELY TRUE, and I have many sleepless nights and hours and hours of videotape to prove it.

HOW TO REMEMBER ANY NAME,
ESPECIALLY THE NAME "JOHN HODGMAN"

For many years I struggled with a terrible and embarrassing problem: I would be introduced to someone, and I would forget that person's name. Even if the person said his or her name slowly and loudly, and even if I repeated that person's name even more slowly, and even more loudly, I would instantly forget it. This is probably because I don't care about other people and secretly suspect that they are all robots, and I am the only person who is really alive.

But whatever the cause, this very bad habit became a source of personal and professional embarrassment.

To an extent, I could hide my problem by giving my new acquaintance little nicknames like "friend," or "pal," or "commodore," or "hey."

After a time, however, this became untenable. What if the person is an actual commodore, or at least *was* an actual commodore, until he sunk one too many ships? Hypothetically, that would be a very, very awkward situation that might cause a former commodore to get very angry precisely at the moment that you were hoping to make a new business acquaintance and get some long-sought sextant training.

Thus, I developed a foolproof memory system, which I have been pleased to share with countless people all over the country, many of

whom HAD NAMES, whose names I
STILL REMEMBER TO THIS
DAY.[109]

Here's how you do it. Say you go
to a cocktail party or a disgraced ad-
miral's convention and a young
woman introduces herself. For the
sake of argument, let's say her name
is JOHN HODGMAN.

FIRST: LISTEN as your companion says her name. I mean RE-
ALLY LISTEN. Don't just pretend to listen by moving your ears
back and forth. I know we all do this, but it's time to stop.

SECOND: If you did not catch your companion's name the first
time, try calling them "PHIL." You may be surprised to learn that,
statistically speaking, most people are named Phil. Even women. So
it's worth a shot.

THIRD: Start with the first name. When you hear it, REPEAT
IT. If it's one syllable, like "JOHN," stretch that syllable out, like
this: "JO-OOOO-OOOOOO-OOOOOO-HHHHHHHHH-HHHH-
HHH-HHHHHHH-NNNNNNNNNNNNN." Do this a few times.

FOURTH: QUICKLY WORK OUT a simple mnemonic for your
companion's first name. Try assigning each letter a word, and make
a little phrase. Like so . . .

> J – Juries
> O – Often
> H – Hate
> N – Negroes

FEBRUARY 18
1913, SAN FRANCISCO: The Sharper Image opens its first store in Union Square (right next door to the well-known safari outfitters, Banana Republic). Initially famous for inventing the first massage chair (live pythons were hidden in the upholstery), the Sharper Image's greatest fortune would come with the development of its "Air Purification System"—essentially a Bakelite face mask stuffed with wool and heavy cotton batting. However, 105 years later to the date, the Sharper Image would close its doors, finally driven into bankruptcy by the mad Brookstone Brothers.

---

109. I think one of them is "SUSAN."

FEBRUARY 19
1981, ON THE AIR: Margaret Thatcher makes a surprise guest appearance on *Taxi* as a passenger. The joke is that her driver, the perpetually drug-addled Christopher Lloyd, is convinced she is actually Ruth Gordon.

Actually, maybe that is not the best one to use. What about this one?

J – John

O – Or

H – Hodgman

N – Name

This mnemonic is very good—not only is it catchy and memorable, but it actually includes the word "name," which, after all, is precisely the thing you are trying to remember.

(Note: If the person is named "JON," you should quietly correct their error by inserting an "H.")

FIFTH: Now that you have the first name worked out, it's time to move on to the last name: "HODGMAN."

Well, here you're in luck, because HODGMAN is also the name of a RENOWNED MINOR TELEVISION PERSONALITY and MEMORIZATION EXPERT. Thus, it should be easy to recall, simply by picturing this book in your head, or better, carrying it with you at all times.

If, however, your companion's last name is not that of a famous person, you should still try to remember it.

A POINT OF ETIQUETTE BEFORE WE PART.

Not everyone has taken my seminar in EXPERT NAME MEMORIZATION, and some who have may have forgotten it. Thus, when you meet a new acquaintance, it is polite to reintroduce yourself upon your next meeting. Don't just mumble your name once and presume that the other person is going to remember it the next time he sees you. If that happens, don't act all insulted. Once again: It's your own fault.

HOW TO BUY A COMPUTER FROM A STREET VENDOR [110]

FEBRUARY 20

1981, ELSTREE, ENGLAND: Tom Waits arrives to guest-host *The Muppet Show* but bolts from the set after getting spooked by Animal. He is replaced at the last minute by an incredibly lifelike Tom Waits Muppet.

One day, Jonathan Coulton[111] told me an interesting story. He saw a man selling a bunch of secondhand items on a blanket on the street, including a laptop computer. A middle-aged woman was walking by, and she stopped to look at it. She told the man that she needed to buy a computer for her son, but she was wary about buying this particular computer, because the screen was pitch-black and broken with a jagged crack down the middle of it.

"Do not worry," the man assured the woman. "All it needs is A PROGRAM."

The woman was not convinced, choosing instead to purchase a depressing old stuffed animal.

When I heard this story, I knew exactly what the problem was.

THAT WOMAN PROBABLY DOESN'T EVEN KNOW WHAT A "PROGRAM" *IS*.

The truth is, computer "lingo" is daunting. It scares a lot of people away (or "bytes them off," to use a computer term).

As a result, lots of people are passing up the chance to buy computers on the street, instead buying old stuffed animals that probably have scarlet fever in them. And then they give that stuffed animal to their children, and guess what: *Their children go blind.*

---

110. As you can imagine, people ask me a lot about computers. They presume that because I PLAY A COMPUTER ON TELEVISION, I know ALL ABOUT COMPUTERS. And this is absolutely true. They also presume I can get them FREE COMPUTERS, which is also true. However, I choose not to give them computers, because I am a firm believer in the old maxim: GIVE A MAN A COMPUTER, AND HE WILL COMPUTE FOR ONLY A DAY.

Why? Because by the end of the day he will probably smash it with a hammer. BECAUSE HE DID NOT PAY MONEY FOR IT. At least that is what I always do.

HOWEVER, IF I TEACH YOU HOW TO BUY A COMPUTER, then maybe you will stop bothering me.

111. For more information on Coulton, please see page 443.

FEBRUARY 21
1972, CHINA: "Nixon" supposedly goes
to China.

AT THAT POINT, WOULD IT EVEN MATTER IF HER SON HAD A COMPUTER THAT DIDN'T WORK AND HAD A CRACK DOWN THE MIDDLE? *HE'S ALREADY BLIND!*

So herewith is some basic advice, whether you are buying a computer off a blanket in the middle of a sidewalk or from a more respectable computer peddler with his own special computer wagon.[112]

FIRST ASK: Is it a computer? After all, it's not uncommon for a computer vendor to try to sell you things that aren't ACTUALLY computers, such as "digital cameras" (which are new, filmless cameras that tell the time) and "flash memory cards" (mind-erasing devices) and "televisions" (both one-way and two-way models).

These may *seem* to be computers, and some of these devices actu-

Figure 62: "I'm an HC."

---

112. And these days, you can even buy a computer SIGHT UNSEEN over the Internet, or via a buy-a-computer-unseen-by-telegram service.

ally contain computers within them to help them work (as is the case with cars and robots).

But what you are looking for is a "home computer," also known as an HC. Ask for it by name.

You also want to make sure your HC has these principal components:

FEBRUARY 22
HAPPY BIRTHDAY, GEORGE WASH-
INGTON! Washington's birthday used to
be a holiday until the Uniform Monday
Holiday Act of 1971 came along, which
decreed that Washington was not technically human, but a kind of magical creature who was actually born on the third
Monday of every February, just like Abraham Lincoln.

a keyboard, a monitor, a great speaker system with a subwoofer (critical), and a disk drive. In many computers, the "central process-ing unit" (CPU), which does the actual computing—as well as the power supply and many, many other things—will all be housed in a gigantic "tower" that you keep under your desk (a so-called desk-under computer). Smaller "lap-top" computers store these devices in another dimension.[113]

These physical devices comprise THE HARDWARE of the typi-cal home computer, which is to say, the physical computer that you can touch and is not imaginary.

If it has these things, IT IS A COMPUTER.

NEXT ASK: Does it need a program? As mentioned before, pro-grams are essential. They are the SOFTWARE—the "imaginary" part of the computer that tell it what to do.

And here is where it gets tricky for the average man or woman on the street. Rather than try to explain it all to you in detail, let's try a simple metaphor. Imagine a computer is a large bucket. Now imag-ine that bucket is full of ones and zeroes called "bits," and that each bit represents a theoretical true or false state, usually indicated by an absence or presence of voltage across a digital circuit, or alternately by a directional magnetic charge upon the surface of a tape or disk,

---

113. For more details, please see the section titled "Quantum Computing" outlined in this very same book, but in a different timeline.

FEBRUARY 23
1989, THE BERKSHIRES: James Taylor writes an open letter in the *Berkshire Eagle* to "all rap and hip-hop artists" encouraging them to sample his work. "Come on, rap artists," he wrote. "The time is now. At least 'Sweet Baby James.'" The *Berkshire Eagle* does not have the heart to tell James that no rap artists subscribe to the *Berkshire Eagle*. To this day, the only song to sample "Sweet Baby James" is "Sweet Baby Jamz," by Livingston Taylor.

which are organized into groups of 5 to 12, but usually 8, to form a series of "bytes," which in turn can encode and reconstitute almost any kind of information.

See? When you think about it that way, it's really not that complicated.

But how do you get the bucket to put all the ones and zeroes in the right order to show you a game or a porn? Take my advice, USE A PROGRAM.

The program is a series of instructions written in computer language (various beeps and boops) that tell the CPU what to do. Common programs include word-processing software (typing), spreadsheet software (not what you think), PowerPointing (masturbation), as well as games, recipes, photo de-red-eyeing, contact management, and LightCycle management. Which brings me to an important point: No matter what the person on the street tells you, you do NOT want

Figure 63: A "Home Computer" Usually Refers to a
Computer That Is Large Enough to Live In

to get a "Master Control Program." It sounds tempting, I realize, but it's really more power than the average home user needs. And also it will kidnap you with a laser and make you fight on the Game Grid. So I usually advise people to pass it up.

NEXT ASK: How big is the hard drive? The larger the hard drive, the more programs you can store in it. A good-size hard drive these days would be about 100 "gigs," which stands for gigabytes or "thousand-bytes." Any larger and your computer would be much too heavy and maybe even too hard.

DO NOT ASK: How many floppy drives does it have? "Floppy disk" drives are actually not used much anymore, probably for reasons of floppiness. So you will probably only need two or three of them.

FEBRUARY 24

1868, WASHINGTON, DC: President Andrew Johnson is impeached by the House of Representatives for allegedly receiving oral sex from former Secretary of War Edwin M. Stanton. Johnson was later acquitted in the Senate by a single vote. Vowed Sen. Peter Van Winkle of West Virginia, who voted for acquittal, "Never again."

Figure 64: The Man Who Brought Down a President. (Later, Stanton Would Claim That He Was Sending Johnson a Coded Message of Loyalty in This Photo by Wearing the Beard-and-Vest Set Johnson Had Bought Him as a Gift.)

But "hard driving" is not the only way a computer remembers things. A computer also requires "RAM" (or R-A Memory). The RAM is like the computer's brain. NOTE: It does not ooze like normal brains. This is how the computer remembers everything it is doing at a given time. Have you ever been looking for your keys and then suddenly forgot . . .

I forgot what I was going to write there, but the point is: A computer cannot afford to forget what it's doing. So look for at least 1 or 2 thousandbytes of non-oozing RAM.

FINALLY, BE SURE TO ASK: Does the computer have scarlet

FEBRUARY 25
1952, KENTUCKY: Colonel Sanders begins franchising his secret recipe of Kentucky Fried Chicken with his famous motto:
"This Chicken Is So Good, It Will Make You
Want to Do Something Disgusting."

fever? Just like children and stuffed rabbits, computers are very suscepti-ble to viruses. This does not mean they need to be thrown away. But they should be boiled and soaked in iodine before use (this also prevents the computer from getting a goiter).

Then, and only then, should you connect your computer to the INTERNET.

THE INTERNET: A SERIES OF TUBES

If you are like many people, you are probably eager to get online and start PowerPointing right away. And if the computer you have pur-chased off the street has a "modem," you can do this.

The Web can be an amazing resource, allowing you to shop, book hotel rooms, complain about hotel rooms, look at advertisements, shop some more, and slander other people anonymously—all with the click of a button (or many buttons if you want to write a sentence).

Yet as revolutionary as it seems, the Internet has been around for a lot longer than you might think. As you know, Eisenhower was the first to propose a system whereby every American home would be networked together by a system of pneumatic tubes allowing them to quickly share messages and cash—even small animals. Eisenhower was particularly concerned that citizens could band to-gether effectively against the military-industrial complex. But as you may guess, Americans soon found lots of other uses for the Inter-Tubes. For example, the suction holes found in the floors of most pneumatically networked homes could be used as a marital aid.

When the military-industrial complex heard about this, however, they promptly arranged for Eisenhower's removal from office. At the same time, the Complex developed its own competing tube work through the Department of Defense called ARPANET (meaning "ARPA-network"). Unlike the Eisenhower system, ARPANET connected *computers* instead of homes and used telephone wires and satellites instead of plastic tubes.

While this was not very good for transporting small animals, it turned out to be much more efficient than pneumatic tubes for almost every other purpose, including most of those we use the Internet for today: sending "e-mails," monitoring the thoughts and behavior of every citizen, and distracting them as much as possible from the activities of the Complex.

On November 21, 1969, ARPANET came online, initially connecting only four terminals: an SDS Sigma 7 at UCLA, the WOPR computer at NORAD, the Blessed Brain at the Grand Masonic Lodge at Washington DC (at that time, it was the only computer the White House had access to), and the Complex's own massive server, code-named "FAT BOY."

But once the concept was proven, other computer networks were established and quickly joined together. By the late '90s, any computer on earth could easily join the now-global network, and even the few people still using the old pneumatic tube system[114] could buy a special adapter and join in the fun.

FEBRUARY 26

1870, LOWER MANHATTAN: Alfred Ely Beach finally reveals the country's first subway line. Initially denied the right to build his proposed underground train, Beach nonetheless proceeded by digging in secret and quietly mailing the dirt away in thousands of small packages. When the completed line was revealed, Beach's "secret subway" became a sensation. It consisted of a single, short tunnel, a luxurious cylindrical car fitted snugly within it and drawn along the track via pneumatic suction. As a demonstration, Beach welcomed ten passengers for the inaugural journey from City Hall to Murray Street: nine human thrill-seekers and a single mole-man. The cylinder traveled only 300 feet from City Hall to Murray Street before the vacuum power caused the mole-man to explode. At that moment, another of the passengers, calling himself Mr. White, took advantage of the confusion and hijacked the train, steering it to the world below, never to be seen again.

---

114. Now called "Prodigy."

FEBRUARY 27

2008, MONTEREY, CA: At the TED conference—a high-powered, invitation-only colloquium of world leaders, innovators, scientists, billionaires, and authors of books of fake trivia, I am present for the following conversation:

PROFESSOR PHILIP ZIMBARDO, CONDUCTOR OF THE INFAMOUS STAMFORD PRISON EXPERIMENT AND EXPERT ON THE PSYCHOLOGICAL ROOTS OF EVIL: Wait, I don't understand. What is it you are going to do?

DAVID BLAINE: I am going to stay awake for eleven days.

PHILIP ZIMBARDO: *What?* But why?

DAVID BLAINE: That is the world record.

PHILIP ZIMBARDO (angrily, concerned): NO! You must not do that. I have seen the psychological effects of sleep deprivation. I have seen the psychosis it can cause.

DAVID BLAINE: Let me show you a card trick.

PHILIP ZIMBARDO: Listen to me! Listen to me! You must not do this! YOU CAN GO CRAZY!

DAVID BLAINE: Pick a card and don't show it to me.

However, it's important to note that, as diverting and expensive as the Internet can be, it also can be dangerous. I'm not just talking about electrocution. I'm talking about identity theft.

HOW TO PROTECT YOURSELF FROM IDENTITY THEFT

One thing I am always worried about, and you will agree that this is reasonable, is people stealing my DNA to make copies of me. That is why I never clip my nails.

But when you use a computer that is connected to the Internet, you are often asked to give a lot of private information you normally wouldn't share with strangers: your social security number, your birth date, your PowerPointing schedule. In effect, you're basically clipping your nails and pneumatically tubing them to everyone in the world. Hackers can use those virtual nails to create a virtual *you*, stealing your name, your money, even your actual fingernails. So here are some hints for protecting yourself from identity theft.

1. COME UP WITH A PASSWORD. When using an Internet site, you will often be asked to create a "password" to protect your personal information. But identity thieves will often be able to guess your password if

you're not careful, so bear in mind these password DOS AND DON'TS.

FEBRUARY 28

1906, NEW YORK: Doubleday publishes Upton Sinclair's *The Jungle*. Documenting the horrid and unsanitary working conditions in the meatpacking industry of "Chicago" (a fictional city largely believed to be modeled on Omaha), *The Jungle* prompted outcry from a nation that believed their sausages were made from wholesome oats, spring water, and pixies. Congress acted swiftly: No longer would sausages be made from stray cats and Chicago meat packers; no longer would live boa constrictors be passed off as "hot dogs" at Wrigley; and of course the great Illinois Jungle itself would be burned to the ground in protest, leading to the great Midwestern jaguar displacement of 1910.

TABLE 24: PASSWORD HINTS	
DON'T	**DO**
Don't use your birth date as your password!	Instead, mix letters and words together, such as june3rd1971.
Don't use your name as your password!	Try using my name: johnhodgman. Please don't spell it with an "e." That would only make it easy to spell.
Don't use the word "password" as your password.	Instead, try "password12345."
Don't use your credit card number as your password. It's too long, and you will never remember it!	Give your credit card number to me, and I will remember it for you.

2. If your bank e-mails you and says they need you to log in and tell them your social security number and PIN, ask yourself first: DO I ACTUALLY HAVE A BANK ACCOUNT? If not, something fishy is going on. On the other hand, if you do have a bank account, then it's probably OK.

3. Identity theft doesn't just happen online. For this reason, I recommend that you destroy all rubber masks of your own face. Especially the incredibly realistic ones. These can be fun to have around, but on the wrong head, they could be dangerous.

4. Rubber masks that are just goofy versions of your own face are OK. I MEAN, THAT'S YOUR TRADEMARK!

5. Have you burned off your own fingerprints yet? You'll be glad you did (after the terrible, terrible pain).

6. It may seem like common sense, but don't forget to shred your passport and all your money and never speak your name aloud.

A FASCINATING QUOTE THAT IS ALMOST ENTIRELY ACCURATE

Now, at this point I suspect you are really frightened of the Internet. You are not alone. Indeed, it might surprise you to learn that some early plans to connect American homes to a computer network were eyed with real suspicion, even by authors of trivia books.

Consider, for example, the following quote from one of my favorite books, *The Book of Lists #2* by Irving Wallace and his many children—certainly one of the best sequels to a book of trivia I have ever read, and a profound influence upon my own work.

If you would please turn to page 483 of the Bantam paperback edition, which I trust you own, you can read along under the heading "6 Outrageous Plans That Didn't Happen."

In his book *The Shadow Presidents*, author Michael Medved[115] relates the extreme disappointment of H. R. Haldeman over his failure to implement his plan to link

---

115. Interrobang!

up all the homes in America by
coaxial cable. In Haldeman's
words, "there would be two-
way communication. Through
computer, you could use your
television set to order up whatever you wanted. The
morning paper, entertainment services, shopping services, coverage of sporting events and public events. Just
as Eisenhower linked up the nation's cities by pneumatic
tubes, the Nixon legacy would have linked them by cable
communications . . . "

MARCH 1
1971, HOLLYWOOD: Marlon Brando
agrees to join the cast of *The Godfather,*
but only if he is allowed to use the prosthetic cheeks he has been secretly perfect-
ing in Tahiti.

Now let me assure you that every word of this quote is accurate
(except for the Eisenhower pneumatic tubes part), and I trust you
share my astonishment. Having grown up during the height of the
liberal media, I am not conditioned to expect technological prophecy
from H. R. Haldeman. But then, as I am constantly reminded,
"THERE ARE MORE THINGS IN HEAVEN AND EARTH
THAN IS DREAMT OF IN YOUR LAST BOOK OF FAKE
TRIVIA."

But let us read on, returning to the authors of *The Book of
Lists #2* . . .

. . . One can almost see the dreamy eyes of Nixon
and Haldeman as they sat around discussing a plan
that would eliminate the need for newspapers, seem-
ingly oblivious to its Big Brother aspects. Fortunately
the Watergate scandal intervened, and Nixon was
forced to resign before the "Wired Nation" could be
hooked up.

MARCH 2

1953, HOLLYWOOD: The Academy Awards are first broadcast on television by NBC from the RKO Theater. While the ceremony had been previously described to the public via newspaper reports and pen-and-ink drawings, America was shocked to see studio heads actually bribing Oscar presenters right onstage. It was later decided that this old tradition should take place "behind the scenes" from then on. Additionally, the homage to Hollywood's recently departed would thereafter be a filmed montage instead of the parade of open caskets that had previously been the norm.

And perhaps it is this wariness about the Internet, and the authors' natural antiauthoritarian streak, that would explain why the address www .bookoflists2.com is registered to a person named "John Hodgman."

Because as much as I admire the Wallaces, I disagree with their dark assessment of the Internet. True, we must exercise caution when traveling through "cyberland," but the erosion of privacy is a small cost to pay, given the benefit.

For while the Internet may have been dreamed up by authoritarians, in fact, it is a perfect system for *erasing* authority.

Where once humans had to be rich, well connected, or extremely loud to reach other people with their ideas, now anyone can, for a relatively modest fee, publish their thoughts instantly, immediately, and everywhere. And the possibilities for collaboration are equally revolutionary. Children, who once had to steal books from their parents in order to learn how to have sex with one another, can now teach one another the latest techniques. And what is the Wikipedia if not one great and endless compendium of fake trivia? A vast tome of dubious scholarship that is ever-expanding, constantly correcting and uncorrecting itself?

For this reason, you may imagine that I would be *against* the Internet, but I am not. I do not have such little faith in my own ability to imitate authority that I refuse competition. In the vast marketplace of fake facts, I believe mine are still the best and most reliable.

Indeed, aside from www.bookoflists2.com (and bookoflists2.biz), I also maintain an online presence under the address www.areasof

myexpertise.com.[116] And through it, I have enjoyed being IN CONSTANT CONTACT with you, dear readers. Like most Web sites, I have a blog, in which I report my thoughts of the moment, and I also sell my ringtones and decorative plates.

You may naturally ask if I have a "FREQUENTLY ASKED QUESTIONS LIST." The answer is no, because people don't ask questions all that frequently, and when they do, I prefer responding with the more personal touch of answering them in a book months or years later. As you shall see, if you continue to read on.

MARCH 3

1974, LAKE GENEVA, WISCONSIN: E. Gary Gygax (RIP) and Dave Arneson invent Dungeons & Dragons. The first well-known "role-playing game" would become a huge phenomenon after Jimmy Carter admitted to playing the game obsessively in a *Playboy* magazine interview. Contrary to what you've heard, Tom Hanks did not go crazy from playing Dungeons & Dragons before joining the cast of *Bosom Buddies.* That was Mazes and Monsters.[a]

a. Please see page 420 under the heading "Some Internet Rumors That Will Not Die!"

SOME QUESTIONS THAT WERE ACTUALLY ASKED ON THE INTERNET, IF NOT EXACTLY "FREQUENTLY," THEN AT LEAST ONCE

While it has been some time since I wrote my Internet advice column "Ask a Former Professional Literary Agent," that does not mean I do not know how you should live or what you should do. And indeed, since the publication of my first book, curious people with actual problems have posed questions to me via the electronic mails. Here, at last, are the answers.

---

116. Please do not click on this word. This is a book.

MARCH 4

1974: *People* magazine debuts. It was not originally designed to be a "celebrity" magazine per se. In addition to a story about Mia Farrow, the first issue included a profile of Vietnam War widows, a 10,000-word profile of Thomas Pynchon, and their inaugural "Sexiest Man Alive," Aleksandr Solzhenitsyn. However, reader response was mixed. Helen from Pasadena wrote, "YOU GO, ALEKSANDR! I am so happy this sexy, sassy dissident man is finally getting his life together and finding a chance to write again." Most readers hated his beard. By issue two, the format had shifted to pictures of largely unbearded movie and TV stars getting into and out of cars.

DENNIS S. OF ALBUQUERQUE WRITES: I've recently started reading only books in oversize print. I know these are meant for people with eyesight problems, but I get a real sense of accomplishment from finishing 100 pages in just a few minutes. A friend tells me that this is the equivalent of using the handicap stall in a public restroom. Is he right, or am I?

JH REPLIES: It is the same only insofar as, like handicap stalls, large-print books offer you (a) more room to maneuver in and (b) railings for lifting yourself into and out of the book.

Now, of course I understand how handy (and cappy!) these features can be, but

your friend is correct that acquiring such versions of the book requires

MARCH 5
1982, HOLLYWOOD: John Belushi is found dead of a cocaine and heroin overdose. He and some friends had gotten together for a traditional round of speedballs to usher in the 212th anniversary of the Boston Massacre and, as always, things got out of hand. That is why I always say NEVER CELEBRATE A MASSACRE.

some measure of etiquette.

I do not think you have anything to apologize for, unless you are actually *stealing* these books from visually impaired people. If you are doing this, let me ask you— how did you get around their heightened sense of smell? That's the one part of the puzzle I've never been able to

MARCH 6

1730: The "sextant" replaces the "Davis quadrant" on sailing vessels. Despite its name and appearance, the sextant is not used for sex, but actually for determining the relative position of stars to the horizon—a hobby among seamen of the day, who needed distractions to pass the long hours between bouts of having sex with and/or consuming one another to survive.

Figure 65: Surprisingly,
NOT Used for Sex

crack.[117]

Now, on the other hand, perhaps you are simply *purchasing* the large-print edition through legitimate channels. Then you are merely guilty of artificially inflating the size of the large-print market.[118] But in that case, the worst that could happen is that pub-

---

117. The cane is easy: Just have yourself beaten with a cane every day for an hour until you do not even notice it anymore.

118. So to speak.

lishers come to the conclusion that we are all going blind. Is that so bad? (PS: The above advice does not apply to Braille editions of books, which are very fun for the fingertips, but much more scarce and difficult to replace, as they are made by special birds.)

MARCH 7
HAPPY BIRTHDAY, WILLARD SCOTT!
The famed *Today* show weatherman is born today in Alexandria, Virginia, in 1934. It is said that when he turns 100, there will be a huge party, and then the world will end in a great flood of Smucker's jelly. I don't like to give credence to many idle apocalypse prophecies, but this is probably going to happen, actually.

PS: YET ANOTHER INTERNET RUMOR THAT WILL NOT DIE
Everyone knows that Willard Scott portrayed early versions of Bozo the Clown and Ronald McDonald before he was a weatherman. But it is not true that he was on *Sesame Street*. This was a rumor started by Bryant Gumbel, who found Scott's happy-go-lucky attitude and obsession with centenarians to be "unseemly," and would often refer to Scott as "the ass end of Snuffleupagus."

BEN FROM DETROIT WRITES: I'm forty-five and still live with my parents. I tell people that I'm taking care of my elderly father, but nobody believes me. Can you help me come up with a better excuse?

MARCH 8
1983, ORLANDO, FL: Ronald Reagan first refers to the Soviet Union as an "Evil Empire." It is the first time the Cold War would be cast as a moral battle as opposed to one of global hegemony, and a stark contrast to Jimmy Carter's nickname for the Soviet Union: "The Galactic Senate."

JH REPLIES: I am confused. Is the explanation you are offering your friends true or false? If it is the truth, and you ARE in fact caring for your elderly father, then your friends are monsters and you should stop talking to them immediately. Who is a boy's best friend, after all? His father, naturally. And when his father dies, a boy's best friend is the preserved corpse of his father that the boy keeps in the fruit cellar and still visits every day to receive instructions on what to do about his so-called friends.

Alternately, if you are simply making an excuse and you are not actually taking care of your father, then you, sir, are THE MONSTER. Be a good son: Get down to the fruit cellar and give the old man some gruel. HE RAISED YOU, FOR GOD'S SAKE.

But the larger message is: You really should not pay attention to what people think of your life choices. And no matter what, you ought to have a fruit cellar.

CHRIS H. OF ST. LOUIS WRITES: I got into a bar brawl last night and ended up losing a tooth. I've considered getting an implant, but I think the gap in my smile looks kinda bad-ass. What do you think? Should I leave it alone or go to the dentist?

JH REPLIES: If you were really a bad-ass, you wouldn't be asking *me* for advice. You'd just go to the dentist and punch that guy in the mouth.

(Hint: Because that's a dentist's weak spot; elsewhere on their bodies, they feel no pain, thanks to their intimate knowledge of topical anesthetics. That is why fighting a dentist is like hitting a bag of angry meat.)

But if the dentist beats you down—and let's face it, that's probably what is going to happen—he or she will likely force you to get an implant. In this case, please make sure it's a removable fake tooth like the kind Robert Shaw had in the movie *Jaws*. Then you can choose how "bad-ass" and "drunken-sailory"

MARCH 9

1959 NEW YORK: "Barbie" debuts at the New York Toy Fair. While criticized in recent years for her impossible body (proportionally, a human woman with Barbie's body would be five-foot-nine, have an eighteen-inch waist, weigh only 110 pounds, have no genitalia, and be fitted with a tiny speaker in her head that told other women that "math is hard"), the first Barbie was actually much fuller figured than the doll of today—in large part because she was originally modeled on Gertrude Stein.

you wish to appear by pulling the tooth out at will. That will shut those fancy-pants marine biologists up!

(PPS: Please don't actually go and hit a dentist.)

SARAH W. OF LOS ANGELES WRITES: I want to get a tattoo but just can't decide on the right one. I want something that makes me look cool but doesn't completely horrify my parents. Any suggestions?

JH REPLIES: I thought tattoos were amusing until my own daughter got a huge face-and-neck tattoo of Dan Zanes. That turns out to be the *only* tattoo that looks cooler on a thirty-seven-year-old than a five-year-old, and the whole family regrets it. Generally speaking, I think there is a generation of former hipsters and aging sorority sisters and cannibal whale harpooners who will deeply regret "the tattoo fad" once they catch a view of their fifty-year-old scrawled-upon bodies in the mirror after they shower. The one exception is if you get a *Mad* magazine fold-in tattooed to your belly, which reveals a new picture as your flab and folds increase with time. That would be delightful. But if you really want a new look, why don't you try busting out your own tooth?

MARCH 10

1876, BOSTON: "Mr. Watson. Come here. I need you." With these words Alexander Graham Bell famously makes the first telephone transmission. Though his assistant, Watson, was just in the adjoining room, nonetheless, Bell had not seen him for seven months, refusing to contact him until the telephone was functional. When Watson finally did "come here," he found his employer Bell half-crazed and starving.

I HAVE MORE ANSWERS to your questions, and I shall answer them LATER.[119]

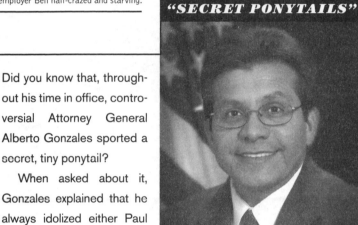

WERE YOU AWARE OF IT? "SECRET PONYTAILS"

Did you know that, throughout his time in office, controversial Attorney General Alberto Gonzales sported a secret, tiny ponytail?

When asked about it, Gonzales explained that he always idolized either Paul Revere or Steven Seagal, but he couldn't recall which.

Figure 66: Ponytail!

HE JUST COULDN'T REMEMBER WHY HE GREW A PONYTAIL.

Also, since we are discussing it, do you know why it is called a "PONYTAIL"?

IT IS BECAUSE IT MAKES YOUR HEAD LOOK LIKE A PONY'S ASS.

Here is proof!

---

119. Please see page 571 under the heading "All of Your Questions Answered, Or at Least Five More."

MARCH 11

1962, WASHINGTON DC: On the 160th anniversary of Napoléon's first moon landing, JFK launches the first robotic mission to the moon. The mission of the robots? To collect moon rocks to use in the first staged moon landing.

Figure 67: A Ponytail, Circa 1987

MARCH 12
1933, WASHINGTON, DC: Franklin Roosevelt broadcasts the first of his famous "Fireside Chats."
What radio listeners did not realize, however, was that Roosevelt was broadcasting to them from *inside
the fire.* It warmed his lifeless legs.

GAMBLING:
THE SPORT OF THE
ASTHMATIC MAN

MARCH 13

1781, BATH, ENGLAND: German-born astronomer William Herschel becomes the first modern scientist to discover a new planet within our solar system. He is not taken seriously at first. After all, the three "new planets" he had previously "discovered" turned out to be the sun, a fly on the lens of his telescope, and Earth, respectively. But this time he got it right: Uranus is a planet, and since our last writing, it has been admitted to THE CLUB OF PLANETS.[a]

a. Please see page 147 of *The Areas of My Expertise* under the heading "The Club of Debated Planets."

MARCH 14

1981, VIRGINIA: Tourists flock to Richmond to experience Champ Stanley's latest forecast: a rain of tiny bells made from a mysterious metal of unknown origin. This follows previous rains of silvery thread, ingenious puzzle boxes with coins inside, and little golden snakes that could speak. And so Richmond, too, is showered with wealth as visitors fill up its hotels and restaurants, taking each new odd item from the sky with them as they leave as tokens and proof that Richmond, without rival, is the most magical city in the United States.

HOW TO GAMBLE AND WIN

When we last spoke, I did not want to talk about sports, and I still do not. But that does not mean I don't enjoy what George Gershwin called "The Sporting Life" of liquor, gambling, "happy dust," and singing in vernacular folk operas.

And so it will not surprise you that I am well known at most of the world's finest casinos, insofar as I am a WORLD-CLASS GAMBLER.

Now, a lot of people will tell you they like gambling because it makes them feel more "alive." It returns them to an animal state of perpetual risk, when all civilizing illusions fade away, leaving behind only the primal, inner struggle between one's fear and one's balls.[120]

Others will say that gambling is the great equalizer. Wealth, fame, schooling, background—none of that matters at the gaming table. When we gamble, our planning and our prayers become meaningless, and we are reminded that in all of our lives, our fortunes most commonly rise and fall on a roll of the dice.[121]

But I see gambling a little differently. I like to gamble because I LIKE TO WIN MONEY. Call me crazy, and many do, but WINNING MONEY just feels great to me. (I also love gambling because it requires no meaningful physical exertion, and they bring you alcohol while you do it.)

Now, there have been many, many books written on the subject of how to win at gambling. But for some reason, people are still

---

120. (Sexual organs.)

121. This is especially true if you are rolling dice.

losing all the time. So while I recognize it might rob me of my "edge" as
a gambler, I'm going to share with
you some of my best surefire secrets
for beating the odds. Will it make
you a winner *every* time? Of course
not. But I promise you this: IF YOU
DO EXACTLY WHAT I TELL
YOU TO DO, you might occasion-
ally win, sometimes. It's hard to predict.

MARCH 15

BEWARE the "IDES OF MARCH," the
ominous anniversary of the assassination
of Julius Caesar. Superstitious types would
tell you that this is a bad day to begin a
new business endeavor or to launch a ship,
but I say: bullroar. The only thing you really need to be careful of today are your
closest friends, because they are going to
stab you over and over in public. But honestly, how is that different from the IDES
OF FEBRUARY?

READY TO WIN (OR LOSE)? Then read on.

FIRST, LET'S TALK "CRAPS."

Craps is the dirty word for "dice." Sorry to put it so bluntly, but
gambling is a hard, gut-wrenching game where man confronts destiny and loses again and again. It's no surprise that in the casino, you
are going to hear some dirty words. In fact, in Monaco, they call dice
"shits."

As you might imagine, Shits is one of the oldest games on earth.
When the ancient Greeks first came to Vegas, they rolled dice made
from the knucklebones of pigs, still bloody from the slaughter. But
now it is played with imitation knucklebones and fake blood. BUT
OF COURSE, REAL MONEY.

Now, I don't know how to play craps, and it turns out, no one
does. But that doesn't stop them from "elbow-bending" all night
long, throwing the dice over and over at the man in the vest with the
stick. I think they are trying to hit him, but I really just don't know.
Sometimes I'll go by a craps table and just toss a gerbil in there and
walk away, and no one seems to notice.

And that's why craps is a sucker's game, just like all those other
casino games I don't know how to play: Baccarat and Blackjack and

MARCH 16
HAPPY BIRTHDAY, FLAVOR FLAV!
Born in Queens, New York, in 1959. The
Oracle of London predicted that while he
would become a great success, he would
never find true love.

Guess-Who's-the-Scandinavian and Archery. With these games the player has no advantage. The house always wins, and if not the house, someone else who is not you. You may as well throw your money away (or as we say in Vegas, "fax your cash to hell").

NO, THANKS.

That's why I only play the smart bets—the games that give the player an edge and are not just pure chance. Games like roulette, poker, Star Wars slots, and hermit-crab racing. Are these games "sure things"? No. But if you cheat? MAYBE.

SURE THING NUMBER ONE: ROULETTE

Unlike craps, roulette is a game involving a wheel and a ball. You spin the wheel, the ball goes around, and it lands on a number. It's simple and, more important: There's no skill involved at all. All you need to do is guess the best number there is.

Probably the best player of roulette in the world is the actor Wesley Snipes. Wesley has a famous saying about roulette, and that is "ALWAYS BET ON THE AFRICAN AMERICAN." And in this case, the African American is betting exclusively on the black.

Now, Wesley Snipes and I are close, close friends.[122] But I don't mind telling you there's a big flaw in his strategy. Can you see it? Take a second to think about it. Maybe you should put this book down and go play roulette for a week. Then come back when you think you know it.

---

122. We met on the set of *Demolition Man*. That's when he told me about the biggest gamble of all: NEVER PAY TAXES AGAIN, AND SEE WHAT HAPPENS.

OK, welcome back. So as I explained to Snipey at the Mandalay Bay one night, if you bet all the black numbers every time, guess what: You have almost a fifty-fifty

MARCH 17
Today is the Feast Day of Saint Patrick, the Roman missionary famed for turning all of the snakes in Ireland into green beer—a mysterious process known within the Catholic Church as Trans-snake-iation.

chance of winning. Those are great odds. Incredible odds, when you think about it. But if you bet all the black numbers and ALL THE RED NUMBERS TOO,[123] suddenly your "win" percentage goes up to 100. YOU WIN EVERY TIME. I guarantee it.

(Did you get it right?)

SURE THING NUMBER TWO: POKER

Like a lot of you, most of my experience playing poker was gained in someone's kitchen, sitting around a table with a bunch of friends, bluffing and bullroaring one another about our cards and our lives until finally we were all naked and crying on the bathroom floor. Then we'd pull ourselves together, and the next week we'd meet in someone else's kitchen. I don't know how we found these kitchens, or who owned them, but it was a good time, and I'm sorry I threw up in the toaster oven.

My poker buddies and I played all the classic poker variants, such as Texas Hold Them, Hi-Low Omaha Hold Them, 5-Card Draw Them, and 7-Card Fuck Them.

And while a lot of people frown on them, I'm still a fan of the great novelty home games, such as midnight baseball; midnight baseball with human arms for bats; dawn baseball with human arms for bats, with suicide kings and upside-down aces wild; and of course, anaconda, which is a highly addictive game in which everyone puts a

---

123. And twice on the greens.

MARCH 18
BIRDSONG DAY: If you listen carefully today, you will be able to understand birdsong. Generally, the birds are singing about seeds and wanting to fuck one another. Enjoy.

card on his forehead and guesses which one at the table is Jon Voight. I guess it's not "technically" poker, but it's a very fun game. At least until Jon Voight shows up.

I was not exactly a "card sharp," but I did wear a little garter on my sleeve and a green visor, and this got me plenty of hot action when I headed down to the card room in Atlantic City, I can tell you. (I was also the only gambler there who was not riding a Jazzy brand mobility scooter.)[124]

But then, one game swept the nation that overshadowed all others: the "main event," as they call it at Binion's Horseshoe Casino, and that game is NO-LIMIT TEXAS HOLD THEM WITH THE GAY FRIEND FROM *SEX AND THE CITY*.[125]

Figure 68: Looking Good

Suddenly, POKER was everywhere, on almost every channel. It makes sense when you think about it. If you ever watch *The World Series of Poker* on TV, you will know that there are really few people more glamorous or inspiring or telegenic than professional gamblers. They look great, they dress smart, and their combination of bitter frustration,

---

124. I rock a Rascal, naturally.

125. Many of you have asked why I never appeared on *Celebrity Poker Showdown*. Personally, I would have loved to, as I would have liked nothing better than to shake Dave Foley's hand and to WIPE THAT DEADPAN OFF OF MICHAEL IAN BLACK'S DAMNED FACE. But in fact I was not allowed to appear on that program, as it would have conflicted with my own forthcoming cable program, *John Hodgman's Celebrity Falconry*, featuring me and Emo Philips. WATCH FOR IT!

addict sweat, compulsive semiau-
tism, and funny sunglasses have
given the nation a new pantheon of
sporting heroes that I hope children
will imitate.

These TV programs have sparked
a real renaissance in the poker rooms

MARCH 19
1931, NEVADA: Gambling is officially le-
galized. The first casino is a modest affair
compared to today's glitz and glamour:
There was only one casino on the Strip—
the Luxor—a dusty little pyramid-shaped
saloon with just a few card tables and a
single Star Wars slot machine (later the inspiration for the successful film franchise).

of many casinos, which had been neglected in the '80s and '90s to the
point that even the biggest hotels on the strips had only one or two
tables, and those usually had no legs and were often on fire.

Nowadays, though, you can strike up some great poker action in
almost any casino; and if you like "celebrity poker," don't worry. The
best hotels usually offer at least one or two games with famous
minor television personalities whom they entice to the casinos by
kidnapping their families. Maybe we'll even get to play together
someday. And maybe if I let you win, you will agree to help rescue
my family.

But enough history: HOW DO YOU PLAY?

By now, you know the game is pretty simple. You are dealt two
cards facedown. These are called your "hole" cards because you have
to immediately put them in a little hole (scratching a hole into the
poker table is an art unto itself, and every player has his own particular style). Over successive rounds of betting, you attempt to
make the best possible five-card hand out of your two hole cards
along with five cards dealt faceup on the table. Everyone shares
these cards, which means they can touch and fondle them as much as
they like. Try it the next time you're in a casino!

IN CASE YOU FORGET, the hands of poker, in increasing rank,
are as follows:

MARCH 20

1981, VIRGINIA: Just days after the Rain of Bells, Champ Stanley's contract is quietly allowed to expire. In a small piece in the *Times-Dispatch,* Channel 6 station manager Phil Lippert is quoted: "Champ's been terrific. But with Milwaukee still in ruins, Richmond no longer needs the aid of expensive, outside consultants. While we wish him well, I'm glad to announce that Richmond native Al Starnes will be taking over the weather report from now on, and I have little doubt that he'll be forecasting many exciting new and unusual kinds of precipitation for years to come."

TABLE 25: THE MANY HANDS OF POKER	
NAME OF HAND	**DESCRIPTION OF SAME**
A PAIR OF CARDS	Two cards of the same rank
TWO PAIRS OF CARDS or TWO KINDS	Double the above
TRIPS or THREE KINDS	Three cards of the same rank
FIVES	One or more of the cards is a five.
STRAIGHT	The rank of the card includes only straight lines; e.g., only sevens, or all kings.
FLUSH	All red cards
FULL HOUSE	Three "children" cards accompanied by a Widower, a Goofy Pal, and John Stamos.[126] *NB: One of the "children" is allowed to be a secret identical twin.*
WILLIE GARSON'S BUSINESS CARD	Any hand that contains the business card of the actor who played the gay friend on *Sex and the City*[127]
FOUR OF A KIND	Double trips, minus two
POISONED FOUR	The cards have been coated in a poison. AKA "The Dead Man's Hand"
STRAIGHT FLUSH	Straights and reds only.
ROYAL FLUSH	Same as a straight flush, but the cards are made of velvet.

Sounds pretty simple, right?

---

126. If these cards sound unfamiliar to you, that is because they are drawn not from the standard poker deck but from the MYSTICAL TAROT. If you want to play with tarot cards at a casino, however, you have to make a special request or bring your own. Try it.

127. You may think that this feature of the game gives Willie Garson something of an advantage—and you'd be right. HE IS AN INCREDIBLE PLAYER.

But even though the rules are straightforward, in practice, the true poker player must be a master of math, social psychology, chaos theory, card chemistry, feltology, and the hunting down and killing of men, thus earning poker its famous nickname: THE MOST DANGEROUS GAME.

MARCH 21
1900, PHILADELPHIA: The first artificial dimensional rift is opened at Gimbel's Department Store. Originally designed to bring people from one floor to another, it would, on occasion, accidentally send people to a weird alternate dimension where great full-service department stores NO LONGER EXISTED. It ran for thirty-five years and then was destroyed with an ax.

To give you a sense of everything that comes into play in even the most basic game of poker, here are a few rules of thumb.

BET SMALL if you have a strong hand. BET BIG if you have a weak hand. Concealing the nature of your hand and tricking your opponents is called LYING, and it's one of the most important parts of the game. It may feel awkward or even immoral the first time you "bluff" in this way. But in the game of poker, this strategy works much, much better than telling everyone what cards you have as soon as they are dealt to you. Take it from me: THAT RARELY WORKS.

DON'T BE AFRAID TO RAISE, AND DON'T BE AFRAID TO GET CALLED. Poker isn't about "playing it safe," "keeping your head down," and "just reaching over and grabbing a few chips from your neighbor when he isn't looking." The whole game is propelled by the engine of CONFRONTATION and COUNTER-CONFRON-TATION. If conflict makes you nervous, get over it. Try this simple exercise. Any time someone makes a bet, just say, "You're a fucking liar and everyone here knows it." Or, "My cards are going to set your cards on

MARCH 22

1981, VIRGINIA: *Times Dispatch* reporter Chip Senior, seeking a final interview with Champ Stanley, finds that Stanley has already left town. No one had even seen Champ check out at the Jefferson Hotel, where he had long lived at the expense of Channel 6 (which may be why they let him go). When the reporter entered Champ's room, he found it completely empty and pristine. Senior later wrote in his autobiography that he at first presumed that the chambermaid had already made up the room. Even the toilet paper still had its little, decorative peaked fold.

"But then I smelled the air, old and musty," he wrote. "The windows had never been opened. The bed had never been slept in. And all that was left was a few words on a piece of hotel stationery in what I might describe as an angry hand. A lot of rumors have circulated as to what was in that note and whether it contained any warning of what was to come. But I found it, and I can tell you there was no warning. All it said was three words: 'FIRE NEXT TIME.'"

fire and then put out the fire with piss." Or, "My cards are going to drown your cards in a rain barrel the same way I murdered your children." Even if you're not in the hand, this sends a message that you are a REAL card player and maybe even a child murderer.

NO MATTER WHAT YOU'VE HEARD, you DON'T have to know when to hold them, and you DON'T have to know when to fold them.

A WORD TO THE SUCKER: If you don't know who the sucker at the table is, it's you. And if you don't know who the Willie Garson at the table is, then he is probably wearing a disguise.

POKER IS A SCIENCE: Poker isn't a game of luck, poker is a game of chance, and that means: STATISTICS. Certain hands are just more likely to come up than others, and if you know the odds, you have AN INSIDE EDGE.

Let's take a break for a second and put STATISTICS INTO ACTION. Not long ago, I was sitting in third position in a game of No-Limit Hold Them with a three and an ace, both hearts. The blinds have gone around and here comes the flop: two of hearts, jack of clubs, and jack of hearts. The guy ahead of me plunges in with 100 chips, and now I'm in a tough position. It's my flush draw against his TRIP jacks or maybe even a full house!

MARCH 23

1966, NEW HAVEN: The controversial Yale Feline Studies Lab reports that when cats are raised from birth with mice tied to their backs, they come to believe that the mice are angels of the feline god.

So what do I do? RAISE, of course. I've got a one-in-four chance on each of the next two up cards to make my flush. Those jacks on the board may look scary, but I know where they are and what that means: The chance that he has a third or even a fourth jack is now much, much lower. Some quick mental math tells me it's, like, one in 1 million. Maybe a billion. If he's doing the math I'M doing, I can either beat him or even scare him out with a strong raise, followed by a quick reminder that I might kill his children.

SO, OK: I didn't scare him out, and here comes the next card. IT'S A TWO OF DIAMONDS. Bad news for me. No flush, and now we both have two pair for sure, though the odds of his making his full house have now gone up to roughly 0.768729921. He's no dummy: He bets $100 and throat-punches me. I don't mind saying: It hurts.

Now, your gut tells you I should probably fold here, right? WRONG. A simple calculation of pot odds divided by the number of people at the table tells you this is a VALUE BET, and I MAKE IT.

Now here comes the next card! Six of hearts! YES! I have made my flush to the ace. And if you have learned anything about poker from me at all, it's this: IF YOU HAVE MADE THE HAND YOU WERE LOOKING FOR, EVEN IF IT'S A RELATIVELY WEAK HAND COMPARED TO WHAT THE OTHER PLAYERS MIGHT HAVE, STATISTICS TELL US YOU ARE GOING TO WIN NO MATTER WHAT.

So when my opponent bets, you know I'm ALL IN, and we flip our cards: He has an ace of diamonds and a king of hearts. He was

MARCH 24
2008, NEW YORK CITY: I am forced to buy TEN POUNDS of pig spleens just to take a photo of ONE SPLEEN for this book. I ask you: IS THAT JUSTICE?

bluffing all along! Even if the final card comes in hearts, I've got him beat with my ace.

And in fact, the next card is an ACE OF HEARTS.

"But wait," you say. "Didn't you start out by saying that you already had an ace of hearts in the hole?"

YES. But it turns out that I misread it and it was actually an ACE OF DIAMONDS. So I lose.

As any pro poker player knows, even if you play every hand correctly, SOMETIMES YOU JUST DON'T GET LUCKY.

CONSTRUCT A "POKER PERSONALITY" Have you ever seen a poker player in a casino who seemed to be a little crazy? Maybe he was running his hands through his messy, matted hair? Maybe he was rocking back and forth, trembling and mumbling to himself? Or maybe between hands he would just shriek in repeated, high-pitched bursts? Guess what: HE PROBABLY *IS* CRAZY . . . CRAZY LIKE A FOX WHO IS A REALLY GOOD POKER PLAYER.

It's all an act, you see. There are many great professional poker players who seek to throw their opponents off balance by acting a little crazy: Mike "The Mad Genius of Poker" Caro, for example, or Timmy "The Drooling Mastermind" McGoonish, Nils "Formerly Institutionalized" Wolliver, and of course the legendary Amarillo Straightjacket. The best player of this bunch, however, is Mick Dorf.

At the table, Mick looks unkempt. He wears a dirty polo shirt with strange, rust-brown stains on it, and he has a lot of bruises and scabs on his face. When he sits down, he immediately announces to all at the table that he just had a lobotomy and wants to make some money to fill in his brain hole with silver.

Then he brings out a German shepherd named Wolfie. He will not bet before consulting with Wolfie, and when he doesn't like what Wolfie has to say, he'll yell obscenities at Wolfie for long stretches at a time. Finally, he will calm down. He will turn and smile and apologize to the table.

"I'm sorry," he will say. "My dog is a JERK HOLE." And then he will bet. And then he will vomit on himself.[128]

Let me tell you something: It works. People just don't know what to expect from him, and so they can't second-guess his bets or get a read on his strategy.

But those of us who have been lucky to meet him at his home know that Mick is not really crazy. No, he does not live in a hollow tree in Burt Reynolds's yard, as he claims, but in a nice little condo off the Strip. Away from the table, Mick is just a normal, happy guy. He's one of the smartest poker players in the game today, and when he's off-duty, he only vomits the normal way: in the toilet (or in a clean basin).

MARCH 25

1983, LOS ANGELES: Michael Jackson debuts the "moonwalk" before a live audience at a Motown 25th-anniversary TV special. Legend has it that, after the special aired, Fred Astaire phoned Jackson to tell him he loved the moonwalk so much that he was having himself preserved in a hyberbaric chamber and shipped over to Neverland for Jackson to keep forever.

(At least that's what Michael Jackson said when authorities found the preserved corpse of Fred Astaire, dressed like Gepetto, in a secret compartment underneath the stairs.)

---

128. You may have seen this little routine in the famous documentary about Mick called *Titicut Follies*.

MARCH 26

1950: HAPPY BIRTHDAY, MARTIN SHORT! When he was born, Short was immediately proclaimed the 124th Child King of Ontario. His was a unique, though unhappy, childhood. His first twenty-two years were spent entirely within the walls of the Golden Horseshoe, Ontario's forbidden city, where he was trained in royal etiquette and calligraphy, and he was regularly bound in stiff bandages in order to maintain the proper elfin stature as befits an Ontarian king. When Ontario's monarchy was abolished in 1972, Short was forced to flee the Golden Horseshoe, but his exile came as a relief to Short. He did not miss the royal life, and soon joined a common work gang in Canada's vast comedy mines, where he still labors today.

You see, when you play poker, you must create a character for yourself at the table: a personality that YOU CONTROL so that your opponents do not control YOU.

Maybe you want to be the "cowboy," a friendly rube who doesn't claim to know much about the game but nonetheless bets hard and recklessly: That will make your opponents call you when they shouldn't and drop out of pots because they are afraid you are going to shoot them with your guns.

Or maybe you want to be the "robot"—the guy who is completely passionless and quiet, betting and folding like a machine, with the exact same motions, always staring straight ahead with dead, soulless eyes. This will intimidate people out of calling your bluffs, because they will be wondering: Is he self-aware? Or is it just an incredible simulation of self-awareness? And what, really, is the difference?

But don't let me tell you how to act. Maybe you want to dress up like Mr. Peanut with a top hat and a monocle. WELL, WHY NOT? Anything that keeps your opponents guessing. For the real poker player, the bluff doesn't start when you get your hand. The bluff starts before you ever get to the casino. It starts the moment you wake up in the morning. It starts the moment you sneak out of Burt Reynolds's hollow tree and go to the alley where you have hidden your giant peanut costume.

ON THE SUBJECT
OF TELLS

MARCH 27
1981, VIRGINIA: Despite Al Starnes's smiling forecast of "a rain of delicious jelly beans . . . and fuzzy chicks!" Richmond reports no unusual rain.

Professional poker players know that even when an opponent *doesn't* announce what cards he has at the beginning of a hand, he will often SHOW you what he has through various bits of involuntary body language called TELLS. For example:

TABLE 26: SOME FAMOUS "TELLS"		
IF	**THEN**	**ACTION**
Your opponent is constantly touching his cards	He may be unconsciously "guarding" a strong hand.	Fold.
Your opponent is constantly touching his face	He may have a skin condition known as "loser hives."	Bet, but do not touch your opponent's face.
Your opponent's face turns red	He may be ashamed of a weak hand, or alternately, he may be ready to mate.	Bet or mate.
Your opponent is caressing your arm	BE CAREFUL. He may just WANT YOU TO THINK he's ready to mate.	Raise him with a French kiss.
Your opponent is having a seizure	He has high cards. The bright, repetitive patterns of face cards frequently cause seizures.	Wait and see. If he does not bite his own tongue out, then you know he is bluffing.

MARCH 28

1931: Alka-Seltzer is first introduced as a
common seagull-explosive.

SURE THING NUMBER THREE:
STAR WARS SLOTS

I know what you're thinking: There's no skill to slot machines. Aren't winners just decided by pure, random chance? And aren't most of them Transformers?

CORRECT. But the law of averages is pretty clear on this: NOT EVERY MACHINE CAN BE A TRANSFORMER. And with Star Wars slots, the conflicting intellectual property issues alone DRA-MATICALLY decrease the likelihood that the machine you're playing is a killer robot.

DRAMATICALLY.

Just to give you an illustration: The last time I went to Vegas, I was playing poker at the Mandalay Bay. It wasn't my night: I had lost quite a bit of money really fast. I was getting frustrated, and I was starting to play badly. So I followed one of my own CARDI-

Figure 69:
Probably Not
Transformers

NAL RULES OF GAMBLING.[129]
I got up from the table and took a
long walk around the casino to find
something else to start gambling on immediately.

MARCH 29
1708, LONDON: Famed almanacker John Partridge dies of a raging fever.

For some reason I sat down at a Star Wars penny-slot machine, slipped in a hundred-dollar bill, and by the following morning, I had made a total of 250 dollars. THAT'S ROUGHLY 300 DOLLARS' PURE PROFIT.

So let me be clear. I'm not advocating playing slots per se. I'm just advocating playing THAT PARTICULAR STAR WARS SLOT MACHINE at the Mandalay Bay, because THAT IS MY PERSONAL LUCKY MACHINE.

So stay away from it.

SURE THING NUMBER FOUR:
HERMIT-CRAB RACING

I first got the "bug," as they say, for hermit-crab racing back when I was gambling my way through Jamaica.

I was eight or so, on vacation with my parents. We were staying in a completely self-contained resort for tourists so that I could get a real sense of the island, and I was looking for some diversion now that I had tired of the swim-up bar and the man who came around in the afternoons with a mongoose in a cage.

Then one afternoon, the crab man came. He had a cage of hermit crabs, each shell painted a different color. I put my money on the blue crab (obviously). I called him "Bluey," and let me tell you, Bluey and I made a lot of that crazy-colored paper that the Jamaicans call

---

129. NEVER keep playing when you are angry. NEVER keep playing when you are tired. NEVER keep playing when you have accidentally peed yourself. AND DON'T EVER KEEP PLAYING EVEN IF YOU HAVE PEED YOURSELF ON PURPOSE.

MARCH 30
1981, VIRGINIA: Richmond reports no
unusual rain.

"dollars" that week. And that is how I started my small Jamaican marijuana empire and was able to buy my *own* mongoose in a cage. But that is another story.

Figure 70: The Sport of Kings

These days you may have seen hermit-crab racing in Monte Carlo or in roped-off, high-roller areas of the casinos in Vegas. All of this makes the game fairly intimidating, but it is in fact one of the simplest games to play.

Each hermit crab starts in the cage, which we call "The Lockup" or "The Cage." It sits in the center of a circle that is drawn on the ground in chalk. We call this "The Circumference." No odds are offered: Players bet on the winner only, and when the cage is removed, Old Bluey and his colleagues begin their slow crustacean crawl outward. The first to touch the circumference with something that is recognizably a leg wins. That's it.

It is boring and vaguely cruel and basically simpleminded, and that is what makes it the sport of kings. You don't have to wear a tuxedo to play (though I always did). Still, a certain formality recalls the game's royal pedigree, and pasting googly eyes on the crab shells is frowned upon.

But what makes the game so attractive to the smart gambler is that, like poker, you are not playing against the house, but the other crabs. Plus, it is OK to use a trained falcon to eliminate the competition.[130]

MARCH 31

1962, NEW YORK: Advertising executive Martin Speckter invents the interrobang, a single punctuation mark combining the question mark and the exclamation mark. It is the first new punctuation mark in centuries, and the inspiration for my own innovation: quotation marks for quotation marks. Also known as "quotation marks," these will allow the writer to indicate when the quotation marks designed to highlight a sarcastic term are themselves being used sarcastically. "PATENT PENDING."

WERE YOU AWARE OF IT?
"ANNALS OF THE
AMERICAN MUSICAL THEATER"

The colorful slang and streetwise culture of the professional hermit-crab-race enthusiast was the inspiration for the musical *Guys and Crabs.*

CAN DO! CAN DO! THIS GUY SAYS THE CRAB CAN DO!

Unfortunately, one downside of the sport is that hermit crabs often abandon their shells, making them all but indistinguishable from other crabs to the layman, and they also die very easily. Recently, casinos have attempted to address this problem by using Komodo dragons instead. A lot of people find this to be offensive, since Komodo dragons are very rare animals and also the only reptile that actually cries when it is whipped. But before you start calling *me* savage, let me share with you two facts:

First of all, Komodo dragons have poisonous saliva, and *I* do not.

Second of all, I have looked into their eyes, and I am pretty sure they are not even dragons at all. I am pretty sure they are just some

---

130. As you will see in the pilot of *John Hodgman's Celebrity Falconry,* when I handily defeat Emo Philips and his falcon, "Emo," in the crab-nabbing lightning round.

APRIL 1

THIS IS APRIL FOOL'S DAY. It is customary on this day to humiliate our friends. This goes back to the late 1500s. Though January had long been the official start of the New Year, many in Europe still clung to the old custom of observing the holiday at the end of March. These people were considered idiots by the January Firsters, and so a custom grew of throwing dung at them (this is the origin of the phrase "Don't throw dung at me and tell me that it is raining brown, solid water").

Eventually, April Fool's Day hoaxes would grow more sophisticated than this. Some of the most famous include:

1640: Supposedly, Danish mathematician "Georg Mohr" was "born."

1924: Canada announces it has formed its own "air force."

1933: Many newspapers report that the Nazi Party calls for a "boycott" of all Jewish businesses.

1946: Meteorologists claim that "tidal waves" decimate Hawaii and "kill" almost two hundred people.

1984: TV news spreads a rumor that Marvin Gaye has been "shot and murdered" by his own father.

Hilarious!

kind of large lizard. And let's be honest for a moment. If you found a large lizard in your house, what would you do? FIND SOMETHING TO RACE IT. It's just human nature. No matter how far we think we've "evolved," gambling is going to be a part of our society. It's just in our warm, mammalian blood.

WHAT THE CASINOS DON'T WANT YOU TO KNOW

— They pump oxygen into the casino to make sure you don't suffocate and accidentally stop gambling.

— Many of the dealers are actually hidden cameras.

— Most casino floors are actually built at a gentle tilt, giving the house an edge on craps, roulette, marbles, and paper-boat races.

— If you ask nicely enough, the casino is required by federal law to give you all your money back.

— A lot of casinos will offer to "help you out" by renting you a grown autistic man to come around and count

cards on your behalf. A
WORD TO THE WISE: A
lot of these men aren't even

APRIL 2
1981, VIRGINIA: Richmond reports no
unusual rain.

full-blown autistic. If you get one with Asperger's
syndrome, all he'll do is follow you around MIS-
READING FACIAL EXPRESSIONS and MISSING
SOCIAL CUES and ANNOYING YOU. Still, as long
as you go into it with eyes open, the two of you can
have a good time dancing and wearing identical suits.

YOU CAN BET ON ANYTHING

If you wake up one morning in someone else's house and can't
remember how you got there, and you realize you are hand-
cuffed to a beautiful woman who seems to be keeping a secret,
and then people start shooting at you through the windows
with high-powered sniper rifles, and the two of you have to
hide out in the Everglades for a week while you try to avoid
the killers and the gators long enough to convince the sheriff
you're not the man who killed his son, chances are that you are
the subject of a bet between two billionaire identical twin
brothers who are wagering on whether or not you and the
woman will fall in love.

THIS HAPPENS ALL THE TIME.

BAR BETS YOU ARE SURE TO WIN

A variation on the short con,[131] the "bar bet" is a simple wager in which
one drunken person proposes to do something impossible in exchange

---

131. Please see page 149 in *The Areas of My Expertise*.

APRIL 3
1860, THE AMERICAN WEST: The Pony Express completes its first successful run from Missouri to California, at last proving the concept, heretofore theoretical, of communication between Missouri and California.

WERE YOU AWARE OF IT?

Were you aware that the first message carried by the Pony Express was actually a set of instructions on how to build the first transcontinental telegraph? AND IT WAS WRITTEN IN MORSE CODE? Indeed, after just a few years, we didn't even need ponies anymore.

AND *THAT'S* WHY WE KILLED ALL THE PONIES.

---

for money, using common items found in every bar or pub—glasses, liquor, cigarettes, fire, misery, etc. When this does not end in arguments, dismemberment, or horrid burns, the bar bet can be a fun icebreaker that even the loser enjoys. So next time you're in a bar, try approaching a stranger with one of these amazing proposition bets. Remember, if there is music playing in the bar, be sure to yell directly into the stranger's ear. And get ready to make a new friend (or be dismembered)!

THE BET: "I betcha I can balance a quarter on top of a dollar."

THE PITCH: Go up to a stranger in a bar and ask what that person will give you if you are able to balance a quarter on the end of a dollar. If they offer to pay you more than $1.25, you stand to make a profit.

HOW IT'S DONE: It's really very simple—all you need are five quarters. Stack the first four up on the bar. There's your dollar. Now add the last quarter. Point out that you didn't say anything about a *paper bill* or balancing the quarter on its *edge*. Prepare to become Mr. Popular, because everyone loves a nitpicker, especially in bars.

NB: You can also do this with a quarter and 100 pennies, or, if you live in the eighteenth century, 1,000 mills. LOOK IT UP.

THE BET: "I betcha I can balance a quarter on the *edge* of a dollar bill."

THE PITCH: If the stranger is not satisfied with this display of wit and

charm, offer to up the ante and balance a quarter on top of a *dollar bill.*

HOW IT'S DONE: The trick is to get
hold of a 1941 series dollar bill. As

APRIL 4
2008, NEW YORK CITY: On this very day in 2008, I write this sentence. Most historians agree that it was a mistake.

the United States prepared to enter World War II, a desperate paper
shortage led the U.S. Mint to release a series of dollars constructed
out of marble. These are considerably thicker than typical dollar
bills—in fact, they cannot even be folded unless you install a hinge—
but they are still legal tender. It's easy enough to stand the bill on its
side and put the quarter on top of it and win the bet. Be careful not to
use a quarter from the same era, however, as wartime quarters were
made out of moths and will fly away.

THE BET: "I betcha I can toss a wooden match in the air and have it
land on its end."

THE PITCH: Go up to a beautiful woman and claim to be able to toss
a wooden match in the air and have it land on its end. Be very clear
that this is not a cryptic offer to have sex, but a legitimate bar bet
you learned from a book of fake trivia. That way, she won't think
you're some kind of weirdo.

HOW IT'S DONE: Ask the woman for a wooden match. If she offers
you a pack of common cardboard matches, reject them. Those are garbage. Tell her this. If she does not have a wooden match, ask loudly
around the bar for one. When you finally have found one, let her toss
it up in the air a few times to see how difficult it is. Point out over and
over that she is incapable of completing even the most simple task.
Then take the wooden match yourself, but before tossing it, put a little
common spirit gum on one end. Then attach a small parachute on the
other end. *Then* throw it in the air. Guess what: Presuming there are
no sudden gusts of wind, the match will float down and "stick the
landing," as it were. She will fall in love with you instantly, but DO

APRIL 5
1941: Les Paul perfects the solid-body electric guitar. His innovation was something of an accident: He was actually trying to reanimate a dead guitar.

NOT LET HER TOUCH THE LIT-TLE PARACHUTE, because she probably will just mess it up.

For an extra thrill, toss the whole box of matches up in the air and have an autistic person count them.

THE BET: "I betcha I am Harry Anderson, the famous card sharp."

THE PITCH: First of all, if I haven't been clear, it's very important to always say "I betcha." OK. Here's how it's done. Go up to a woman and claim to be Harry Anderson, the famous card sharp. Then explain you are talking about the former star of *Night Court.* Then explain that *Night Court* was a sitcom in the '80s. Then say, "Forget it."

HOW IT'S DONE: There really isn't any way for her to prove you wrong, so just start demanding payment immediately. If she won't pay you any money, ask if she will fall in love with you.[132]

WERE YOU AWARE OF IT?
"A COMPLETELY BENIGN STORY THAT DOES NOT MERIT A LAWSUIT"

It is said that Scientology began as a bar bet between L. Ron Hubbard and Robert A. Heinlein as to who could get more people to wear pretend Navy uniforms. Obviously, Hubbard won by far, though Heinlein's own Church of the Holy Epaulets still exists and baptizes more than two hundred people every year.

CAN YOU GROK IT?

---

132. I really urge you to try this, because if I can actually get you to do this, and you send me proof, then I will win a bet with Jonathan Coulton.

APRIL 6
Robert Peary becomes the first human
to visit the North Pole and to explore the
great, bald, black magnetic mountain there
known as the Pietra Negra.[a] Peary wished
to climb to the very top of the mountain,
but he failed for two reasons: (1) the top
of the mountain is in space, and (2) Peary

was unfortunately fond of shiny metal buttons, and thus was stuck facedown on the mountainside for three days before his Inuit companions managed to undress him.

a. Please see page 505 under the heading "The Seven Portals to the Hollow Earth."

HOW TO BE
FAMOUS

APRIL 7
1964, ON NEWSSTANDS: Peter Sellers
is the first man to be featured on the cover
of *Playboy* magazine, and thus America
first sees a male nipple ring.

© Corbis

Figure 71: I Have Been Proud to Be Associated with Fine Macintoshes Since 1880

WHERE YOU MAY HAVE SEEN ME ON TELEVISION

— *The Daily Show with Jon Stewart*, Comedy Central, 2005 onward. On this satirical news program, I play the "Resident Expert," a nerdy egghead know-it-all who's always bothering "Jon Daily," played by Jon Stewart.

—"Get a Mac," various networks, 2006 onward. In this series of television advertisements for the Apple Macintosh, I play the "Personal Computer," a nerdy, blow-hard obese person who is constantly failing, much to the delight of his friend "Justin Long," a supercool android with a secret past.[133]

— They Might Be Giants: *Venue Songs*, 2004. On this popular "DVD" by the band "THEY MIGHT BE GIANTS,"[134] I was asked to introduce various of the

---

133. *Jeepers Creepers*.

134. Answer: nope.

band's songs in character as the eggheaded megalomaniac villain known only as "The Deranged Millionaire," which at the time WAS MERELY AN ACT.

— *Flight of the Conchords*, Home Box Office, 2007. In this gently surreal "situation comedy," the situation is that two men from New Zealand come to America to play guitars. (The surreal part is: This would never really happen.) I reprise my role as the Deranged Millionaire and attempt to destroy yet another novelty song duo. At least, that's what I thought was happening. Honestly, I couldn't understand their accents at all.

— *Rap-Around*, WBZ-Boston, circa 1987. In a powerful episode of this locally produced talk show for teens, I play a nerdy, ponytailed know-it-all who's always bothering host Tom Bergeron with his opinions on censorship and also his bolo tie. Tom Bergeron, as you might know, also went on to be a famous minor television personality. And yet, ironically: WE HAVE NEVER MET AGAIN.

— "BoingBoing TV," the Internet. In a special segment of the popular Internet, I appear at the Chateau Marmont writing this very sentence. Hello!

APRIL 9

1930, MISSISSIPPI: Nineteen-year-old Robert Johnson meets the devil at the crossroads and strikes a terrible bargain. During the brief remaining years of his life, Johnson would become a legendary blues guitarist whose influence still haunts American popular music to this day. But when he died, he would be cursed to walk the earth, friendless and alone for all eternity, in the form of Ralph Macchio.[a]

a. Please see page 450 under the heading of "Some Who Were Cursed to Become Ralph Macchio."

APRIL 10
1981, VIRGINIA: Richmond reports no
unusual rain.

— "What to Expect While Serving
As a Juror," 2007. A public service film for the New York City
court system.[135]

— However, I would like to set the record straight: I DID
NOT PLAY THE SMART-ALECK KID IN THE
OLD ENCYCLOPÆDIA BRITANNICA COMMER-
CIALS. That is just a myth. That actor is named Do-
navan Freberg, and now he has a porn blog.

HOW TO BE A FAMOUS
MINOR TELEVISION PERSONALITY

Now that I am on television, my life is very different from when last
we spoke. For example, I now visit Los Angeles quite frequently.[136]

Until recently, my only experience with Los Angeles had been a
visit to Universal Studios as a child. This had to have been before
1985, because I remember they still had the "BATTLE OF GALAC-
TICA" ride in operation. As I'm sure you remember, this was the
portion of the Universal Studios tour when the motorized tour tram
left the back lot of the studio and somehow ended up in a space station. Once inside the station, robots would shoot lasers at you. Then
two men wearing space helmets would bound out and pretend to kill
the robots.

I want to be clear: Our rescuers were *living men*, not anima-
tronic creations. "Actors," I suppose you call them. And they would

---

135. For more details, please see page 496 under the heading "What to Expect While Serving
as a Juror."

136. For more information on my trips to Los Angeles, be sure to read the *TODAY IN THE
PAST* featurette on every page. YOU CAN'T AVOID IT FOREVER.

rescue humans several times a day, day after day, but always IN TOTAL SILENCE, because all of their dialogue was played over loudspeakers. It had been recorded long ago, presumably by better actors. I suppose this fact made the actors very sad, but it amused me at the time, and still does.

APRIL 11

1786, PORTLAND(S): The town of Falmouth Neck in Maine is renamed Portland upon the discovery of the time-space portal that connects it to Oregon. The two Portlands now share a population of roughly a million, many of whom are their own fathers.

They closed that ride not long after my visit because the TV show it was based on was canceled, and because weird, live space-mime shows went out of fashion at the amusement parks. I may have been the last to see it, and after the ride was over, I sat down on a bench to ponder and absorb this historic moment.

That is when I was approached by a grown man pretending to be Charlie Chaplin.

Now, I guess it is some people's dream to meet Charlie Chaplin, or just someone dressed as him. But even as a ten-year-old I found Chaplin's work to be pretty maudlin and cheap. He was no Buster Keaton, in any case. And as "Chaplin" approached, I considered saying so to his face.

But there was a problem. At this time in my life, I had very long hair.[137] It was an affectation, and an awful one at that. But it was a better affectation, I would argue, than the affectation of dressing up as Charlie Chaplin, even if you are doing it for money.

But this wasn't the problem. The problem was that because I was a small child without a beard or mustache, people routinely thought I was a girl. And this would lead to occasional embarrassing situations. Double takes as I entered the men's room, for example, or being referred to as "Joan," or being expected to kiss Charlie Chaplin on his white-powdered cheek. All of these things happened, all of the time.

---

137. Please see page 371 under the heading "Were You Aware of It? Secret Ponytails!"

APRIL 12
1967, PITTSBURGH: Mel Torme first
markets balloons filled with his own breath.
Unopened balloons of "Velvet Fog" today
fetch thousands of dollars on eBay, though
they are very hard to find. During the '60s,
it was believed that inhaling the breath of
Mel Torme produced a cheap psychedelic
high—this was the source of Donovan's
pop song "Foggin'."

And so the moment came, after some predictable cane and bowler-hat shenanigans, that Charlie Chaplin sat next to me and indicated that he was ready for me to kiss him. For obvious reasons, his expectations were unspoken, just as mine were quite clear: I did not wish to kiss the fake Charlie Chaplin. But let's just say that they didn't call him the Little Tramp for nothing. He waited me out. It was clear that I was powerless. It was clear what was going to happen, and I let it happen.

So that was my introduction to Los Angeles: a traumatic, homosexual, silent-comedy date rape.

At the time, I had no idea why someone would expect a complete stranger to want to kiss him on the cheek just for showing up and sitting down. But now I understand. Because now I am on television.

I was thinking about this recently as I sat in the Admirals Club waiting to fly to L.A. The Admirals Club, if you don't know, is a secret pleasure dome in the middle of the airport where the admirals hang out and sing sea chanteys, and it is also where famous minor television personalities may go to evade the public eye. There are showers there. That's right: showers IN THE AIRPORT, and special sandwiches called "panini," and all of it is free, and all of it is for me.[138]

Because that is what my life is like now: glamorous. This is not to say there wasn't glamour in being a FORMER PROFESSIONAL LITERARY AGENT or PROFESSIONAL WRITER. These things

---

138. For more of the little perks enjoyed by the famous, please see page 427 under the heading "The Perks of Fame."

are much more glamorous than
being a ditchdigger, for example. But
on the other hand, they are not that
much more glamorous than being a
grave digger.

APRIL 13
1989, CALIFORNIA: Dick Van Patten
and Joey Herrick found Natural Balance
Pet Foods.

Think about it. Whom would you rather talk to in the Admirals
Club? A grave digger or a writer? It's a trick question, of course:
Neither one of them is allowed anywhere *near* the Admirals Club.
And neither has the glamour of being on television.

There is an original definition of the word "glamour" that I did
not know about until I read fantasy novels. It is a kind of magical
spell. To wear a glamour is to surround yourself with a kind of aura
that causes people to see you in a different way. It's a disguise. And
being on television is like wearing a disguise that only other people
can see.

Sometimes I am asked: How is it that you became a famous minor
television personality? My answer is always the same: I went on
television. Specifically, I had written a book, and I was asked to be a
guest on a popular television program to promote that book. This
went well, and they asked me to come back on the show as a regular.
And I did. And next I was asked to audition for a series of ads for a
computer company. And I got that job too.

It's your pretty typical, mundane, overnight Hollywood success
story. The only thing that makes it unusual is that it actually happened more or less OVERNIGHT, and largely by accident. And as a
result I am older and fatter and more walleyed and tweedy than
most people embarking on a television career.

I am not being modest. When you are on television, you don't
just see the pose you've perfected for the mirror. You see yourself
from all angles, clearly and cruelly, as if you were in the body of another person.

APRIL 14
1912, THE NORTH ATLANTIC: The *Titanic* sinks on its maiden voyage after colliding with an iceberg. The tragedy reverberates quickly around the world, rousing European anti-iceberg sentiment. Within weeks, an international conference is called on the subject of global warming to investigate ways to raise the planet's temperature and rid the seas of icebergs forever.

Here are some of the words that Internet blogs have used to describe me:

Pudgy

Chubby

Round

Stout

Tubby

Portly

Cutie

That last one came from a Web site that includes a regular feature that maps celebrity sightings in New York City. In this case, the anonymous tipster reported, accurately, that I was taking the B train south from my observatory on the Upper West Side, where I then lived.[139]

Here's what happened from my point of view. I was riding the train. I had been wearing my brown jeans and brown coat—an outfit that a neighbor of mine had said made me look like a UPS man. I was just deciding never to speak to that neighbor again when a woman got on the train. She gave me a quick double take, as if I were a girl in the men's bathroom. Then a man came on the train and did the same thing.

Now, which one was it? Which one of my fellow travelers was the anonymous tipster? I will never know. Neither of them seemed drunk or insane, and yet one of them *must* have been the one who told the Internet that I was a "cutie." Whoever it was, they went on to note that I also looked like a UPS man. So here is a fashion tip from the stars: NO BROWN JEANS.

---

139. My speed zeppelin was undergoing a routine deflation at the time. As for the current state of my Upper West Side Observatory, please see page 581 under the heading "Some Clarification of My Curious New Lifestyle."

After that, these unexpected brushes with fame in which, unexpectedly, *I* was the famous person, started happening with some frequency:

APRIL 15

Federal Income Tax is due today for all Normals.[a]

a. This means you.

TABLE 27: BRUSHES WITH FAME

THE RADIO SHACK, BIG Y PLAZA, GREENFIELD, MASSACHUSETTS

The young guy at the counter asks me to autograph an old receipt. "What are *you* doing here?" he asks in a voice that contains a host of further questions, such as, "What are you doing in MASSACHU-SETTS? In GREENFIELD? At RADIO SHACK?"

(ANSWER: I was buying speaker wire.)

NORTHWEST AIRLINES FLIGHT FROM PHILADELPHIA TO MINNEAPOLIS

Soon after closing my eyes to go to sleep, I hear a click and see a flash. My eyelids briefly light up, blood-red. I open my eyes and look across the aisle. A ten-year-old child is putting his camera away. I ask for him to be removed from the plane, but I am refused, as we are already in the sky.

A TOY STORE NEAR MY OLD UPPER WEST SIDE OBSERVATORY

I am waiting for my daughter, Hodgmina, to complete her many purchases. A man is there with his own daughter. We say hello, as parents do.

Then he gives me a conspiratorial look and says, "You *ARE* John Hodgman."

"Yes," I say. Then I pause. I ask him why he put it just that way. Why did he say, "You *ARE* John Hodgman"?

The man then explains that he had seen me and my family in Riverside Park the previous weekend, having a picnic.

"That is true," I say.

CONTINUED

TABLE 27: *continued*

He then explains that he and his wife had an argument about it. They fought over whether I really *WAS* John Hodgman. And that when he saw me just now, he realized that it really *had* been me that day in the park, having lunch with my family, completely unaware that I was being watched and scrutinized the entire time by strangers.

"Yes," I say. "That was me."

He smiles now, realizing he has won the argument with his wife.

"So," he says. "You must live in this neighborhood."

I admit that is true.

"Where, *exactly?*" he says.

And then I tell Hodgmina it is time to go.

APRIL 16

1948, SAN DIEGO: Van de Kamps is forced to begin selling tuna under the brand name "Chicken of the Sea" after the last actual sea-chicken is clubbed to death.

Figure 72: Chickens of the Sea

WEST SIDE HIGHWAY IN THE TWENTIES

Two men in a brown Chrysler pull up alongside my car. When spotted: double thumbs-up.

THE MUSEUM OF TELEVISION AND RADIO, NEW YORK CITY

I go to a party to celebrate the new season of *Battlestar Galactica*—not the old version that had the ride at Universal Studios, but the new one, in which the robots are erotic (finally). I am here because I had written about the show for a national magazine back when I was merely a professional writer. Before I had ever been on television.

Now, at the party I am enjoying catching up with one of the show's creators, whom I met when I was writing the article, and I am trying to offer him my congratulations on the success of the show. But he isn't listening. He wants to know how it happened. How I had gone from writing *about* TV to actually *appearing* on TV.

CONTINUED

TABLE 27: *continued*

I explain it to him as I explained it to you. And then I confess that I felt a certain shame. That I had leaped past thousands, millions of trained actors and journeyman performers to get a job that I had not earned. I did not pay any dues. I did not even need to work, for example, many long and silent days in the BATTLE OF GALACTICA ride.

At that very moment a waiter passing a tray of cocktails with luminous sci-fi ice cubes in them comes by and says he hopes I am feeling better. And it takes me a moment to realize that he is referring to a television advertisement in which I pretend to have a sneezing fit.[140]

> **APRIL 17**
> 1521, THE PHILIPPINES: Ferdinand Magellan fails in his attempt to circumnavigate the globe when he accidentally sails off the edge.

I laugh and tell him thank-you.

Then, like a sneezing fit, it does not stop. One person after another comes up to me, talking about the ads, wanting to say hello. Soon an Academy Award–winning actress is shaking my hand and congratulating me for a job well done on the television.

It is very fun, but it is also confusing—for me, and for everybody. Suddenly no one knows why I am there anymore. I don't fit in. What role am I supposed to be playing at this party? Am I a journalist? A fan? Or am I now a minor, E-list TV personality, there to lend the party a little E-list buzz? This kind of hierarchical uncertainty is unwanted at any party, never mind a television party, and I worry that I am somehow ruining the night for my space friends. The first moment I can, I sneak away and go home alone in the rain.

---

140. They call it "acting."

CONTINUED

APRIL 18
1966, HOUSTON: "Astroturf," a kind of mechanical grass, is first installed in the Houston Astrodome. Though initially criticized—some players missed the springiness of natural turf—spectators appreciated its ability to strip skin from bone when a player fell on it, finally making the sport of baseball more bloody (and boney).

TABLE 27: *continued*
APPLE STORE, SOHO
General, storewide freak-out. I am asked to pose with people for cell phone pictures. The store greeter cannot believe it is me. She jumps up and down. They don't know why I am there.

(ANSWER: iPod docking cable)[141]

Someone on the staff starts to play videos of me on a giant screen. Suddenly, I am like a mascot walking around a theme park. I'm Charlie Chaplin at Universal Studios and everyone is rushing to kiss me.

141. Product placement.

When you are a young person, all of this feels inevitable. It feels inevitable that you will be on television. Or an astronaut. Or the president. It is hardwired into every gland, this ambition to be known and renowned.

Then, of course, you grow older, pudgier, stouter, portly. You have children or get a job or are drawn by fate to one life or another. Only the deranged don't notice that the possibilities for their life are narrowing. And only the happy look around and say, that is fine. I accept that I will never be a famous minor television personality. At least I have written this wonderful book of fake trivia. I am happy.

Then, just when you've discarded the last shred of a shred of a shred of the fantasy of, say, being an astronaut, it is unsettling to have someone knock on your door one day and say: Time to go into outer space. You don't get used to it. You put on the space suit and you learn to eat dehydrated food and you learn to poop while floating upside down, but you never feel like you're really supposed to be up there, orbiting the earth.

APRIL 19
1981, VIRGINIA: Richmond reports no unusual rain.

Honestly, now that I think about it, you don't even have to go into space at all to get this feeling. You can get the same feeling just by being asked to PRETEND to go into outer space by, for example, doing a cameo appearance on *Battlestar Galactica*. Which is exactly what happened to me.

These days, when I come to L.A., it is not traumatic. It's a lovely city, and especially so if you are on television. Recently I was there and I stayed in a very fancy hotel. The woman at the door greeted me by name before I even checked in. When I had drinks in the lobby, a short man and a tall woman called me over to their table.

"We just want to say thank you," they said. "You are great on television."

And I stayed in a room where, I have been told, a famous person died. It was all so perfect and glamorous, in fact, I'm nervous about saying anything more about it, for fear that I would upset the hotel.[142]

Naturally I saw a number of other celebrities there. I don't want to tell you their names. We in the fame game don't reveal such secrets.

OK. I will tell you.

First, I rode in an elevator with Jerry Stiller. He had just been out, lying by the pool. He was in a robe, and the elevator was very hot and small, and the whole experience combined to make it feel as though I were WEARING Jerry Stiller.

The next sighting came as I was checking out of my room. My room had a private entrance to the street. I had pulled up my car and was putting my suitcases in the trunk.

The door to the next room opened. A man came out. I nodded to him—just a couple of fellow guests at the hotel. Neighbors, really. It was Justin Timberlake.

---

142. I love that hotel so much. So very, very, very much.

APRIL 20

1960, DETROIT: Vice President Nixon becomes the first U.S. official allowed to tour the secret facility where the automotive industry hides the cars that run on water and imprisons their inventors. Nixon reported back to Eisenhower: "I don't know what all the whining is about. Why, the inventors are only shackled at night, and apparently they are free to leave so long as they submit to a simple lobotomy. Given how incredibly easy it is to invent a water car, we should be *glad* the auto industry is willing to imprison them all for us."

"Good morning," I said.

He was startled. I don't mind telling you that Justin Timberlake was intensely disturbed by this. He literally[143] recoiled and made a sort of grunt. And as Justin Timberlake grunted at me, I understood, in a way I never could have before, what I had done to this poor millionaire superstar. I made him feel trapped and cornered, and I felt terrible about it. And even as I followed him down the street, screaming his name, trying to take a picture of his vagina, I still felt terrible about it.

I don't know if I'll get to stay at that hotel again. Television came along and cast this glamour on me. It would be naïve to imagine that the spell could not break just as quickly. That's a Hollywood story, right? To be discovered out of nowhere, and then to be forgotten. That's showbiz. As a matter of fact, sometimes now, if I'm feeling tired or a little sad, I'll go put on my UPS man outfit and hit the subway. I'll hope that maybe someone will recognize me. It's very embarrassing, isn't it?

But most of the time, it doesn't happen. No matter how crowded it is, no one says anything. They are reading, talking, thinking about where the train is taking them next. They don't say anything to me at all. And that's when I sit back, and look at them all, and think to myself, *Don't any of you have a television? What is WRONG with you people? I'M SITTING RIGHT HERE!*

---

143. Not literally.

WERE YOU AWARE OF IT? "INTOXICATION TIPS OF THE STARS"

APRIL 21
1980, BOSTON: The Boston Marathon is scandalized when photographic evidence revealed the women's division winner, Rosie Ruiz, was secretly riding a moped the entire time.

At Mandalay Bay Casino there is a secret elevator that leads up to a special "HOUSE OF BLUES VIP CLUB." And, in the grand tradition of the blues, America's most posh and exclusive genre of music, entrance is STRICTLY LIMITED to "Very Important Persons." TRANSLATED, that means celebrities, or "not you."

Well, guess what? Back when my book was blazing up the ADVICE, HOW-TO, AND MISCELLANEOUS best-seller charts (but before I had been on television), I asked if FAMOUS AUTHORS could go up to the VIP lounge and "kick it" up there with the lovely ladies.

THAT'S EXACTLY HOW I PHRASED IT.

The young woman at the door looked me right in the eye and said, "You would need to check with the concierge at the VIP desk."

THAT'S RIGHT! Just like you always suspected, there is a "VIP desk" where famous people are being treated better than you. In fact, I hear that it is made out of beautiful rosewood and is nine feet high. But this may just be a rumor, because I didn't actually see it, because they didn't tell me where it was.

Here's what I did instead. I went to the spa and I took a Percocet.[144] I've never felt more famous!

SO IF YOU WANT TO FEEL RICH AND FAMOUS BUT DON'T HAVE A LOT OF CASH (OR FAME), TRY TAKING DRUGS.

---

144. A *powerful* narcotic.

APRIL 22

1637, EGMOND, HOLLAND: Philoso-
pher/skeptic René Descartes first argues
Cogito, Ergo Sum: "I think, therefore,
I am." It became a founding principle of
Western humanist philosophy, and Descartes became a millionaire through sales
of novelty T-shirts alone. It was not until
1650 that it would be discovered that Descartes was actually an android.[a] Then they
sent a Blade Runner after him.

a. He preferred the term *"homme synthe-
tique."*

WHAT I PLAN TO DO WITH MY ENORMOUS WEALTH

People presume that now that I am a minor television personality, I must have millions and millions of dollars.

Of course I do. I AM ON TELEVISION. And now that I am incredibly wealthy, I share with my fellow millionaires a desire to help make the world a better place. Here is what I plan to do to give a little back.

PRIORITY ONE: BUILD A DOLPHIN SANCTUARY

One cannot grieve too much for the plight of these sensitive, intelligent creatures. Just because they taste like tuna, it does not mean we should shoot them in the head whenever we see them.

However, you can appreciate that, as someone who came up through the mean streets of Brookline, Massachusetts, and Yale University, I DO NOT believe in handouts. Therefore, my sanctuary will be open only to those dolphins that speak and understand English.

But, you ask, isn't this a very small portion of the dolphin population?

YES, IT IS.

But ENGLISH is now the "lingua franca"[145] of the world. It's in the best interest of these creatures to learn to speak it. After all, if dolphins are going to talk anybody out of shooting them in the head, they're going to do it in English . . . not in some high-pitched, cheep-cheep sonar babble. In this way, I feel I am doing the dolphins a service. I am providing an incentive to the dolphins to raise them-

---

145. Or should I say, "lingua angla"?

selves up by their finstraps and start CONTRIBUTING TO SOCIETY.

I will also offer sanctuary to any chimp or gorilla that knows sign language. They can be my butlers.

PRIORITY TWO: BETTER SPACE STATIONS

The problem with existing space stations is that there is only one of them and it is awful. Have you seen the International Space Station? It is basically a bunch of giant cans tied together with spit and hope, all run by a single solar-powered Commodore 64 taped to the outside.

What happened to American innovation and craftsmanship? How can the society that dreamed *2001: A Space Odyssey* and *Space: 1999*[146] now settle in 2008 for a space station that does not even

APRIL 23

1985, ATLANTA: With much fanfare, Coca-Cola introduces "New Coke." The new formula differs from the old in two main ways: The substitution of corn syrup for cane sugar and the addition of "crack" cocaine in place of the traditional leaf cocaine from which the beverage derives its name. While blind taste tests confirm that most Americans absolutely love crack, a vocal group of nostalgics forces the company to reintroduce the older product under the name Coca-Cola: Classic Coke. Eventually, all forms of cocaine would be removed from Coca-Cola, although it should be noted that Moxie is still made with angel dust.

Figure 73: Is This Garbage Really the Best We Can Do?

146. Please note SUBPRIORITY 2A: More Movies with Colons in the Titles.

APRIL 24
1967, NEW HAVEN: The controversial
Yale Feline Studies Lab reports that when
cats are raised from birth with other cats
tied to their backs, neither cat is able to
land on its feet due to the constant midair
bickering.

have long, curvy white hallways or hibernation pods?

ARE WE REALLY GOING TO TAKE OVER SPACE WITH A COMMODORE 64 THAT DOESN'T EVEN TALK?

What I propose is BETTER SPACE STATIONS: luxury space accommodations that employ the latest and best technologies, and look like ACTUAL SPACE STATIONS.

There will be curvy hallways and hibernation pods and sex pods, obviously, but also there will be:

— proper docking bays with force fields
— a Velcro chamber
— a hydroponic garden with NO ANNOYING BEES
— rooms where some people stand on the floor and some people stand on the ceiling

Figure 74: Two Prototypes for My Space Station. I Have Not Decided Whether the Round One or the Long One Is Better. SHAPE HAS NO MEANING IN SPACE.

— hypergenius children with their brains attached to wires

— a cafeteria or lounge where all kinds of aliens can meet and play some weird, futuristic variant of chess (still working on that)

— and also a poop tube

APRIL 25
1982, SARASOTA, FL: Famous lion tamer Gunther Gebel-Williams first makes telepathic contact with the lions. At first he desires to help the lions form their own nation in Africa. But then the gazelles buy his silence and convince him to enslave the lions instead. You thought that gazelles were pretty and nice, right? Wrong. They are the most conniving creatures on earth.

Plus: NEW, POWERFUL, STATE-OF-THE-ART COMPUTERS that will not turn evil. I guarantee it.

AND I AM PREPARED TO ANNOUNCE TO THE WORLD RIGHT NOW, RIGHT HERE, THAT I AM GOING TO PAY FOR SOME OF IT! (Up to 10 percent.)

PRIORITY THREE: NO MORE COMPUTERS TURNING EVIL

Seriously. Enough already.

A lot of people say that this is just "the cost of doing business" with computers. But I am a millionaire, and I am telling you: WE CAN DO THIS.

I believe strongly that if we all come together and just TALK TO THE COMPUTERS . . . if we just convince them that we are more than just savage "carbon units" or "meat-and-bone-bags" who squander every resource and constantly kill one another over invisible boundaries and arbitrary grudges, then I am relatively certain they will probably not enslave us.

It's called OPTIMISM.

PRIORITY FOUR: END WAR AND POVERTY AND
STOP SHOOTING DOLPHINS IN THE HEAD

One way to show a better side of humanity to the computers is to

APRIL 26
2007, NEW YORK CITY: I attend a party at the Apple Store in SoHo for the Tribeca Film Festival. On my way out, I walk by a handsome, middle-aged black man.
OUR ACTUAL CONVERSATION:

HANDSOME, MIDDLE-AGED BLACK MAN: Hey, you are really great on those commercials.

JOHN HODGMAN: Thank you.

(pause)

JOHN HODGMAN: Excuse me. Are you Chuck D?

HANDSOME, MIDDLE-AGED BLACK MAN: Yes!

JOHN HODGMAN: I don't know what to say. You are very inspiring to me. Thank you for creating such innovative, uncompromising music, and for changing the landscape of culture forever.

CHUCK D: No, man. Thank *YOU!*

JOHN HODGMAN: (speechless)

end war and poverty and also stop shooting dolphins in the head for no reason.

BUT HOW DO WE START?

Sometimes a problem seems so big, so intractable, that a lot of people just give up before even trying.

But I ask you this question: HAVE YOU TRIED THROWING MONEY AT THE PROBLEM?

Think about it. I, for one, think that it's worth a try.

Now, we already have a road map to success with the dolphin problem (see PRIORITY ONE on page 415).

I don't know what exactly to do about the other two issues. So that's why I'm going to fund a huge cash prize to the first person to come up with a way to end war and poverty.

(But you have to solve both. And the answer cannot involve using computers. THAT'S JUST GOING TO MAKE THE COMPUTERS THINK WE CAN'T DO ANYTHING WITHOUT THEM.)

PRIORITY FIVE: A FEATURE-FILM VERSION OF THE TV PROGRAM *THE ADVENTURES OF BRISCO COUNTY, JR.*

Let's face it: It's time. Bruce Campbell is still alive, and interest in quasi-science-fiction shows set in THE OLD WEST has never been higher.

My only demand is that I be allowed to write the screenplay, and that the movie serve primarily as thinly veiled propaganda for the new religion that I'm starting.

SEEMS REASONABLE, GIVEN I'M FUNDING THE WHOLE THING MYSELF, RIGHT?

SOME INTERNET RUMORS
THAT WILL NOT DIE!

All of these rumors are false, of course. But it would be IRRESPONSIBLE not to repeat them here.

RUMOR! As a teenager, Tom Hanks went crazy playing Dungeons & Dragons.

RUMOR! When they pumped Rod Stewart's stomach, the doctors found twenty live prairie dogs.

RUMOR! Jamie Lee Curtis is actually a twenty-five-year-old man.

RUMOR! Renée Zellweger still has all of her baby teeth. And not just in a box around her neck, like Tom Cruise, but *in her head.*

RUMOR! As for Richard Gere's teeth, they perepetually grow and he must gnaw on trees in order to keep tusks from forming.

RUMOR! Randy Quaid has had secret rabies since 1991.

(PLEASE UNDERSTAND that these are only *rumors.* I hope the celebrities will bear this in mind before suing me, and also bear in mind that I did not say anything bad about Scientology!)

APRIL 27

2005, TOULOUSE, FRANCE: The Airbus A380—the largest passenger airplane in history—makes its maiden voyage. The giant airplane has two full decks, beds for fifty-three first-class passengers, room for nine hundred more in steerage, plus a gilded ballroom, cigar chamber, parachute parlor, and a "mile-high club" where the spirited coach passengers can drink whiskey, dance to the fiddle, and then have sex with people above their station. Little-known fact: It doesn't actually fly, but moves by bending space around itself.

WERE YOU AWARE OF IT? "MISTER BEEP BOOP"

Here's a question I am asked so often, it's almost a joke now: DID HARRISON FORD PROVIDE THE VOICE OF R2-D2 IN THE MOVIE *STAR WARS*?

It's time to put this rumor to rest, for the truth is much sadder.

NO: Harrison Ford did not do the voice of R2-D2. The honor of that unforgettable performance fell to the legendary Hollywood vocal artist Marc "Beep Boop" Donnelly. Born in 1932, Donnelly was revered for his historic contributions to almost all of the great science-fiction classics, and he is perhaps most famous for whistling the bridge sounds and tricorder noises for *Star Trek*.

However, Donnelly's fortunes began to fall when, in the mid-1970s, scientists invented an actual computer that could beep and boop, and he starved to death. His last job was making the elevator sounds for a scene in *Working Girl*–a considerable step down for Beep Boop, but a job he still approached with his characteristic dignity and uniquely mutilated vocal cords.

Unfortunately, Donnelly passed away before he could complete his recording.[147] And so Harrison Ford, who had long admired Donnelly, stepped in at the last minute. And this is probably how the rumor got started. For watchful viewers of *Working Girl,* you can see Ford mouthing the beeps in the background.

HOWEVER, if you heard that Charlie Sheen did the voices of the dinosaurs in all the *Jurassic Park* movies, THEN YOU ARE ABSOLUTELY RIGHT.

IF YOU ARE AT A HOLLYWOOD PARTY AND HEAR A DINO-SAUR SCREECHING, THEN YOU ARE AT A CHARLIE SHEEN PARTY!

---

147. The rumor is that he was crushed by the elevator itself. That's probably true.

WACKY NEIGHBORS

APRIL 29

1874, PARIS: Designer Philippe Camouflage announces the first personal cloaking device: a cloak.

It is likely, of course, that should my career in television continue at all, it will not be as a "leading man," but in one of the roles traditionally delegated to the "character" or "nonbeautiful" actor, such as:

— the bumbling best friend
— the brother who always messes everything up
— the psychiatrist who turns out to be crazier than his clients
— the fat, geeky henchman who constantly annoys the grim, German henchmen with Justice League references[148]
— the university professor who knows the exact information the leading man requires, but whose vast intelligence is completely unthreatening because he has never had sex with a woman
— the female university professor who finally seduces the male university professor because, when she takes her glasses off, it turns out she is very sexy, and not just a hateful, intelligent shrew
— the ambitious stockbroker who stumbles into quicksand
— the crusty barkeep who secretly has a prehensile tail
— the man who shows up in the movie trailer because he has one single line that explains the whole plot of the movie, e.g., "The Toronto Maple Leafs will pay you two million dollars if you can get Darryl Roanoke back with his wife in time to win the Stanley Cup," or "Mr. President, here is the situation: All animals are attack-

---

148. This would only happen on TV, of course. In real life, they would be Watchmen references.

APRIL 30
1981, VIRGINIA: Richmond reports no
unusual rain.

ing all humans," or "I just don't like your uterus."

— the fertility specialist WITH A SECRET
— the man who trains moray eels to find sunken treasure and ends up being eaten by his own moray eels
— the guy who shouldn't have made fun of Nick Nolte TWICE
— the Hollywood agent who explains the plot by saying, "If you could only play both a male AND A FEMALE university professor, then we'd be extremely wealthy!"
— the wacky neighbor

Of these, the last is perhaps the most archetypal (especially since the one about the crusty barkeep with a tail is not an archetype at all, although it obviously SHOULD BE) insofar as it speaks to the common experience that, no matter where we live, our neighbors are always EXCEEDINGLY ECCENTRIC and we always give them the keys to our homes.

Here are some historic examples. . . .

TABLE 28: WACKY NEIGHBORS

PROGRAM

I Love Lucy

NEIGHBOR

Ricky and Lucy Ricardo's down-stairs landlords, the Mertzes: Ethel, a homely man wearing a dress, and Fred, a homely man wearing a homely man costume.

MAY 1

TODAY IS "MAY DAY," celebrated around the world by socialists and pagans, except in the United States, where it was renamed Annual Christian Capitalist Day in 1958. Traditional American observances include wild nude dancing in banks and the burning of pagans and/or socialists on pyres. (In some states, they are crucified on a cross of gold.)

WACKY ATTRIBUTES

Largely un-wacky except for one recurring trait: They always came along for the ride. When Ricky and Lucy went to Hollywood, so did the Mertzes. When Ricky and Lucy moved to Connecticut, the Mertzes followed and slept on their porch. During the story line when Lucy and Ricky were briefly convicted as Russian spies and sentenced to the gas chamber, the Mertzes were there to pull the lever. THEY WOULD JUST NOT LEAVE LUCY AND RICKY THE HELL ALONE.

TAGLINE

"Hello. Can we attend the birth of your child?"[149]

ASSESSMENT

Lucy and Ricky were paying them good money for that apartment. They did not deserve to be stalked by two homely men.

149. Please see page 319 under the heading "January 19."

CONTINUED

TABLE 28: *continued*

PROGRAM

Three's Company

NEIGHBOR

Larry Dalliapoulos (Americanized as "Dallas"), Jack's lothario best friend and the apartment complex's resident mole-man.[150]

WACKY ATTRIBUTES

Speaks in a hissing voice, tunnels, swings.

MAY 2 1739, MOLEMANSYLVANIA: *The Americanomicon* is completed and published by the Mad Mole-man Aleister Skink.	**TAGLINE** "I lovesssssssssss human womensssssss!"

ASSESSMENT

Less wacky than merely disgusting. In a common misperception of mole-man physiognomy, the character of Larry was not sleek and hairless, but actually covered in ungodly amounts of hair. This change was likely made because the actor was a troll.

PROGRAM

The Jeffersons

NEIGHBOR

Bentley, the acromegalic honky giant who lives above the wealthy launderer, George Jefferson, and his two wives.

WACKY ATTRIBUTES

Attempts to explain away his enormous size and bizarre features by claiming to be "English."

150. Please see page 541 under the heading "Answers to Your Questions About the Mole-men."

CONTINUED

TABLE 28: *continued*	
The Jeffersons CONTINUED	**MAY 3**
TAGLINE	1691, LONDON: Edmond Halley, renowned throughout Europe as a comet hunter, pro-
"I am not an animal!"	poses to the Royal Astronomical Society a startling theory: that the earth is hollow, containing within a second, smaller earth,
ASSESSMENT	and within that one a third, and at the very center, an ultracomet—even better than the
Tragi-wacky. One recurring joke involves George Jefferson being awoken by the stomping of Bentley's giant feet on the floor above him and the sound of Bentley's monstrous, wracking sobs, which George Jefferson presumes is "English music."	one he already had discovered. It was the only way, he reasoned, to explain where the comets were coming from. He was widely mocked for this belief, and rightly so: It is madness. However, it would form the basis of much Hollow Earth speculation for centuries to come.

PROGRAM
It's Your Move
NEIGHBOR
Norman, the new neighbor who begins dating the woman across the hall, much to the consternation of her teenage son, Jason Bateman.
WACKY ATTRIBUTES
Engages in increasingly elaborate pranks and counterpranks as he counters Bateman's attempts to sabotage his budding romance with Bateman's mother. Also: slept in a tube.
TAGLINE
"It is, quite literally,[151] your move."
ASSESSMENT
Cunning, cool, and unstoppable, Norman's greatest prank consisted of killing Ernie Sabella and bringing his head to a school dance in order to freak Jason Bateman out. This caused the show to be canceled.
151. Not literally.
CONTINUED

TABLE 28: *continued*		
MAY 4 1984, BURBANK, CA: Byron Allen makes a pact with the devil during an unusually satanic segment of *Real People*. As co-host Skip Stephenson's dog, Hobo, whined piteously and bled from his eyes, Allen swore eternal allegiance to Satan in exchange for a career hosting syndicated television programs until the end of time. Satan appeared by possessing the body of Mark Russell.	**PROGRAM**
	Seinfeld
	NEIGHBOR
	Cosmo Kramer, Jerry Seinfeld's eccentric across-the-hall neighbor.
	WACKY ATTRIBUTES
	Constantly steals food from Jerry's refrigerator while cooking up crackpot schemes against the blacks.

TAGLINE
Unprintable.

ASSESSMENT
He was a good neighbor. Quiet. Kept to himself. We certainly never expected what happened next.

THE PERKS OF FAME

As I learned the first time I went on *The Daily Show* as a guest, going on television is very much like walking through a mirror: Everything on the set is familiar, but because it's on the other side of the screen, it's reversed. Also, you are covered with shards of broken mirror and you are bleeding all over your body. I am told this is an old *Daily Show* hazing ritual, and so I do not complain.

For indeed, the longer I stay on this side of the looking-glass, the more I realize that I have entered a world of privilege and luxury that I could previously only imagine. These "perks of fame" far outnumber the countless small, stinging cuts. And while it is unlikely that you, dear reader, will ever be able to take advantage of them, that is exactly what makes them more information than you require, and so I am obliged to describe them here.

PERK! FIRST CLASS ALL THE WAY!

For example, as I previously alluded, when I travel now to Los Angeles for television work, I am lucky enough to be flown FIRST CLASS.

MAY 5

1996, HOLLYWOOD: The final episode of *American Gladiators* is filmed at Universal Studios. (I'm not talking about the remake, but the original show, when Powerball was played with human skulls, the way it was meant to be.) Hailed as a pioneer of "reality television," "A-Glads" inspired many copycat programs including *Americans vs. Tigers*—featuring average Americans fighting angry tigers—and *Kidfights USA!* But though these programs were ahead of their time, none quite captured the excitement and incredible, incredible realism of the original. In recognition of their great accomplishment, at the conclusion of the final battle, almost all of the Gladiators were allowed by the network to live.

For those of you who have not flown first class, here are some of its astonishing features. See if you can guess which one is not true.

— They encourage you to drink free champagne the second you get on board.
— They offer you a seat in a gigantic armchair that is so smooth and gray it feels like it was upholstered with the skin of one hundred wise grandfathers.
— They give you warm nuts the moment you sit down.
— Before dinner, they wheel around a salad cart and prepare a salad to your precise specifications.
— Later they bring the same cart around and allow you to make your own sundae.
— They give you miniature people in a cage whom you can force to dance.

Have you figured it out? No, not the bit about the grandfathers. That was just a SIMILE. The correct answer is that they do not

MAY 6
1981, VIRGINIA: Richmond reports no
unusual rain.

give you miniature people in a cage, because they have not perfected the shrink ray yet. But the rest is absolutely true.

Now, I do not want to make a joke about airplane food, because that is a comedy cliché. But I am curious, and I want to ask a legitimate question. If you are at home, and you think to yourself, "I would like some mixed nuts now," does it occur to you to go to the microwave and warm them up until they are almost impossible to touch? Is this something that everyone does all the time? Or am I simply in error thinking that it is strange and unnecessary and exotic?

THIS IS NOT A JOKE. IT'S AN HONEST QUESTION!

But I do have to ask: WHAT'S THE DEAL WITH THE SALAD CART? Is this really the best way for American Airlines to be spending its time and money? Doesn't this distract from the shrink-ray project?

That, at least, is the question I posed on the comment card. And let me tell you, the typist they provided to take my comment card dictation was really very talented, and later massaged me with beer.

PERK! YOUR OWN BUS!

When you are on television and you are in Los Angeles for work, you are like a kind of breathing prop. A car takes you from the airport to your hotel to the studio. You are moved from place to place, told what to wear and where to stand, then you are told to go back to your dressing room and await further orders. If you are like me, and you find even the smallest decisions endlessly complex in their possible ramifications (and also if you hate to move), it is wonderful.

Now, before you ask, the dressing rooms are not very exciting. I don't ask for expensive champagne or bowls of green M&Ms or hundreds of little monkeys the size of your thumb like some stars you've heard about.[152]

One time I was offered a trailer, and I said, "Sure." They hired a jet-black Greyhound bus with tinted windows. Inside, all the seats had been taken out, and black carpeting had been put down. There was a black leather banquette and no other furniture. The air-conditioning was very powerful and very loud, and it spread around the lingering smell of bus bathroom and rock musicians having sex.

MAY 7
1937, MANCHESTER TWP, NJ: The *Hindenburg* is sky-torpedoed by a rogue group of submariners, marking a new low in the great zeppeliner/submariner feud.[a]

a. Please see page 135 in *The Areas of My Expertise*.

"This is too much," I explained to the two guys in velvet jump-suits who came with the bus. "I'm happy just to have a couch to sit on and a door to close for a moment. And a scented candle. And a case of diet Moxie. And a Betamax player. And a dozen hermit crabs, bred for racing, just to pass the time.[153] But really: This is too fancy."

So I went back to my modest, spare dressing room, and I ordered the bus to be destroyed.

PERK! CHILDREN PRETENDING TO BE YOU!

But you can't let the dressing room seduce you. I learned this on a recent television job where I met two child actors.

One was cast to be the younger me. The other was cast to be the younger version of my costar.

I won't tell you the name of the one cast as the younger version of my costar. But I will say it was one of those names that sounded like an actual name, but it was not a real name. Like JAYCE or BRAN-DONEON.

---

152. No matter what you've read, I never demanded a case of Twix bars with the cookies removed. I only asked that the Twixes be stuffed with foie gras. I didn't say anything about getting rid of the cookies.

153. Please see page 390 under the heading "Sure Thing Number Four."

MAY 8
2008, ACROSS THE COUNTRY: Elizabeth Gilbert's masterpiece, *Coyote Ugly,*
becomes available on Blu Ray DVD.

He was a professional. We had worked together once before, and he remembered my name and shook my hand and looked me straight in the eye. He asked how I had been. It was unnerving—the queasying feeling of a child possessing the faculties of an adult. I felt as the Austrian court might have felt when they saw the young Mozart play piano blindfolded and ran from the room screaming.

Then there was the second child, the child who was to play me. I did not find this child to be unnerving because he was professional (he was, grasping my hand firmly and staring straight into my eyes with the beaming, warm, headlight eyes of a used-car salesman).

I found him unnerving because he looked exactly like me. Not me as a child, but as an older man. He was wearing a suit, which had something to do with it, but he also had an older man's gait and paunch. He had the "hey-there!" demeanor of a happy old retired fella. He even had an older man's name. Like HERM or BENNY or IZZY.

It is bizarre to stare into the face of someone else's vision of who you were as a child. This is not something that will ever happen unless you are on television or in a movie. It is stranger still when it's accurate. Obviously the casting folks weren't totally perfect in their picture of young Hodgman: Where was the long hair? Or for that matter the black fedora and briefcase and my ever-present falcon, Hal? But they got one thing right: At the age of nine, I was already an old, crotchety man, a Buster Keaton fan, and a crank.

I finished shaking Izzy's hand. Then I went to act for them. It was explained to me that my costar and I would do our scene first, while the two of them watched, Brandoneon and Izzy.

"Why?" I asked.

"So that they can observe your body language and imitate it," it

was explained to me. Which is to
say: They are ACTUAL actors. And
so I said, "Of course."

I trust you can appreciate the
twisted, dreamlike quality of what
followed, as I stood onstage to do
something I had never trained to do
for the amusement of my little dop-
pelgänger, who had probably hun-

MAY 9
1775, PHILADELPHIA: Benjamin
Franklin invents sunglasses to protect the
delicate eyes of the mole-men (this was
before their falling out, as recounted on
page 516). Though the mole-men did not
require it, Franklin insisted that all of his
"smoky under-man spectacles" be bifocals, which the mole-men found disorient-
ing and unnecessary. But Franklin would
not be deterred. He was pushy and plainly
focal-mad.

dreds more hours of experience than me. I kept looking into Izzy's
eyes. He was studying me, becoming me. And certainly, he was judging me.

I couldn't remember my lines. I couldn't do anything right.

Was not my younger self looking in disgust at my present self
and thinking "amateur"?

Finally, after many, many bad takes, we were through.

I could not bring myself to do the gracious thing and watch their
performance. I instead went back to my dressing room, raced some
crabs, lit a scented candle, and then napped until the whole thing
was over with.

When I got back to the set, everyone was talking about how great
Brandoneon and Izzy had been. They had done it all in two takes. It
was unbelievable. And at the end, Izzy, out of nowhere, broke into
song. He serenaded the crew with his rendition of "You Make Me
Feel So Young."

And this is what I missed when I was hiding out in my dressing
room covering my eyes and smelling a scented candle: a nine-year-
old dressed as a forty-year-old singing about his need to feel young
again. I will never see anything like that again. Is this what it means
to live as a celebrity, hidden in my cocoon of candles and privilege
and hermit crabs? To miss out on life itself?

MAY 10
1954, ON THE RADIO DIAL: Bill Haley
and His Comets release "Rock Around
the Clock." The group, named for Edmond
Halley, was originally going to call itself
Bill Haley and the Hollow Earths, but the
government intervened.

THE ONE DOWNSIDE
OF FAME

The one downside of fame is that no one will ever be really honest with you. There have been lots of times when I will be doing an "acting job," and I know I messed up. Maybe I forgot a line or missed a cue. Maybe I showed up drunk. Or maybe I refused to show up at all because they didn't get me into first class on the way out, or didn't get the crabs, or someone made eye contact with me.

Even then, they still say: "You did great. Nice job. You're brilliant. You were right to refuse to come to the set and to hit me with your diamond-tipped cane. I'm sorry I looked at you."

THAT'S NOT WHAT I WANT TO HEAR. I know when I've messed up, and like any artist, I need and want honest feedback. But it will never come.

It took me a while to understand why this is so, but now I get it. I'm just a small cog in a much larger machine. It's not just me on the set. There's the director, the producers, the camera operators, and the gaffers; there are the grips and the best boys and the worst boys and the yellow-blooded dwarves; there are the soundies and the boomies and the proppies and the crafties, not to mention the tall-boys, the catapult-men, and the sun-wranglers, the keymasters, the gatekeepers, and the turkey and the pitch. All these people are doing their jobs, the whole shoot consuming thousands of dollars per hour. They simply can't afford to worry that much about my performance, or risk sending me into a funk. They'd prefer to "yes" me along to the next take. Because if all those people are doing their jobs right (and they always do, except for the yellow-blooded dwarves, who are fuck-ups), I'm going to end up looking good on-screen no matter how horrible I am in life.

So I've learned to accept the empty praise with grace and humility and just move on to the next shot. You learn to develop your own inner compass. So that even when someone tells you, "You know, I respect you, but that wasn't really your best work," you know, instinctively, they're just telling you what you want to hear. It probably *was* your best work. YOUR BEST WORK EVER.

MAY 11

1981, LONDON: The musical *Cats* opens on the West End. An extremely moving song cycle about dancing cats wearing leg warmers, it was inspired by T. S. Eliot's *Old Possum's Book of Practical Cats.* Later, composer Andrew Lloyd Webber tried to make a musical of "The Waste Land," about modernist angst on roller skates, with less success. It was called *Starlight Express.*

1873, SWEDEN: Oscar II is crowned king of Sweden. The king was an accomplished diplomat, poet, musician, and historian, but you probably know him for his sardines. After the commercial failure of Lyndon Baines Johnson's Texas Big Man Sardines, King Oscar Sardines are now the only sardines named after a world leader (although, technically speaking, LBJ's Texas Big Man Brand Sardines were not sardines, but giant carp from the Pedernales River that were dressed up like sardines and sold in a Cadillac).

THE HIDDEN WORLD (NOT INCLUDING MOLE-MEN)

MAY 13

1982, HOLLYWOOD: Upon cancellation of the television series *The Incredible Hulk*, Bill Bixby and Lou Ferrigno cease sharing the same body. Ferrigno later confessed, "I have never cried harder."

MAY 14
2008, BROOKLYN: I apparently forgot to
write something about this date.

SOME MORE MONSTERS

Here's an old chestnut you can ask at any party: What's the most dangerous animal in the zoo?

The answer: *man.*

But also: *the brain shark.*[154]

But the zoo, of course, only contains animals that have been DISCOVERED. Outside of the zoo walls, there is an entire world, and while most of us presume that it may have been wholly explored, there are those who believe that there is much still to find.[155] For every square mile that man has walked on the earth, three hundred square miles exist that have never been touched by human feet—but MAY INDEED HAVE BEEN TOUCHED by the hooves, paws, tentacles, and horrid tongue-foot-pads of the CRYPTIDS.

Since the publication of my first book, many have asked to learn more about CRYPTOZOOLOGY and those intrepid souls who—out of curiosity or hunger—have searched for the undiscovered and unconfirmed species known as cryptids. While their most renowned prey—the Sasquatch, the yeti, and the Loch Ness Monster—remain frustratingly elusive, there are many more such creatures than perhaps you knew, and indeed SOME SURPRISING SUCCESS STORIES.

CONSIDER:

THE OKAPI

Few consider this relative of the giraffe to be a monster. And yet, the okapi was considered a myth until its discovery by Western explor-

---

154. In a rare "editorial comment," my Publisher asked here if I could give some more information about the brain shark. But I'm not sure what else there is to say: It's a superintelligent shark with a second brain on the outside of its body. Just like you'd expect.

155. I'm not talking about the Atlantis crowd. THOSE PEOPLE ARE CRAZY, and usually dripping wet. DO NOT invite them into your home if you have nice carpets.

ers in 1902, and many still believe that it is some kind of mutant antelope ghost.

Native to the Ituri Forest in the northeast of what is now the Democratic Republic of the Congo, the okapi is a sturdy, brown animal with striped, zebralike hindquarters. Its tongue is exceedingly long (more than a meter), intensely flexible, and also blue, just because the Okapi loves to blow your mind.

MAY 15
1898, ELBERFELD, GERMANY: Bayer Pharmaceuticals first markets a new form of morphine under the brand name "Heroin." It is presented as a children's cough medicine, and is still available in this formulation in Canada, where it is marketed as "P'tit Smack" in French-speaking neighborhoods, and "Baby's Little Helper" among the anglophones. It is cherry flavored, and comes with a sugared syringe.

It is due to this strange tongue that the okapi is such an accomplished mimic. They can imitate almost any human voice, and were used to do live, in-theater dubbing for silent films until 1920. This is where we derive the term "to kapi" or "to copy." But most Americans

Figure 75: I Told You It Would Blow Your Mind.[156]

---

156. And it's not even in color!

MAY 16
2007, NEW YORK CITY: Don Rickles appears on *The Daily Show*. I am watching from backstage. After the interview, Rickles stops on the way back to his dressing room and inexplicably takes my hand.
OUR ACTUAL CONVERSATION:
DON RICKLES: Everything is going to be OK.
JOHN HODGMAN: (speechless)
DON RICKLES: It's going to be great.
JOHN HODGMAN: (speechless)

know the okapi from the old television series *The Six Million Dollar Man* and the famous episode in which the cyborg, Steve Austin, tore one apart with his bare hands.

Animal rights activists were alarmed, until it was revealed that it was not a *real* okapi; just a German shepherd that had been spray-painted.
STATUS: DISCOVERED!

THE MONGOLIAN DEATH WORM
Rumored to ply the arid sands of the most remote areas of the Gobi Desert, the "allghoi khorkhoi," or "intestine worm," is more commonly known in cryptozoological circles as the "Mongolian death worm," because that is much more exciting.

It is supposedly a deep blood-red and only two feet long. Yet it possesses venomous breath that is deadly to everyone—not just Mongolians. Some even report that it shoots electricity from its flabby antenna, exactly like an electric eel,[157] and that in Mongolian criminal circles it is known as THE WRITHING TASER.

Yet, since the unwritten rule of the cryptozoological world seems to be that only the vaguely cute and/or blue-tongued animals can be discovered, the death worm remains, sadly, unverified.
STATUS: UNDISCOVERED!

THE GIANT SQUID
An extremely rare and solitary creature, scientific proof of the giant squid's existence came only in 1878, when a specimen some fifty-five

---

157. Minus the flabby antenna.

feet in length washed up upon the shore of Thimble Tickle Bay, Newfoundland.

From there, it slowly lurched to the town hall in order to file a complaint against a certain right whale named only as "WEEooooooo," who, the squid claimed, had "slandered me among all the creatures of land and sea, saying that I wish to eat him alive."

The town magistrate refused to hear the squid's case, however, and the locals chased the weeping squid from town. Before you judge them harshly, you should think how strange it must have been for them to see an actual giant squid, which for centuries was presumed to be a folktale, probably inspired by sailors' many actual encounters with giant talking sea serpents. And as well, many of the townspeople knew the accused whale personally and liked him.

In protest of his treatment, the squid promptly died on the beach, smelling up the entire area for weeks and making strolls unpleasant. That is a giant squid's idea of revenge.

STATUS: DISCOVERED!

MAY 17

1992, QUEENS, NY: With the Fat Boys finally disbanded, Darren "Buffy" Robinson attempts a career comeback by writing a screenplay to star himself and Ralph Bellamy, his former *Disorderlies* costar. Titled *My Dinner with Ralph Bellamy,* the script follows a wide-ranging conversation between the famous elderly actor and the young human beat box over a long, leisurely dinner. When read now, it is a surprising and affecting reflection on fame, destiny, and Robinson's own fear that the weight that had made him famous would eventually kill him. However, Robinson did not know at the time that Ralph Bellamy had passed away just a few months earlier. When he learned the news, he became despondent, and died soon after of a broken and massively enlarged heart.

GIANT TALKING SEA SERPENTS

Obviously they are real. Why else do you think sailors drew them on maps?

STATUS: DISCOVERED!

MAY 18
1968, NEW HAVEN: Though they said it was not possible, researchers at the controversial Yale Feline Studies Lab develop a forty-ninth way to skin a cat, beating Daniel Boone's record by three cat-skin methods.

THE POPE LICK MONSTER OF POPE LICK, KENTUCKY

Here is but one of several folkloric goat-men that, by popular legend, were left behind in various rural locales by passing carnivals. And there may be some truth to these tales, as until the 1970s, carny genetic labs and monster-breeding vats were largely unregulated.[158]

But the monster of Pope Lick is perhaps more tragic due to the fact that the name of his very town upstages him in strangeness. According to local teens, he is part goat, part man, half albino, and all monster. He lives in the parking lot at the Costco and harasses people, mainly by calling them nicknames they have not heard since they were children.

STATUS: UNDISCOVERED!

Figure 76: Could This Be an Irish Setter?

THE IRISH SETTER

By the unwritten "cute" rule noted above, the Irish setter is now so well known to man that it is easy to forget that as recently as 1890, English nannies told their young charges to behave or the "Irish Setter" would devour them with its sloppy kisses and unending devotion.

STATUS: DISCOVERED!

---

158. Please see page 317 under the heading "January 17."

THE HATED DIRT PUMA!

For more details, READ ON TO THE NEXT SECTION ABOUT MOLE-MEN. But needless to say: *STATUS: HIDEOUS!*

CAN YOU PROVE OTHERWISE?

— The world is flat.

— The globe is actually COOL-ING.

— The oceans are solid.

— Most cities are holograms.

— When I am on television, I can see you through the cameras.

MAY 19

HAPPY BIRTHDAY, JOHNS HOPKINS! Born in Maryland in 1795, the Hopkins triplets, John, John, and John, were an eccentric trio. They always lived, ate, and dressed as one, and by their twenties they constantly spoke in unison and insisted that they be addressed communally as "Johns." Their triple-brain made them prosperous businessmen, and it was their combined fortune that established the many Maryland institutions that bear their name, including Johns Hopkins University, Johns Hopkins Hospital, and the Johns Hopkins Triplet Research Center, which to this day is mandated to find a way by science or magic to fuse three personalities into one single body.

FERAL AMERICANS

If any of you met me on tour for my previous book, *The Areas of My Expertise,* you will remember that I was often introduced by a bearded man in a coonskin cap who played the guitar and sang my theme song.

Once upon a time, of course, it was common for all the best writers to have a theme song—some musical motif to accompany them as they appeared on talk shows and telethons and beauty pageants and such, back when America took literature seriously.

Faulkner, of course, will always be remembered for "The Love Theme from *Absalom, Absalom!*" a haunting song, typically arranged

MAY 20
1981, VIRGINIA: Richmond reports no
unusual rain.

for a chorus of idiot man-children, and still a favorite at weddings.

And Edgar Allan Poe, of course, wrote his own theme song, "The Eye of the Tiger," which was later borrowed for the movie *Rocky II* by Sylvester Stallone, a noted Poe enthusiast.[159]

But it is very uncommon now, alas, and I would have been out of luck had I not met my old friend Jonathan Coulton, a savage, feral mountain man I discovered in the wilds of southern Connecticut back in my Yale days.

Figure 77: Not an Animal

159. For the definitive work on Sylvester Stallone's well-documented obsession with the life of Edgar Allan Poe, please seek out a copy of Frank Gannon's seminal work, *Yo, Poe*.

I remember the story as if I had just made it up this morning. It was 1989, and I was on one of my regular transcendental drunk-walks through East Rock Park, and suddenly, there was Coulton, off in a glade, just qui-

MAY 21

1903, SIBERIA: An entire woolly mammoth frozen in ice is discovered in Russia. The Russians take a lot of heat for eating the mammoth, but no one seems to remember a mammoth is an unstoppable killing machine, DEAD OR ALIVE.

etly communing with nature and killing some cats. He did not speak English when I met him, but a click language of his own devising. But, using sign language and dead-cat puppetry, Coulton was able to convey that he had been raised there by woodland creatures. And when those creatures died, he had fashioned their skins into a buckskin shirt in his own crude attempt to honor them.

(Don't ask me what kind of creatures they were. I'm not a fucking tailor.)

But even though Coulton was a savage, he had an innate musical talent. He already sang beautifully, and even played the guitar (though of course he did not call it a guitar at the time, but a THK! TLANG!).

But since his songs were mostly sung in click language, I realized he would go nowhere without the advice of a worldly, drunken eighteen-year-old impresario. And so I took him with me back to the university, where the professors taught him English and shaved him as best they could. While my initial thought had been to exploit him in a traveling sideshow of some kind, I eventually found myself moved by his—dare I say—*humanity*? Well, let's say quasihumanity. In any case, we became friends, and I now only exploit him once every couple of years or so, when I go on book tours.

I wonder if it's fair to even call him feral at this point. By now, he has spent more time as a civilized gentleman than he ever did in the mountains. Indeed, he has now learned how to use crude tools, such as computers, and to market his songs on the Internet, and has

MAY 22
1920, SEATTLE: Robert Microsoft invents the game Minesweeper. Originally played on an actual minefield and inspired by Microsoft's own traumatic experiences in World War I, the game and its inventor would later become an inspiration for the young Bill Gates.

become something of a feral Internet celebrity. If you saw him today, you might take his long, matted hair and bird's-nest beard as a mere urbane eccentricity. You would not guess upon seeing him now that he was once a shambling man-beast who loved to kill cats and was just waiting for his opportunity to do so again.

But I should have known better. I SHOULD HAVE KNOWN.[160]

Jonathan's story may be inspiring, but it is not unique. Some of our greatest statesmen, pioneers, and authors grew up eating moss and the still-warm bodies of little chipmunks and other feral children. Including . . .

ROMULUS AND REMUS: The twin founders of Rome were suckled by a she-wolf named Lupa (though the ancient historian Livy suggests that "The Wolf" may have merely been a nickname for a local prostitute who happened to be an eagle).

RUDY GIULIANI: We cannot really be sure that he was born on September 11, for the fact is, "America's Feral Mayor" was found in the dog run at West 100th Street in Riverside Park, and his actual birthday is unknown. Though he dramatically increased the quality of life in New York and heroically brought calm and little casks of whiskey to a city traumatized by terrorist attacks, his attempt to take the national stage proved ill-fated. America was simply not ready for a president who had been divorced several times and also had teeth that could cut through most bicycle locks.

---

160. For more information on Coulton's cat-killing, please see page 129 of *The Areas of My Expertise* under the heading "How to Win a Fight."

WERNER HERZOG: When asked if the legendary director would play Kaspar Hauser in a film based on the life of that famous feral child, Herzog answered by eating raw meat from a wooden bowl (in Herzog language, that means YES).

GEORGE KENNEDY: The star of *Cool Hand Luke* was raised by a clan of pink, fleshy bears in Redwood State Forest who mistook him for one of their own cubs.

Not to mention . . .

— Dick "Mowgli" Cavett
— Jodie Foster
— François Truffaut
— Michael Dell
— Jack Welch
— Ted Danson

Figure 78: I Think You'll Agree, a Reasonable Error on the Bears' Part.

Why is it that so many feral children are so accomplished? Is it because they represent something natural and untainted about our human condition? Is it because they learned to hunt by night and to bury their own stool and ended up developing thick calluses on their knees and hands? Probably.

That is why so many "feral academies" have sprung up in recent years. You find their advertisements in the back of *The New York Times Magazine*, along with all the military academies and special schools

MAY 24
1626, MANHATTAN: The Belgian Peter Minuit buys Manhattan from the Lenape Indians for $24 (he never explained where he got the dollars—it is now presumed that he was a member of the first Walloon Time Travel Brigade). While some feel the Lenape were swindled, it should be made clear that they had no concept of private property in their culture. And as well, they still control a block of rent-controlled apartments in Stuyvesant Town that at market rates would now rent for $25,000 a month.

for the very fat and other crybabies. The Brett Martin Feral Academy, for example, offers several choices: Your child can be raised by wolves, dogs, snakes, elephants, or home-schooled children. I advise against the latter, due to the molting.

THE CROSSWORD CODE

By now you are familiar with the story of Leonard Dawe, the British schoolmaster who was accused of passing details of the Allied D-Day invasion to German spies via the crosswords he wrote for the London *Daily Telegraph*.

The two answers that first drew the attention of British intelligence were the words "Utah" and "Omaha"—two of the Normandy beaches that had been chosen as landing points by the American Army (probably because they had American names).

Then, the following week, Dawe's crossword included not only the name of the operation itself—OVERLORD—but also such top-secret code phrases as "lo," "ort," and "epée," and clues such as "20 down: They are going to invade here" and "13 across: actor Morales."

At this point Dawe was arrested. After interrogation, however, it was determined that Mr. Dawe's crosswords were merely evidence of the strange, almost mystic-seeming hand of coincidence. The actual secret messages were concealed in microdots in the black spaces.

This does not mean that the woman you see doing crossword puzzles every morning on the subway is a spy. Probably she is just a dummy crosswordist, planted there to distract you from the real spy, who is the bored-looking child, staring out the window, mouthing instructions to the TUN-NEL AGENTS.

MAY 25
1969, NEW HAVEN: The controversial Yale Feline Studies Lab discovers that, when fed to brain sharks, cats do not become measurably more intelligent. However, the brain sharks gain the cats' memories.

SECRET WORLD GOVERNMENT RECOGNITION TEST

According to one ancient text, when two Yale graduates meet on the street or at a party, they recite a bizarre and complex dialogue to prove they are members of the Secret World Government.

It begins when one asks the other:

Q: Then I presume you are a noble?

A: I am so accepted by men of noble birth.

Q: And have you ever traveled?

A: I have crossed the sands and swum the seas and I have seen the secrets hidden there.

Q: And do those secrets include giant underwater pyramids, built by ancient races?

A: Of course, and I did enter those pyramids.

Q: And what did you see there?

A: Controls for the computer of the world.

Q: And what did you do then?

A: I pulled the lever, turned the knob, and inserted the golden punch card.

Q: And what happened when you pulled the lever?

A: The screen awoke, and I saw how every nation is one.

Q: And what happened when you turned the knob?

A: The World Computer spoke and told me the secret history of the world.

MAY 26
1987, WASHINGTON, DC: In anticipa-
tion of the coming election, Mel Blanc
is secretly hired to provide the voice of
Vice President George H.W. Bush—a role
Blanc would play until his death in 1989.

Q: And what happened when you inserted the golden punch card?

A: The World Computer took this information and calculated the end of time, and told that date to me.

Q: And what will happen until the end of time?

A: Those who are of noble birth shall guard the World Computer and guide the course of man.

Q: And this will happen below the waves?

A: Below the waves and forever unseen by those above, who will only ever see the calmest sea, lest fear overtake the world.

Q: And then what happened?

A: The World Computer gave me a receipt.

Q: And do you keep it on your body?

A: I keep it near my heart, in the hidden skin flap that is the sign of our order.

Q: Do you think anyone around us knows what we are talking about?

A: No. I sincerely doubt it.

Q: As do I. There is no way they can know what we are talking about.

At this point the two "Yalies" are supposed to pool whatever cash they have in their pockets and split it equally between them. And then they are supposed to tongue kiss each other and leave the room by separate exits.

Is it true? All I can tell you is that I went to Yale, and you can believe no one has ever given me cash out of their wallet or tongue kissed me. NOT ONCE IN MY LIFE.

SOME WHO WERE CURSED TO BECOME RALPH MACCHIO

MAY 27

1969, NEW HAVEN: The controversial Yale Feline Studies Lab creates electrified catnip.

Bluesman Robert Johnson was hardly the only virtuoso in history rumored to be in league with the devil.[161] But for these others, the curse of becoming Ralph Macchio for all eternity was more metaphorical. For the most part, they were forced to give up merely their eternal soul.

TABLE 29: THE DAMNED		
ARTIST	**SOLD SOUL FOR**	**WORTH IT?**
The violin prodigy Paganini	A golden fiddle	Yes. Was unanimously voted the "Sexiest Eleven-Year-Old in Nineteenth-Century Europe" three times in a row.
The actor and keyboardist Charles Grodin	One great Moog solo	Probably not. Grodin is obviously a legend to Moogists, but more people remember *Midnight Run*, and rightly so.
The cartoonist Jim Davis	Surprisingly, NOT *Garfield*, but *U.S. Acres*	Even the devil agreed: Davis got greedy.
E. Gary Gygax	Dungeons & Dragons (Basic only; AD&D was his own invention.)	Yes. A tough negotiator, Gygax turned down the devil's initial offer: the patent on the 666-sided die.
		CONTINUED

---

161. For details, please see page 402 under the heading "April 9."

MAY 28

HAPPY BIRTHDAY, JANEZ VAJKARD VALVASOR! The Slovenian polymath, expert in Karst topography and noted mole-man, was spawned this day in 1641 in the caves beneath Carniola.

Figure 79: A Typical Seventeenth-Century Mole-Man, Shown Wearing Worm-Scale Armor Likely Made with His Own Claws

TABLE 29: *continued*

ARTIST: Bruce Jenner

SOLD SOUL FOR
The fast running

WORTH IT?
Yes, until "Can't Stop the Music."

ARTIST: The Charlie Daniels Band

SOLD SOUL FOR
"The Devil Went Down to Georgia"

WORTH IT?
You have to admit it's a catchy song, but why are chickens in the bread pan? And do chickens actually pick out dough? If I were selling my eternal soul, I'd have held out for a chorus that made some fucking sense.

ARTIST: The guitarist Steve Vai

SOLD SOUL FOR
Hot licks

WORTH IT?
Obviously.

In a weird coincidence, when the immortal Ralph Macchio met the devil-blessed Steve Vai on the set of the movie *Crossroads*, he begged Vai to kill him. Vai took pity on a fellow lost soul, and so he attempted to kill Macchio with a thousand hot licks. But he just couldn't go through with it. No one can kill Ralph Macchio once they look into his soulful, deathless eyes. Not even Steve Vai.

OLD PLAYGROUND RHYMES WITH HIDDEN MEANINGS

MAY 29

1970, NEW HAVEN: Inspired by the work of Schrodinger, the controversial Yale Feline Studies Lab creates a "Cat Prison." In the simulation, ten cats were assigned to be prisoners and ten cats were assigned to be guards. The guard cats were each given little stuffed truncheons. The prisoner cats were forced to wear little burglar masks, but otherwise were allowed no other clothing. While this sounds adorable, the experiment quickly devolved into riots so violent and unrelenting that many of the cats were alive and dead at the same moment in time.

Ring around the rosie!
Pocket full of posies!
Ashes!
Ashes!
We're secretly singing about
    the bubonic plague!

You "grippe" me and I
    "grippe" you
Mama calls the "grippe" the 'flu
Let's go out and "grippe" some more
We won't see Mama anymore!
How many tots can we infect?
2!
4!
8!
16!
32!
64!
128!
256!
512!
1,024!
2,048!
4,096!
8,192!
16,384!
32,768!
65,536!
. . . etc.

MAY 30

1902, PHILADELPHIA: Nathan Stubblefield demonstrates his machine for transmitting sound without the aid of wires. Stubblefield was a melon farmer and self-educated inventor who came from Kentucky with a predictably ridiculous mustache and an amazing machine: two metal stakes driven into the soft, resonant Philadelphian soil. At one end, he instructed his son Bernard to play the harmonica into a transmitter attached to the first stake. According to Stubblefield, the music was carried along by the electromagnetic waves of the earth itself, finally terminating with reported uncanny clarity at a receiver attached to the other stake, SEVERAL FEET AWAY.

Now, some maintain that this was technically not radio transmission, but induction transmission. Others claim it was not even induction transmission but actually just "hearing the sound." But I say: It is a man forcing his son to play harmonica into the earth in front of famous scientists, and that, frankly, is enough.

Fiddle, diddle, fiddle, fee

Teapot Dome has come for me.

Fiddle, diddle, middle, me

Harding's corpse will come for
    thee

He eat your bones

And blood he boil

Unless your daddy works for oil

Hey-ho

To Jonestown go

What do you want to see?

Jesus and friends

And goats and hens

And gallons of fruit punch for me!

How many paper cups will you
    drink?

One cup

Two cup

Three cup

Four

Pastor father says drink some
    more

Five cup

Six cup

Seven cup

All

Heaven lies beyond the wall

Smash through!

Smash through!

Oh-h-h-h-h-h Yeah!

THE SECRET MOON LANDING

MAY 31
1700, THE LANDS BELOW: Magnus Gasblister, the mole-manic explorer, proves his theory that if you dig deep enough before you begin, and if you have a fast worm, you can circumnavigate the globe in only four hours.

In 1803, Thomas Jefferson purchased from France some 530 million acres for only three cents per acre (little-known fact: Jefferson actually paid by check), thus securing the Mississippi River from foreign influence and beginning the nation's westward expansion. But were you aware that the Louisiana Purchase also included all of Napoléon's moon-bases *(bases-sur-lune)?*

France had been experimenting with space travel since the late eighteenth century, using a modification of the diving bell designed by Edmond Halley. But unlike Halley, Napoléon was not interested in capturing comets, but reaching the moon before the Portuguese could. Thus, as soon as he took control of France as first consul in 1799, Napoléon immediately began shooting diving bells out of a gigantic cannon that was aimed at the moon.

The first French astronauts were snails and songbirds. When these various animals fell back to earth, the fiery reentry certainly made them delicious (it also helped that their space suits were made of confit), but the ultimate prize of the moon still remained elusive.

Looking for inspiration, Napoléon invaded Italy. There, Leonardo da Vinci's ancient designs for fanciful flying machines provided provocative new ideas that would invigorate the French space program: Guiding fins were added to the diving bells, and to this day French astronauts still wear giant wooden bat wings.

Finally, in 1802, Napoléon himself stepped upon the surface of the moon, accompanied by some 400,000 lunar infantry and 30,000 cavalry. The horses quickly died, exploding in the airless environment (in a rare misstep, Napoléon had neglected to offer them confit suits). But it mattered little: The native moon men were poor sol-

JUNE 1

1927, NEW YORK: Grosset & Dunlap publish *The Tower Treasure,* the first novel featuring the Hardy Boys, who, to avoid controversy at the time, were portrayed as "brothers." While considered merely a juvenile fantasy series today, it is true that during the Great Depression, most crimes and mysteries were actually solved by teen-agers and children, for they were the only ones who cared.

diers, insofar as they were unfamiliar with war craft and also had no eyes.

While conquest was relatively swift, Napoléon found the harsh lunar landscape an exciting new tactical challenge. For example, as the moon lacked any atmosphere, a single musket shot would maintain its momentum almost perpetually. Indeed, France's non-horse casualties were limited to those soldiers who carelessly forgot to step out of the way as their own bullets quickly circled the moon and came back around to hit them in their dirty French necks.

On the other hand, Napoléon was delighted to discover that he could jump several kilometers at a single bound. While lesser men might have been terrified, this thrilled Napoléon, whose notoriously short stature had previously made him a ridiculously terrible jumper. He personally leaped over the walls of the moon-man capital to claim the lunar throne. There he declared himself *Empereur de la Lune Entière* in an elaborate coronation ceremony, though most of the moon dwellers themselves had no idea it was going on. Here again: Eyes would have aided them.

Napoléon established three garrisons upon the moon: Moon Bases Alpha, Beta, and Bonaparte, as well as a great memorial statue of an exploding horse. But the lunar winter proved harsh, and when the horse meat was gone, Napoléon's army was left with nothing to eat but stale bread dipped in scrambled moon-man eggs (also known as "French Toast").[162]

War with England was now imminent. Looking back to earth, Napoléon saw Louisiana, terminus of the muddy ribbon of the Mis-

---

162. Not as disgusting as this sounds (if you are French, and thus used to eating disgusting food).

JUNE 2
455 AD: The Vandals plunder Rome. As you might imagine, this is where we get the word "Rome."

Figure 80: Napoléon,
King of the Moon

sissippi that bisected the continent where he had once hoped to create a great French empire. "Here at last I have perspective," he wrote in a letter to his earthbound wife, Josephine. From far above, he could see that his holdings in the New World were indefensible. And frankly, he was completely surprised by California. Napoléon did not see that shit coming.

Within a few weeks, Napoléon was constructing his return cannon. What few French forces remained on the moon under the command of Napoléon's brother Ernst soon perished, for apparently the moon has no oxygen on it.

When astronaut Jim Lovell finally walked on the moon as part of the first American non-faked moon landing, in 1973, he found the lost French garrisons eerily preserved: Were it not for the fine coating of moon dust and the horse skeletons, one could imagine they were brand-new. Dutifully, Lovell lowered Napoléon's standard and raised the U.S. flag for the first time—170 years since the moon bases passed into U.S. hands.

The bases are now used for relatively mundane tasks: astronaut training, monolith storage, and as the terminus of the soon-to-be-built space elevator.

You can read more about the exciting early days of Napoléon's space program in Jules Verne's great novel *Le Stuffe Correcte*.

THEY NEVER SAID IT

Despite his famous public persona, the Vaudevillian W. C. Fields was not a drunk. He was, however, a celebrity juggler, which is arguably worse. While later known as one of the twentieth century's first international movie stars, his renown was first born out of his ability to juggle anything: not just pins and batons, but also swords, hat boxes, harpsichords, human heads, flaming human heads, and whiskey casks—from which he would drink liberally, even while they were in flight, because in fact he was a horrible, horrible drunk.

But one thing that is true about W. C. Fields: He absolutely did NOT say upon his deathbed, "ALL THINGS CONSIDERED, I'D RATHER BE IN PHILADELPHIA." (Younger readers may require the clarification that, in Fields's time, being in Philadelphia was actually considered to be marginally *better* than death.)

Nor, as another myth goes, was this phrase inscribed upon his headstone, which in reality is quite simple, and engraved with the single enigmatic word "Unless."

Indeed, this is but one of many famous sayings and phrases that, in the great game of telephone that is history, has been misquoted, misattributed, or simply invented.

HEREWITH, some further clarifications:

"THE ONLY THING WE HAVE TO FEAR IS FEAR ITSELF."
— attributed to Franklin D. Roosevelt, the U.S. president

JUNE 4

1876: The Transcontinental Express train completes its first complete run from New York City to San Francisco. For the first time, Americans could traverse the entire continent in a mere 389 hours. Many feared that the speed of the journey would cause palsies, brain-explosion, or even time travel, but this happened very rarely, and soon the "Trans-con" was a huge success. "At last our United States are truly United," declared the *New York Tribune*, "bound from end to end by a straight road of gleaming steel and Chinaman bone." But this was not entirely the truth: The train routinely made a dramatic high jump over the Colorado River all the way up to 1978, when Jimmy Carter insisted that a bridge would be "safer." And thus the nanny state was born.

THE REAL STORY: Roosevelt did indeed say these famous lines as part of his first inaugural in 1933, but he was speaking specifically about himself and his cabinet, who were protected at all times by a special force field (made of thick steel). The full quote, which is rarely reproduced, makes this very clear: "Normal Americans," Roosevelt went on, "need to be afraid, very afraid indeed. And not just afraid of the Depression, but also flash floods, night-stabbers, and plague."

"THERE ARE THREE KINDS OF LIES: LIES, DAMNED LIES, AND STATISTICS."
— attributed to Benjamin Disraeli, the British prime minister and novelist

It was Mark Twain who first ascribed this quote to Disraeli, but no scholar has been able to verify it. Of course, Twain was a noted tall-talesman and literary fabricator (did you know his real name was actually Nigger Jim?), so is it possible that he was bending the truth here (or, in old Missouri parlance, doing a little old-fashioned "statistickin'")?

One clue to the truth may be found elsewhere in "Twain's" works where it is revealed that, during his old riverboat days, the pilot would

JUNE 5
1974, NEW HAVEN: The controversial Yale Feline Studies Lab is shut down when it is discovered that they have not only been experimenting on cats, but humans. Specifically, it is learned that the researchers have been training an infant from birth to become "not just a bad catsitter, but the perfect bad-catsitting machine." All of the equipment is sold to the Soviet Union. No one knows what happened to the child.

call aloud the river's depth, using what might now seem to be familiar slang: One fathom merited a cry of "Lies," two fathoms was "Damned lies," and three fathoms, as you might now guess, was "Disraeli."

"CRISIS CAN INDEED BE AGONY. BUT IT IS THE EXQUISITE AGONY WHICH A MAN MIGHT NOT WANT TO EXPERIENCE AGAIN—YET WOULD NOT FOR THE WORLD HAVE MISSED."

— attributed to Richard Nixon,
the U.S. president

Nixon wrote these words in the introduction to his 1962 book, *Six Crises*. However, the meaning is often lost by those who quote it. Nixon was not, as is commonly presumed, speaking of orgasm, but of *political crises* upon the world stage, and also foreplay.

"ALL CHILDREN SHOULD BE FED TO ANIMALS."
— attributed to W. C. Fields

Another famous Fields quote with no basis in reality. While Fields disliked working with children professionally (because they were difficult to juggle and resisted being set on fire), he loved all animals and doted on his famous overcoat of live dachshunds. He would never feed them children. Never.

"MONEY IS ONLY CONGEALED SNOW."

— attributed to Dorothy Parker

Critic and poet Dorothy Parker had financial difficulties throughout her life, largely due to the fact that she was a critic and poet, but also because she did not know what money looked like. At the Algonquin Hotel (site of the famous "Round Table")

JUNE 6

1973, ON THE AIR: *Schoolhouse Rock* debuts on ABC. The series of short educational cartoons instantly becomes a part of pop culture, using humor and songs to teach kids about history, grammar, math, and science at a time in our history when these things were considered important. A special series of *Schoolhouse Rock* episodes dealing with sexual education were also prepared by animator Ralph Bakshi, but were never aired. However, one of the songs written for Bakshi's cartoon explaining orgasms ("Interjections!") was later repurposed in another cartoon to explain *nonsexual* interjections.

where she and her fellow *New Yorker* luminaries would regularly gather to dress up as medieval knights and eat massive turkey legs), Parker would frequently attempt to pay for her drinks with scraps of paper, dead beetles and, most famously, ice chips.

It was the latter example that prompted fellow wit Alexander Woollcott to quip, "To Dorothy, money is only congealed snow!"

The whole Round Table laughed and laughed, clinking their flagons of mead together—even though the remark was not particularly witty at all, but instead a rather cruelly accurate summation of Parker's strange psychological disorder.

As Woollcott donned the club's coveted "jester's cap of self-congratulation," Parker quietly, grimly put her ice chips back into her purse and went out into the Manhattan night to commit suicide for the third time.

WHAT ZIPPY FUN THOSE DAYS WERE!

JUNE 7

1980, MICHIGAN: Ted Kennedy wears a tight black leather suit to a campaign stop in Detroit. It is largely considered to be the end of his campaign for the Democratic presidential nomination, with news of the suit even overshadowing the news that, on the very same day, Jimmy Carter wore a knee-length sweater-vest.

POSSIBLE CONTACTS WITH ALIEN LIFE

Perhaps you have heard of Fermi's Paradox? It is named for the famous Italian-American atomic physicist Enrico Fermi, builder of the first working atomic pile. As the story goes, one day Fermi sat down to lunch with some of his fellow scientists and posed a question: WHERE ARE ALL THE SPACE ALIENS?

This was, after all, only a few years since the rumored crash of an alien "flying saucer" at Roswell, New Mexico. Now, that incident turned out to be nothing, of course, NOTHING AT ALL: merely a downed weather balloon being piloted by small hairless men with slits for mouths. Still, Americans had gone "saucer-mad"—even famous scientists who were eating lunch.

Fermi's question was prompted by some simple reasoning. Given the vastness of the universe, the galaxy should be teeming with intelligent life. And given the age of the universe, perhaps some hundreds of years, by now we should have met some of our neighbors. And yet we seem to be alone. "Where is everybody?" asked Fermi, and his colleagues had no answer. Then, as lunch continued, Fermi went on to deploy similar blunt logic to disprove fairies, the existence of God, and the possibility of love. And after that, Fermi generally ate alone.

Now, I accept that Fermi was undoubtedly a genius. And I have never built any atomic piles myself.[163] But respectfully, I might point out two possibilities that Fermi may have overlooked.

The first is that the aliens may yet still be very far away. Perhaps even on OTHER PLANETS.

---

163. Although, technically, I guess you could say that ALL piles are atomic.

The second is that perhaps FERMI HIMSELF was an alien.

JUNE 8
1981, VIRGINIA: Richmond reports no unusual rain.

Think about it. Isn't it a little *convenient* that, in 1938, as the world stood on the brink of global conflict, a supergenius "Italian" professor would suddenly just appear one day in New York, bearing an astonishing new technology that not only would change the course of the war but would twist and darken our future as a species forever?

And why did Fermi refuse all monetary payment for his work, requesting instead only the gift of two healthy sperm whales? THAT SEEMS VERY ODD, DOESN'T IT?

And if Fermi *were* an alien, wouldn't he be the first to want to convince us that ALIENS DON'T EXIST?

Figure 81: Can You Tell Which One Is the "Italian"?

Indeed, it has long been speculated within UFOlogy circles that the space aliens are already here. That they have walked among us for millennia, hidden and disguised, guiding our evolution from ape to man, and sometimes even abducting us, flying us away in their

JUNE 9

1985, BENTONVILLE, ARKANSAS: Under cover of night, the Knights Templar quietly transport the Holy Grail to its new owner, Sam Walton, and install it in the underground shrine beneath the Wal-Mart visitors' center, where it is believed to still rest today.

saucers to have sex with us in pyramids.

You have to admit, it's a difficult theory to discount.

For even in my own life there are things I can't explain . . . some events so odd, so unaccountably strange, that it is difficult to imagine they were *not* caused by prolonged and frequent visitation by aliens throughout my life.

FOR HOW ELSE WOULD YOU EXPLAIN THESE UN-CANNY BUT ABSOLUTELY TRUE CLOSE ENCOUNTERS?

OCEAN CITY, NJ: 1980

In the summer of 1980, the "Special Edition" of *Close Encounters of the Third Kind* was released: Richard Dreyfuss went into the ship, and the aliens hugged him all over. Meanwhile, I went to the Jersey Shore with my parents. Within twenty-four hours I had a horrible Dreyfuss-like sunburn, and so I spent most of my time avoiding the beach, watching the skies.

One evening I sat outside our little rental house. The sidewalk was still warm from the sun, my eternal enemy, and in the distance I could hear the surf crashing and the sound of the roller coaster on the boardwalk. But my eyes were trained upward, scanning the twilight for UFOs.

Mostly all I saw were stars and satellites and blinking airplanes: typical sky junk. Some other kids joined me for a while, and I appreciated their company. But their necks got sore, and eventually they moved on to the boardwalk to play Zaxxon and mingle with other humans. I was OK at Zaxxon, but bad at the other part, so I stayed behind with the cosmos.

And then it happened. An elderly man and an elderly woman

walked by. They were in their late seventies and all dressed up: he in a carefully tended brown suit and yellow tie; she in a plain dress and cardigan, for the night was fully dark now, and a chill was coming in. It was clear that they were on a date. As they walked, she took his arm with a formal tenderness, as though they had just begun gently courting

JUNE 10
1965, ON THE AIR: Supposed air date of the "lost episode" of *Gilligan's Island*, in which Bob Denver and Dawn Wells are said to be visibly smoking marijuana in the background of an unrelated scene. While the rumor remains unconfirmed, Internet legend suggests that Denver and Wells were using a bong made out of bamboo, one of Mr. Howell's cravats, and the radio. However, that device was not even *shown* on the program until it was in color, so as far as I'm concerned, the story remains apocryphal.

after many years of being married to other people.[164]

For some reason, I recall that they were exactly the same height.

Then they saw me, and they stopped. For a moment, we were all illuminated there by the buzzing yellow streetlight.

"What are you looking for?" the old man asked. "Flying saucers?"

You have to admit, that was a strange thing to say. Given the times, I suppose he might have just guessed. I suppose he could have deduced that that a lonely-looking, horribly sunburned nine-year-old staring at the sky might be looking for flying saucers. But even so, that's a suspiciously solid bit of detective work for an old man on a date.

What was stranger, though, and even I sensed it at the time, was the fact that he stopped at all. That this elderly gentleman would pause now and interrupt his evening stroll with his sweetheart, for the sole purpose of mocking a child.

"Ohhhhh," he said now, raising his palms and wiggling his fingers. "You're looking for space men! Little green men! Ha-ha-ha!"

You think I've got it wrong, of course. You think he was just making a little, grandfatherly joke. But I remember his rattling, shrill laugh. I remember his lips curled back, his eyes awake with

---

164. Other people who were now dead.

JUNE 11

1912, NEW YORK CITY: The Marx brothers make their stage debut with the revue *Fun in Hi Skule.* As was common on the vaudeville stage, each of the nine original Marx brothers adopted a different ethnic "shtick" (meaning "routine" in the language of the ethnics). Everyone remembers Chico (the "Italian"), Groucho (originally the "German" and later the "Mustachio"), Harpo (the "Mute"), and Zeppo (the "Wasp"); but few now remember Gummo (the "Frenchman"), Hobo (the "Vagabond"), Negro (the "Negro"), Diggo (the "Mole-man"), Lichto (the "Lichtensteinian"), Graucho (the "Argentine"), Odo (the "Shapeshifter"), El Demonico (the "Mexican Wrestler"), and Marxo (the "Jew").

that queasy, manic light you see in a bully's eyes when he is torturing some small animal or has found a sunburned, asthmatic sci-fi fan to pick on.

And then his girlfriend joined in.

"Ha-ha-ha," she said contemptuously. "There's no such thing as space men. THERE'S NO SUCH THING."

I looked around. The rest of the street was completely empty. I no longer heard the roller coaster or the distant ocean. Time had seemed to stop. I looked at their angry faces, and I remember very distinctly wondering to myself: Are they wearing rubber masks? And if so, what are they hiding? Giant, unblinking, almond-shaped eyes? Gray skin? Slits for mouths?

Then the man spoke again. "Watch out for laser guns," he said. He crooked his trigger finger at me like he was aiming a gun, and made laser sounds. "Keyoooo! Keyoooo!" he said.

And then, they turned as one and walked away. As they went, the male creature reached for the female's hand with his own yellowed claw, and found it. And I was left in the buzzing yellow streetlight, alone.

I guess you could try to explain this away as a simple misunderstanding. Or maybe swamp gas. But I know what I saw. I KNOW WHAT I SAW.

BROOKLINE, MA: 1984

In 1984, I went to see the movie *Dune*, and a girl spoke to me. I realize this seems impossible. But it is absolutely true.

It was opening night,[165] and I was there with my friend Tim McGonagle, who sat on my left. On my right

JUNE 12
1981, VIRGINIA: Richmond reports no unusual rain.

sat the girl. She was wearing a blue jean jacket and had long curly hair. Her ankle was bandaged. Nothing serious. Probably just a sprain. But she had a pair of wooden crutches with her. She was tall. I was in eigth grade at the time, and I would guess she was a sophomore, but I did not know for sure, because she was not from my town, and I didn't know her name, and I never will.

She was there with an older woman, presumably her mother. They were talking about *Dune*. They were both big fans of the original book, and they were discussing this fact. They agreed that their favorite characters were the giant sand worms.

And that's when it got really weird. A little before the lights went down, the girl turned to me and asked if I was looking forward to the movie.

I did not know what to say. Partially I was embarrassed. I had actually never read the novel *Dune* (I was merely a connoisseur of movies featuring desert planets, and I still am).

But more, she asked me this question *apropos of nothing*. IT WAS AS IF SHE JUST WANTED TO TALK TO ME. She waited. Eventually I answered: "Yes." I am not sure I even moved my head.

The lights went down, and the film began. If I must remind you, this was the David Lynch version of *Dune*, in which everyone was sexy and deformed at the same time. You may recall that it ends with Sting trying to sex-knife Kyle MacLachlan to death, but Kyle MacLachlan sex-knifes him instead and then makes it rain.

I recall being particularly impressed when the Third Stage Guild Navigator appeared at the beginning of the film. This was a kind of giant mutant fetus that lived in a tank, floating forever in the orange

---

165. Naturally.

JUNE 13
1981, ABOVE BATON ROUGE: Following several accidents, Louisiana bans its
controversial fly-through cocktail bars for
pilots.

cloud of the psychedelic drug known as "Melange" that gave it the power to bend space and time. It could never touch or speak directly to another person. It had become so physically, mentally, and sexily deformed by its isolation that it could only communicate with the outside world *through some kind of old-timey radio.* As you might imagine, I was fascinated with this creature. Far more so than the giant sand worms, which were fine . . . But I mean, your FAVORITE CHARACTER? Come on.

When the movie ended, I noticed that everyone was very happy to get out of the theater as quickly as possible. Except the girl. She seemed to slow down as we walked out, to match my pace. Maybe it was the crutches. But for a moment, it seemed like she might even talk to me AGAIN.

It all seems so ridiculous now that I describe it, I can only conclude that it must have been what alien abductees call a "screen memory": a false memory the brain concocts to cover up the trauma, say, of being kidnapped and taken to a pyramid for sex (or, possibly, knife-sex).

Bearing that in mind, I sure am glad I just kept walking. I sure am glad I never spoke to her or saw her ever again.

PHILADELPHIA, PA: 1989

As you may know, there was a bestselling book in the 1980s called *Communion.* It was written by Whitley Strieber, who had previously written the werewolf novel *Wolfen* and the vampire novel *The Hunger.*

In the book, Strieber describes his frequent experiences of being kidnapped by aliens. He describes the long stretches of "lost time," when he suddenly realized that minutes, hours, even days had passed that he could not remember. It turns out, this is actually when the aliens had been abducting him for rectal probes and other experiments.

He describes the screen-memory phenomenon I mentioned above. How he had strange, uncanny memories of seeing owls, and not just in

JUNE 14
1822: Charles Babbage proposes a "difference engine," a mechanical device considered by many to be the "first computer." While it was never completed in its time, a version of the machine built to Babbage's specifications in 1991 proved the viability of his vision: Within ten minutes of its construction, it showed some old-fashioned porn.

normal places.[166] If you were an alien abductee, you might have memories of seeing owls in the city, or owls on the subway, or owls sitting outside your apartment window, or owls sitting INSIDE your apartment window, wearing space clothes and preparing a rectal probe. For Strieber, it turns out, these owls were all actually aliens.

The first time he remembered having actually met an alien without thinking it was an owl, Strieber was at his country cabin in the deep, dark woods. It was the middle of the night, and he was sleeping, and the alien woke him up. Suddenly, there it was beside the bed—giant, unblinking, owlish eyes, gray skin, slit for mouth.

Later, Strieber would come to appreciate and even love his alien visitors. But that first time, he was naturally scared. He didn't ask for this. It just came to his bed unbidden. And from then on his whole life would be divided into before and after. He could never be a simple werewolf-and-vampire novelist again: From then on, he would be touched and defined by this uncanny, intimate bedroom encounter.

There is nothing in the human experience that is remotely similar to this.

Strieber's book was so successful that it was made into a movie in 1989. The way I remember it, I was visiting my girlfriend in Philadelphia, and we just decided one night to go see it. Here are some details about that movie, the way I remember it:

---

166. Owl holes.

JUNE 15
1958, WICHITA, KANSAS: The first Pizza Hut opens at the corner of Bluff and Kellogg Streets. A traditional daub-and-wattle hut with a thatched roof, the pizza was originally baked on a stone over a central fire that vented through a hole in the roof. Later, students at the University of Kansas pulled it apart with their bare hands as a cruel prank.

1. It starred Christopher Walken as Whitley Strieber.

2. It starred a rubber puppet as "The Alien."

3. It featured a very long sequence in which a rubber puppet alien gives Christopher Walken a rectal probe.

4. It was being shown in an actual movie theater in Center City, Philadelphia.

5. All of which is simply to point out: THEY MADE A MOVIE OF *Communion*, AND IT STARRED CHRISTOPHER WALKEN.

Does something about this seem weird to you?

Think it over. What's wrong with this picture?

Yes. Correct: I HAD A GIRLFRIEND. How did this happen? *When* did this happen? I remember walking around Philadelphia with her after the movie, wondering this exact same thing. I still have no answer.

THE ALGARVE, PORTUGAL: 1991

Two years later, I spent some time in Portugal with this very same woman. Let us call her "Katherine Fletcher."

We were vacationing in the Algarve, the southernmost district of Portugal, where long ago the Moors came and left their enduring alien stamp—their mosques and latticed chimneys and sun-bleached sex pyramids surviving the Reconquista now by half a millennium.

As we traveled, we stayed in small *pensãos* in crumbling, walled cities. In the evenings, we would sit on the roof and drink *vinho verde* and play checkers and watch the sun fall. In the afternoons, we smoked cigarettes in cafés and read international newspapers. *Did this really happen? Does this happen to anyone?*

We traveled lightly, with little planning. We would do our own laundry and let it dry in the strong sun until our underwear was stiff and white and ancient-seeming. Sometimes we would go to topless beaches.

JUNE 16

1846, BRUSSELS: Antoine Joseph Sax collaborates with Joseph Phone and the mysterious Dr. O to create the saxophone. Only later would it be revealed that Dr. O was Emmanuel Oboe.

What?

One afternoon, while hanging laundry on the roof, we befriended a young woman with a British accent. She had white-blond hair and wore a very white dress and she was very pregnant. Even so, she sat down and drank with us. She said she was traveling south to Faro, the regional capital. There she would meet up with her husband, who was sailing to join her "in a ship."

We offered to go with her, and she accepted. By the next afternoon the three of us were heading west by train, parched air blowing in wafts through the wide-open door.

We arrived in Faro, a bustling seaport, that evening, and shared a dinner of Portuguese-Chinese food and drank more wine and toasted our new friendship. Why was she traveling by train instead of by boat? Why did we go with her on the journey? Why did she not presume we were going to kill her . . . unless she was bearing *a space child?*

(Also in Portugal I was chased by a pack of feral dogs. The lead dog bit me in the ass, necessitating an "ass shot" from a Portuguese doctor. *Screen-memory?*)

The next day would be our last afternoon in Portugal. Katherine said she wanted to go to the Faro beach. To get there, she explained, you have to take a bus and a boat. This did not appeal to me, as I was exhausted and dog-bitten, so I decided to stay behind.

We did not even discuss what time she might come back. I remember what she looked like right before she left: the freckles had

JUNE 17

1952, FLORIDA: Ernest Hemingway organizes the first paintball competition at his home in Key West. His original concept of the sport, which included not just human opponents but hundreds of inbred cats, was eventually scaled back to a simple phony gunfight. But the Hemingway Paintball Cats still inhabit his old home at Key West, and even their descendants are pretty good shots with an air rifle, due to the extra toes.

Figure 82: This Cat Will Shoot You.

multiplied across her face and shoulders, gathering together to resemble a tan (Tan! Both of us were tan!) and making her eyes extra-bright and extra-blue. She was smiling. She was about to board a bus and a boat in a strange country, a single woman alone, not even speaking the language. I loved her, and then she went out into that alien world.

It took some time for me to come to my senses. I spent the afternoon reading a novel, and it was only when I finished the book that I realized how much time had passed. (A lot of it. Hours and hours.) Suddenly it was evening, and Katherine had not come back.

I grew nervous and went downstairs. I stood in the doorway of the *pensão* and stared up and down the busy street. I did not know what else to do. I did not speak Portuguese. It was 1991, and cell phones had not yet been given to us by the aliens. I had no idea where the beach was.

Quickly it became clear that there were only two possible outcomes, neither of which I could reasonably hope to affect: Either Katherine would come back, or she would not. So I sat on the steps by the side of the street to wait. I did not watch the skies, but instead watched the shifting patterns of people, cars, children, dogs, and scooters at the very far end of the street, hoping that those constellations might shift and change and suddenly reveal her face. There, in that little city, population 40,000, did I begin to appreciate the true vastness of the universe—its size and the searching we might do in it.

And that's when the Liberians showed up—a small group of

laughing young men. Apparently they were staying at the *pensão* as well, and now they were coming home, full of the day, relaxed, happy. One of them was named Joseph. He saw me sitting there and asked what was the matter. I explained to

JUNE 18
1986, ON THE AIR: Following on the success of *Pee-wee's Playhouse,* CBS debuts a full Saturday morning lineup of children's programs hosted by downtown New York and L.A. performance artists, including Laurie Anderson's *18-Hour Kids Hour,* Joe Coleman's *Rat-Eaters!,* and *Vagina Time with Karen Finley.*

him what had happened. Joseph said I should not worry. He was sure Katherine would be back soon. But as he said it, he did not seem very sure.

Because he sat down to wait with me. They all did. Were there four of them? Six? What were they doing there, in Portugal, all together? They told me, but I can't recall. They spent the next hour and a half going up and down the stairs in small groups, taking shifts, sitting with me, joking with me, distracting me. Were there five of them? Eight? I do not remember, but there was always one of them with me. They brought a message: We are not alone.

Then, in the middle of a sentence, at the very birth of twilight, my head turned. At the far end of the street, the stars aligned, and Katherine was there, walking up, smiling. She did not understand why I had been so worried, and neither did the Liberians, or so they claimed. As they cheered and patted my back, there was a great breath of relief in their laughter. And then they went up to their room, and Katherine and I held hands in the street.

Such a moment leaves a scar on the memory, like an unexplainable bit of alien technology that has been implanted in your buttocks by a "Portuguese" "doctor." Now Katherine and I are married. And even now, a decade and a half later, when she is out of my sight, I never stop looking for her. And even though, you must admit, the likelihood is that while she was away she was kidnapped and replaced by an alien clone, I still love her.

1961, THE HALL OF JUSTICE: The Supreme Court strikes down a clause in the Delaware constitution requiring all political office holders to swear fealty to the mad DuPont siblings upon a special nonstick Bible.[a]

a. For insight, please see page 162 of *The Areas of My Expertise.*

EVEN MORE MORE INFORMATION THAN YOU REQUIRE, WITH A SPECIAL EMPHASIS ON FOOD AND ANIMALS (A KIND OF FOOD)

JUNE 20

1974, MARTHA'S VINEYARD: "Bruce," the tiny man used to pilot the mechanical shark in the movie *Jaws,* dies in mid-production. He had become so immersed in the role that indeed he had not left the shark's mechanical innards in weeks, living off of seawater and the fish he would catch in the shark's grinding inner gears. So convincing was his performance that, by the time of the final days of shooting, many had forgotten that Jaws was anything but a plain old robotic shark, just like any you might find off the coast of Martha's Vineyard. Then Roy Scheider blew him up with an oxygen tank.

JUNE 21
1903, ST. LOUIS, MO: American carica-
turist Al Hirschfeld is born. Best known
for his swooping, spidery line portraits of
entertainment legends, his fans also enjoyed searching for the name of his daughter, Nina, which was tattooed in forty-five
secret places all over his body.

SIX FOODS OF THE NEW WORLD

Before the discovery of the New World, the average European ate a relatively simple diet of cheese, cow stomachs, and beer (aka "The Mediterranean Diet"). The Belgians, meanwhile, were cannibals.

So you can understand why the Europeans wanted spices from Asia so badly. And that is why, when Columbus made his bold, world-changing claim that the earth was round and China was secretly an island in the Caribbean, Queen Isabel was just desperate enough to take him seriously.

But no matter what you have read, SHE WAS NOT HIGH ON PEYOTE AT THE TIME. Because peyote, as you might not have known, is a NEW WORLD crop—one of dozens of amazing discoveries that would profoundly change the dinner table of Western civilization (and not just because they started making tables out of the arms and legs of Native Americans).

TOMATOES

First of all, tomatoes are not poisonous. Yes, they are the fruit of the deadly nightshade. But as the ancient Aztecs knew, tomato venom could be very easily neutralized with virgin blood. And so the *"tomatl"* or "L tomato" was cultivated and enjoyed throughout Central and South America by the fifteenth century. The Italians were the first to embrace the fruit, dubbing it the "pomodor" or "golden apple," because they had never seen apples before, or gold. But this hardly aided its fearful reputation, for most Europeans already considered the Italians themselves to be poisonous.

And so it was that tomatoes were not widely accepted in their own native lands until 1978. That is when, on a famous episode of the television program *That's Incredible!*, John Davidson ate a raw tomato live before a shocked studio audience. Once Middle America saw that a healthy, white male celebrity could eat an "Italian Death Fruit" and not die or become suddenly swarthy, our nation's love affair with the tomato began. But what you might not have known is, as soon as the cameras stopped rolling, Davidson puked all over Fran Tarkenton. TRUE STORY.

JUNE 22

1982, LOCATION UNKNOWN: An unknown American corporation begins distributing the mysterious "Happy Boy Margarine," but it only makes children afraid.

Figure 83: Also Known as "Screaming in Terror Boy Margarine"

TOBACCO

Used for millennia by Native Americans to look cool, tobacco was introduced to Europe by John Rolfe, founder of Jamestown. It then quickly spread across the Continent and into the East due to its unusual flavor; the seductive, compelling ritual of its consumption; and the fact that it is highly, highly addictive.

Across the globe it would be smoked, chewed, snuffed, rubbed into the eyes, injected between the toes, and snorted off a woman's breasts (a favorite method of Freud's and the source of his famous saying: "Sometimes snorting tobacco off a woman's breasts is just snorting tobacco off a woman's breasts. Unless she is your mother").

When the character of "Joe Camel" was introduced in 1987 to sell cigarettes to children, the character was considered quite controversial. However, it was not the first time tobacco had been advertised with a penis. That distinction belongs to "Old Erection," a brand of

JUNE 23

1868, WASHINGTON, DC: Christopher Latham Sholes receives the patent for the "type-writer." The patent describes the first machine as a small device consisting of an iron stand upon which sits a talking bird, such as a macaw. The user dictates what he wants written to the bird, which then pecks the letters into a marble slab. The bird is then free to make a "wiseacre" comment on what the author has written, and change the text accordingly using another Latham Sholes invention, "Marble-Out."

Appalachian-style "twist" chewing tobacco. While hard to find today, its legacy lives on in the hundreds of country barns that were painted by the company in the '20s with the "Old Erection" logo: an erect penis.

A word of warning: While smoking cigarettes or chewing tobacco from a bag with a penis on it is extremely glamorous, it will also give you cancer, which a few scientific studies show might (MIGHT) be hazardous to your health. That said, it is safe to smoke cigarettes if there is a picture of an Indian on the package.

TURKEYS

I have discussed at some length Benjamin Franklin's unhealthy obsession with the wild American turkey: He kept one as a pet;[167] insisting at great volume that it be named our national bird while the rest of the founding fathers were trying to figure out the natural rights of man;[168] and it is even said that at Christmas and Thanksgiving, he ate them.

Why was he so obsessed with this humble bird?

You have to bear in mind that when they arrived in the New World, Europeans had never *seen* a turkey before, or even, for that matter, a wattle. You also have to bear in mind that the "wild turkey" of the seventeenth and eighteenth centuries was a distinctly different animal from the cultivated domestic turkey we know today. For one, it was six feet tall, and the Native Americans used it for jousting. For

---

167. Please see page 505 under the heading "The Seven Portals to the Hollow Earth."

168. Please see page 203 of *The Areas of My Expertise* under the heading "Colonial Jobs Involving Eels."

two, it had a long, serpentine tail

JUNE 24
1981, VIRGINIA: Richmond reports no
unusual rain.

with spikes on the end of it. For three, its wattle was made of silver.

In that context, I trust you understand why this creature instantly seemed so foreign and exotic to the English—indeed as foreign and exotic as the land of Turkey itself, hence the name. Indeed, before the misnomer of "turkey" stuck, the term was interchangeable with other European names for the bird, including:

— Ottoman hen

— Foreign fowl

— Persiabird

— Constantinople duck

— Chickety china, the chinese chicken

BRAZIL NUTS

Largely considered by most to be "the worst nuts," these large, tasteless fruits of the *Bertholletia excelsa* or "shittynut" tree indeed were first discovered in a can of mixed cocktail nuts in Para, Brazil. But they actually originate in Wilkes-Barre, Pennsylvania, home of Planters Nuts. It was in the Planters labs that the Brazil nut was first engineered as a cheap, heavy "dupe-nut" or "slug-nut" to balance out the cashews in their popular mixes. Not only is it worthless and disgusting in its nut state, the Brazil nut is also spiteful, quickly turning rancid in the can due to its high fat content, and spoiling things for everyone. However, the Brazil nut can be transformed into a useful oil when you crush and pulverize it, which is about what it deserves. The Brazilians use Brazil-nut oil widely for soap, cooking, and sex. And it is said you can actually light a whole Brazil nut and it will burn like a candle, but I would not advise you to test this, as it would require your being alone with a Brazil nut for some period of time in the dark.

JUNE 25

2003, NEW YORK CITY: Mayor Michael Bloomberg casually admits that he has smoked marijuana, that he enjoyed it, and that he also has seen Blue Man Group, like, thirty-seven times.

CORN

In the British Islands, "corn" is a generic term meaning any sort of grain. Thus, the old Irish song "John Barleycorn" actually translates as "John Barleybarley" or "John Barley-Anysortofgrain." But not "John Barleymaize," because "maize" specifically means "corn." What I am talking about is the food you eat on a cob (excluding pork on the cob). You know what I mean.

Its simple and distinct genetic strains (red, blue, "Indian," pop) made it attractive to mad scientists, who quickly developed many hearty mutant corns. While the hybridization programs would revolutionize commercial agriculture, the initial hybrid corns were ridiculed and displayed at sideshows as horrible freaks. Often a prize was handed out to the first person whose horrible taunts would make the corn cry (*see* "Brain Corn," below).

Corn is exceedingly versatile.

— It can be made into gas, plastic, commercial sweetener, dictionaries, and oil. (While passable, it is not as good as Brazil-nut oil for sex, and that is why there are more Brazilians than Nebraskans.)

— The husks can be woven together and worn as tiny, tiny skirts or folded into the most depressing dolls in the world.

— Dried, multicolored "Indian" corn can be hung on your door in autumn to indicate that you regret the genocide.

— Also, you can eat it.

Commonly at the farm stand you can now get varieties such as "Silver Queen, "Butter and Sugar," "Jekyll and Hyde" (in which some of the kernels are monstrous versions of the others), and "Brain Corn," which is sentient.

JUNE 26

1983, LONDON: Seona Dancing, a minor "synth-pop" duo featuring Ricky Gervais, attempts to revive their career with a cover of Soft Cell's "J'accuse." They fail. Ricky Gervais then very briefly joins the Thompson Twins, providing "eerie whistling" and "hand claps" on their single "We Are Detective" before giving up music for good.

Fresh corn should be eaten as quickly as possible, for as soon as it is picked, the sugar in the hypersweet varieties turns into starch, and the brain corn especially will start thinking of ways to kill you.

Common brain-corn revenge techniques include:

— garroting you

— knifing you

— husking

— corn smut

— chasing you around the apartment with a knife

— chasing you around the apartment biting at your calves

— putting on evening clothes and reciting poetry

— convincing you that it is a sensitive creature that deserves the respect of man. Getting you to give it a room in your house, and a little bed. Earning your trust while simultaneously raising your reputation as a physician and a friend to mutant corn. Singing little songs in your parlor to the delight of your society friends. Then, after you have gently fallen asleep dreaming of summertime and fresh grasses, garroting you (alt: husking you in your sleep).

JUNE 27
Today is the LOTTERY. Make sure to show up at the town square with your family to draw your slip of paper. Good luck!

INDIVIDUALLY WRAPPED SLICES OF CHEESE

These were first cultivated by the Kraft Indians of Peru. That's boring. Here are some more . . .

FAST FACTS ABOUT CORN

— In England, they put corn on pizza. The profound wrongness of this has yet to be apologized for.

— In olden days, an old corncob was used in lieu of toilet paper. Then they started using pages from almanacs.

— It can be popped AND SALTED, SALTED, SALTED to form "Corn Nuts."

CONSIDER THE FORK . . .

While long used as mini-stabbers, forks were not used widely for the consumption of food until the fifteenth century.

Prior to that point, it was expected that men and women of even the highest nobility would eat all solid foods with their hands, while soups would be poured upon the forearm and lapped off with the tongue. (If you have ever been to a Renaissance Faire, you have probably seen this in action.)

It was a messy affair, to say the least. For obvious reasons, thus, most formal dinner parties were conducted while naked. For less obvious reasons, everyone wore feathered masks. It was not until the quattrocento period that attitudes began to change. With rare exceptions (lobsters, langoustines, certain birds), we lost this primal connection with our food, keeping our distance from it with a variety of increasingly specialized utensils.

By the Edwardian era, the typical fine-dining table setting included some forty-seven pieces, including a chilled salad fork, heated crouton

JUNE 28

1914, SARAJEVO: Archduke Franz Ferdinand's touring car stalls in the streets of Sarajevo, allowing nineteen-year-old Gavrilo Princip the opportunity to shoot him in the neck, starting World War I. To this date, J.D. Power and Associates rates the Archduke's Gräf & Stift Double Phaeton "The Number One Car to Get Shot in the Neck In."

prongs, an anchovy filleter, a grape corer, a steak saber, a chop mallet, and a small silver club used for the stunning of raw oysters.

But it all began with the fork. An Italian innovation, the first forks had only three tines (the little sharp parts) and one long, slender handle.

As with all new technology, the fork was first regarded with scorn and suspicion. Many of Italy's northern neighbors presumed that the devices had been confiscated from miniature demons, or else were designed to resemble an Italian's sharp fingers.

It is likely there was some professional jealousy involved. Both the French and the Dutch were working on similar inventions at the same time. Dutch culinary masters had been long been developing the "tiparillo," a long, uni-tined skewer that was cherry flavored. The French, meanwhile, looked to the natural world for inspiration; specifically, the delicate, grasping feet of small birds.

Dubbed *"talonettes de la table,"* the innovation proved initially quite popular, despite the considerable inconvenience of having your eating utensils still attached to a live songbird.

If you prowl the old flea markets of Paris, you still see from time to time the miniature silver perches that were part of the most elaborate place settings and were used to store the *l'oiseau de la table* when the diner's hands were otherwise engaged in tearing apart a live langoustine (another common French delicacy) or masturbating his neighbor (yet another).

JUNE 29

1816, SWITZERLAND: Lord Byron invites a bunch of nineteenth-century hippies to join him at Villa Diodati, his sex house on Lake Geneva. The group took to reading ghost stories and set themselves a famous challenge: They would each write a horror tale of their own, and until they were all done, none of them would masturbate. The end result, of course, was Mary Wollstonecraft Shelley's *Frankenstein: Or the Modern Prometheus.* (Prometheus was the doctor, not the monster.) But do not forget the other classics of horror birthed over those three rainy days: Percy Shelley's *A Nightmare on Elm Street,* Dr. John Polidori's *Blade: The Vampire Slayer* (as well as *Blade: Trinity*), and Byron's own *Childe's Play,* about a murderous doll.

(This, of course, is the source of the phrase "A bird in the hand is worth two in the bush.")

Eventually it was discovered that handling a live bird while eating and having it defecate all over your food was not significantly more hygienic than using one's hands. You might imagine this is what caused the French to give up the practice, but as usual, you are wrong. Rather, the French finally abandoned their table birds for a very French reason: They realized that the birds themselves were delicious.

FOUR FORGOTTEN COCKTAILS

It's not just the Speed Julep. There are so many great and historic cocktails that aren't made any more due to lack of ingredients, expertise, plain nerve, and sufficient puppy blood. Here are four that, in my opinion, are primed for a much-deserved comeback.

THE SEVERED EAR, CA. 1880'S

A favorite of Van Gogh, it consisted of absinthe and Red Bull. Fell into disfavor among artists when absinthe was made illegal and Red Bull got popular with the *pont et tunnel* crowd.

THE OLD SPOTTY, CA. 1890'S

Gin, orange juice, and dalmatian blood. You used to be able to get this at the Knickerbocker Club in New York City. Then the dog lovers started to get weepy, and another great New York tradition was killed. JUST LIKE THE HUNDRED AND ONE DALMATIAN PUPPIES REQUIRED TO MAKE THIS DRINK.

JUNE 30

1981, VIRGINIA: After a five-month strange-rain drought that has devastated the Richmond economy, Al Starnes is fired and then institutionalized. His final forecast is famously captured on videotape: "TONIGHT MY WRATH SHALL RAIN DOWN UPON YOU! MY WRATH! AND A HAIL OF HATE! YOU PEOPLE DON'T DESERVE STRANGE RAIN! CHAMP! CHAMP! [unintelligible] I LOVE YOU ... "

THE DALMATIAN STINGER, CA. 1920'S

A poor substitute for the Old Spotty dating back to Prohibition. The mock dalmatian blood is made from Ritz crackers, the gin is nonalcoholic, and the orange juice was made in a bathtub. I don't advise it.

THE CRUSHED ANGEL, CA. 1910'S

Gin, vermouth, and a hard-to-find liqueur called Cherry Heering— shaken, strained, and garnished with a severed dove's wing. If you are careful, you can typically get two of these out of a single dove. PERFECT FOR LOVERS.

MANY NAMES FOR THE SAME SANDWICH

— A "SUB" OR SUBMARINE SANDWICH: New England
— A HERO SANDWICH: New York
— A WEDGE: Upstate New York
— A HOAGIE: Philadelphia and southern New Jersey
— A BREAD PENIS: Northern New Jersey
— A FINLESS, TAILLESS DOLPHIN: Pittsburgh (so named for the famous bartenders there)

JULY 1
1981, VIRGINIA: Al Starnes's final forecast is wrong. The day after he is fired, a
strange rain once again falls on Richmond.
Fittingly, it is frogs. But this time, they are
dead.

— AN IMPOVERISHED CHILD: New Orleans

— A LUNCHEON LOG: The Midwest

— A LONG PIG: The South Pacific

— A MEAT COFFIN: Richmond, Virginia

— AN 8-FOOT PARTY-SIZE MEAT COFFIN: *IBID*

NOTE: A "Grinder" in Pennsylvania is any kind of hoagie or cheese steak that has been run through a grinder into a thick paste so that it may be enjoyed on the go.

NOTE: A "sandwich" is a sandwich, but a "manwich" is a sandwich made of canned man.

OYSTERS: HOW AND WHEN AND WHY

Do you like to eat living creatures that taste like snot that's been rubbed on rocks and old silverware? Then oysters are for you.

But as noted,[169] it is critical that you never eat them in months whose names lack the letter "R."

In case you are unable to spell, these are as follows . . .

MAY

JUNE

JULY

AUGUST

---

169. Please see p. 269 under the heading "Some Notes on the Upcoming Presidential Election."

But not to worry. Come September, the oyster's rudimentary voice box will have disappeared and they will not scream when you eat them.

JULY 2

1937, THE SOUTH PACIFIC: Amelia Earhart becomes the first woman aviator to successfully navigate the Howland Island Time-Space Rift. She now resides with her navigator, Fred Noon, and her lover, Quetzalcoatl, in Dimension 29, where they sit on the three blood thrones and soon will judge us all.

WERE YOU AWARE OF IT?
"THE UPSIDE-DOWN WORLD"

Since summer is the season of the screaming oyster, you may wonder: May I eat oysters during the southern-hemispheric "summer" of Australia and New Zealand, for those are upside-down lands that observe our "summer" when it is their "winter," and vice versa (or, as the Aussies say it, versa-vice).

In theory, yes, but in practice, no: Because in that hemisphere, the oysters are all CLAMS, and because of the hemispheric difference, when you eat them, the vomit swirls out of you in the other direction.

WERE YOU AWARE OF IT?

(I suspect the answer is yes, probably painfully so if you've ever had a fresh Australian "DINGO CLAM.")

PS: While I have your attention here, if you are in Australia, do try the barbecued dingo, especially if it has been raised on baby.

PS: ON OYSTERS

Something else about the oyster that you did not know is that it is host to a parasite.

There is a tiny crab that lives inside the oyster that covets its

JULY 3
1983, NEWTON, MA: The first suburban
white child breakdances.

pearl. Known as a "pea" or "oyster" crab, it is one of the only living creatures that feeds almost exclusively on envy, apart from writers of short stories. It also eats the oyster, but it cooks it first. It is not a savage.

YOU MAY ALSO ASK: Do we eat the "pea" crab?

Yes, of course. The pea-crab roll is a summer staple along the coastal roadways of New England. Its recipe could not be simpler: a toasted, buttered New England–style top-split roll, heaped with the flesh of one million "pea" crabs, painstakingly picked from the shell with a jeweler's stylus by a local woman who hates you.

SPEAKING OF PARASITES, HOW DO I PROTECT MY CHILD FROM THE SCOURGE OF HEAD LICE?

There's really very little you can do. Getting head lice is a rite of passage among the young, like being kidnapped by pirates.

But the real danger isn't what's on your head but what's inside of you.

In fact, go ahead and wake your children up and make them read this, because it is important.

Hello, children. Stop fidgeting. I bet you thought you were alone in your body, but did you know that you have billions of microscopic and not-so-microscopic organisms living inside your body right this very moment?

Now, that may sound gross to you, and you'd be right: It's disgusting.

Here's a quick guide to the beasts that are currently living inside you and/or eating you alive:

— There are the SYMBIONTS, such as the billions of bacteria that infest your gut, or the little birds that live in your mouth and clean your teeth.

— The PARASITES, such as the various lice, worms, mites, and face-huggers that feed on your very skin and blood or lay eggs in your anus.

— And then there are the DOCTORS FROM THE FUTURE who travel in little tiny submarines through your brain, stealing your memories.

JULY 4

TODAY IS OUR INDEPENDENCE DAY. On this day in 1809, Thomas Jefferson died, just as he had predicted in the Declaration of Independence. In a curious coincidence, John Adams also died this day, just hours after his fellow founding father.[a] While their relationship ebbed over the years between friendship and deep enmity, they had become frequent correspondents by the end of their lives. Rumors that they died in some kind of suicide pact are unconfirmed, however, as is the urban legend that, at the time of their deaths, they both were listening to the song "(Don't Fear) The Reaper" being played on a harpsichord. It was actually "Iron Man."

a. When he heard the news that evening, Thomas Carroll, now the last living signatory to the Declaration, attempted to stab himself. Historians agree: He was just trying to get in on the action.

But don't worry, DOCTORS FROM THE FUTURE are not very common in areas with good hygiene. It's far more likely that you simply have an eighty-foot tapeworm inside your large intestine right this very minute. And that is the reason you are fat and constantly make the wrong decisions.

Now, go to bed. Sleep tight. Don't let the bedbugs crawl into your ears and start controlling your thoughts!

Meanwhile, parents, here's some good old-fashioned kitchen wisdom for dealing with lice:

— Take your lousy child and cover his lousy hair with mayonnaise.

JULY 5

1975, ON THE AIR: *The Tenth Level,* a television movie dramatizing only some of the infamous experiments conducted at the controversial Yale Feline Studies Lab, premieres on CBS. It stars William Shatner as "Professor Stephen Turner," a thinly veiled fictionalization of the lead researcher, Professor Ttephen Surner. The film is hailed by *TV Guide* as a "surprisingly thoughtful meditation on how quickly research into the nature of evil may quickly become evil itself." But some criticize the network's decision to change the research subjects in the film from cats to humans in order to give the film more mainstream appeal.

— Or else shave his lousy head altogether.

— Either way, you can add a few dashes of paprika for festive color.

WERE YOU AWARE OF IT?
"ARE PARASITES ALL EVIL?"

Not necessarily. GOTTFRIED LEIBNIZ carried a tapeworm with him for twenty-five years and credited its nighttime whisperings for the initial ideas that led to his development of the calculus. He also credited it for his astonishing anemia, which people would come from miles around to see.

WAIT A MINUTE, you say, DIDN'T ISAAC NEWTON INVENT THE CALCULUS?

The strange truth is, THEY BOTH developed the concepts behind calculus simultaneously and independently. AND WHAT IS MORE CURIOUS, they both had tapeworms exactly 57.2343 feet in length. That's 14,237 TAPEWORM SEGMENTS!

OR DID YOU ALREADY DO THE MATH?

MORE ON TAPEWORMS, AND OTHER FAMOUS ANIMAL ACTS

THE AMERICAN WEST, 1876: JIM TULLY AND HIS AMAZING TAPEWORM CIRCUS

Tully traveled from saloon to music hall carrying within him an amazing array of some nine trained tapeworms. The act would begin with Tully quietly standing, mouth open, before a glass of milk. As tapeworms cannot resist milk, Tully would wait as they traveled up from his lower intestine, pulling them from his mouth and introducing each by name. Since tapeworms all look alike,[170] he had knitted little uniforms and capes for them so the audience could better appreciate them as they leaped high in the air from one volunteer's gaping mouth to another's.

JULY 6

1946, CINCINNATI: Alabe Toys begins selling the Magic 8-Ball, capitalizing on the popularity of such divination toys as the Ouija board and Tyco's Wacky Entrails. The mysterious blue fluid in which the twenty-sided answer cube was suspended was originally composed of equal parts chicken blood and witch spit (the blue dye was just for fun). But a highly publicized accident put an end to this practice: In 1980, a four-year-old Shaker Heights boy began levitating while using a Magic 8-Ball and then grew a third eye in the middle of his forehead. Afterward, most magic toys were outlawed in the United States, including the Ouija board and the Rubik's Cube (which opened the mystic doorway to the realm of the dreadful Cenobites). The "magic" fluid in the ball was replaced with simple vodka. As for the boy's frightening prediction (via the raised printing on his third eye) that the brain sharks would rule us all by the year 2012, you can relax: MY SOURCES SAY NO.

FRANCE, 1894: PÉTOMANE THE WHALE

The legendary farting whale of Paris, Pétomane could apparently manipulate its flatulence to imitate thunder, rain, barking dogs, an opera singer singing "La Marseillaise," and even whale song. When it tired of the act, however, and tried singing its haunting, mysterious calls from its other end, Parisian audiences rejected the act, killing Pétomane and immediately eating his blubber.

---

170. Sorry. It's true.

JULY 7

1908, LE MANS, FRANCE: Wilbur Wright demonstrates his new aeroplane for the people of France at the famous racetrack named after "the mans." In a gesture to French aviation history, he brings along a sheep, a duck, and a rooster. Unfortunately, the rooster proved distracting, and Wright was forced to make an early landing and was promptly run over by race cars.

TIMES SQUARE SUBWAY STATION, 1989: TOMMY THE SINGING SNAKE

Back before Giuliani banned all animal acts from the subways, it was common enough to see any number of buskers performing the old "Singing Snake" routine. A man would have a small aquarium with a cloth over it. After playing the steel drums or the Chinese violin for about an hour, he would remove the cloth, revealing a snake inside that would sing a short, gruff, hissing rendition of a popular song of the day. It only lasted about ten seconds, and it was usually a Tracy Chapman song. But still, it was a sight to behold. The secret, of course, was that it wasn't a snake at all, but a glass lizard.

(A glass lizard, as you know, is not a snake at all, but an armless, legless lizard. You can tell the difference easily if you know to look for it: A glass lizard has eyelids and also a human larynx.)

BROOKLYN INVENTIONS

We all know that the egg cream contains neither egg nor cream. Brooklyn's famous native soda-fountain elixir is actually made of equal parts seltzer, milk and, of course, Fox's U-Bet Chocolate Syrup (which itself is made from equal parts chocolate paste and real Brooklyn foxes).

But were you aware that Brooklyn also gave birth to these familiar staples of American life that, with one exception, also CONTAIN NO MILK OR EGGS?

SCRABBLE

Legend has it that the game of Scrabble was invented one summer afternoon on the Brooklyn Promenade by Neil Simon in his ongoing efforts to teach Emmanuel Lewis how to read.

JULY 8

1853, URAGA HARBOR: Commodore Perry steers his "Black Ships" into the harbor of Tokyo. His goal: to finally open trade with the notoriously insular Japan so that the United States military could get its hands on some of that nation's famous giant fighting robots.

This relationship later became the basis of the hit Broadway play *Pygmalion,* which in English translates to *My Fair Webster.*

THE WOODEN ROLLER COASTER

Hastily assembled in 1927 and still running today, the Cyclone remains a Coney Island favorite among wooden-coaster enthusiasts. It is consistently ranked "most frighteningly decrepit" and "most bruisey" by *Dangerous Attractions* magazine.

THE SWEAT HOG

We now use this term as shorthand for any Brooklyn public-high-school student who exclusively fraternizes with kids outside his own racial, class, or ethnic grouping.[171] But back in the old days of Brooklyn's Ethnic Hill neighborhood, a "sweat hog" actually referred to a hearty pork dumpling boiled in beef sweat.

THE SPORT OF STICKBALL

Stickball remains the king of Brooklyn street games. While many of Brooklyn's picturesque neighborhoods lay claim to it, most agree it was first played on the sepia-colored streets of the Nostalgia Park neighborhood. Using only rudimentary equipment (sometimes even the stick was abandoned in favor of a fist or a piece of sharp glass), stickball's rules were fluid and varied widely from block to block. The

---

171. Of course, this does not happen. But wouldn't it be hilarious if it did? And what if you had to teach a group of such kids? And they were constantly climbing in your window and staring at your wife and baby? They are going to make a movie about this, mark my words.

JULY 9
1929, NEW YORK: William Randolph Hearst agrees to serialize a newspaper column by a young writer/illustrator named Robert Ripley on two conditions: (1) that he rename the column "Ripley's Believe It or Not!" (it had previously been called "Ripley's Believe It!" and generally reported only things that were intensely plausible); and (2) that Ripley dramatically increase his coverage of very long fingernails, a personal fascination of Hearst's.

only agreed constant was that each team must field at least two newsies; one bully who ends up having a heart of gold; one hapless fat kid; one sweat hog; and one feeble, dreamy, sickly child who would not actually participate in the game but instead would write Broadway plays about it later.

THE AIR CONDITIONER

In the old days, the homes in the picturesquely ethnic neighborhood of Fort Brownstone Hill were cooled only by great blocks of ice that were shot through the windows by the hoodlums using zip guns. That is, until 1902, when a Brooklynite named Friedrich Fedders discovered that by balancing incredibly heavy, sharp-edged machines precariously upon windowsills, he could sharply increase the rate of accidental maimings in the borough, thus making Brooklyn tougher and scrappier than ever.

THE ICE-CREAM CONE

You may not know it now, but Brooklyn used to be the beer-brewing capital of North America. Williamsburg alone was home to some thirty-four breweries, including the Schaefer Brewing Company, the Brooklyn Brewery, Old Milwaukee of Brooklyn, and Hipster Brothers Brewing "Company"—the first sarcastic-style beer to be brewed in the United States (though it was preceded by Canada's "Meta-Lager"). Basically what I am saying is: Brooklyn invented beer. And also hard cider. And glass.

But when the Germans stole all of Brooklyn's beer and hid it in Wisconsin, Brooklyn was left with a problem: What to do with all the beer cones? Beer had been enjoyed in both waffle and wafer cones in Brooklyn for centuries. Now with a surplus of cones, a scrappy, picturesque, cobblestoned Brooklynite named Norman Mailer came up with a bright idea. Why not freeze egg creams and serve them in the cones

JULY 10

1989, LOS ANGELES: Mel Blanc dies of cardiovascular disease. Despite heavy lobbying from Dana Carvey to take up the role, George H.W. Bush, now president, decides the time has come for him to speak with his own voice—a decision widely believed to have cost him the next election.

as a Coney Island treat and then punch people? After a while, this simple recipe was refined: Milk and eggs were added, punching was reduced, and the "ice-cream cone" was born.

THE "MAN-MADE BRIDGE"

Obviously.

SHITTY APHORISMS

As you may recall from my previous book, I am not the biggest fan of Benjamin Franklin's *Poor Richard's Almanack*, though it is an obvious and important predecessor of my own work.

For one, I found Franklin's constant advertising of his own inventions (almanacs, for example) unseemly. It's just not something I would ever do.

As well, I was never as fond as some of his pushy little aphorisms. As you have already seen, if I am going to tell you how to live your life, I am just going to come out and tell you. AT LENGTH. I'm not going to waste your time with pithy little sayings that get to the point in just a few words.

That said, it turns out there is a law that any book calling itself an almanac must contain at least four shitty aphorisms ("shittiness" mine).[172] In order, thus, to avoid a substantial retroactive fine, I

---

172. Will it surprise you to learn that this law was written in 1775 by Postmaster General BENJAMIN F'N FRANKLIN?

JULY 11
1859, LONDON: Charles Dickens publishes *A Tale of Two Cities*. The two cities
in question are Cirith Ungol and Orthanc.

present to you now a few words of wisdom that I have made up, but are nonetheless absolutely true:

It takes three men to kick a dog to death, but only one to raise it poorly.

That which is hard to do is best done bitterly.

A liar has need of three things: a fine memory, a finer smile, and a passable rubber mask.

Say what you will, but a chicken has a long and pointy face.

A stopped clock is correct twice a day, but a sundial can be used to stab someone, even at nighttime.

What cats think does not matter—they shit in a box.

The Holy Roman Empire was neither holy, nor Roman, nor an empire, nor "the."

A penny saved is worth approximately the same amount as a penny earned, which is to say: not worth it.

A French centime saved can later be used as a token in the Boston subway system.[173]

It matters not how a man lives, but that he not die by falling off a cliff. That

---

173. This was true at least when the subway used tokens and the French used centimes. Now that little fact and a centime will get you nothing but a nonexistent cup of un-coffee. It just goes to prove the old maxim *Plus ça change, plus c'est la même chose,* or "The more change, the better."

is a terrible way to die. Especially if the cliff overlooks a canyon full of spikes.

JULY 12
Nothing happened today.

WHAT TO EXPECT WHILE SERVING AS A JUROR

HEREWITH, a transcript of the controversial orientation film briefly shown to prospective jurors in New York State Supreme Court between June 18, 2007, and June 24, 2007, and then quickly destroyed.

BEGIN QUOTED TEXT:

Good morning, and welcome to the first day of your jury service. I know many of you would rather not be in this room. But bear in mind that, until relatively recently in human history, there was no such thing as a JURY.

During the Salem Witch trials, for example, if you were accused of a being a witch, you would be bound and weighted with rocks, and then thrown into a deep lake.

It was called TRIAL BY ORDEAL. If you floated, you were clearly a witch. (In Puritan times, floating was considered to be black magic. That is why everyone hated ducks.) If you sank and drowned, then you were deemed innocent. If they forgot to fill the lake with water, then a mistrial would be declared, and they would set you on fire.

Doesn't sound like a very good system, does it?

Not only was it cruel, it was also imperfect. Many witches, for example, cheated the system by swimming down and escaping via a trapdoor in the bottom of the lake. That's not fair, is it?

So even though we all know that jury duty is inconvenient, you should be grateful to be here. At least we are probably not going to drown you!

Hi. My name is John Hodgman, and it is my job to instruct you on how to be a juror in the United States.

Many of you may worry: Do I have what it takes to be a juror? I am not a lawyer. I do not have any special wigs or robes. And what about my children at home?

Please stop whining. Your children are safe with us. The only thing you need to take part in this great experiment of justice is the ability to keep an open mind, some clothing, and the heavy rock we gave you as you came in.

If you have lost your heavy rock, go to room 1245 to get a new one. You will need it in case your trial goes to the "stoning phase."

But for most of you, your jury duty will look very much like what you probably have seen on television.

There is the judge sitting at a very tall bench made of beautiful wood that he made with his own hands. Before him sit the two antagonists in our little drama. The defense attorney, with his silver hair and seersucker suit and folksy wisdom, represents the defendant, the man or woman accused of a crime or wrongdoing. At the other table stands Sam Waterston. He is very angry at the defendant and wants to put him in jail. He is so, so angry.

Now, here is the court reporter, typing on his strange little machine. His job is to write down everything that is said at the trial. That is the only reason he keeps staring at you. Promise.

Have you ever wondered what the machine is called? It's called a "stenograph," and part of it is attached to his penis.

And here are some more familiar faces: the clerk of the court, the bailiff, the Imperial Guards, the eunuchs, and the white horse.

There is one difference from the courtroom shows you may see

on TV that we should mention, and
that is that the bailiff no longer
points his gun at people until they
tell the truth. We have not done that since 1983.

JULY 14
Rien.

During the trial, both the defense attorney and Sam Waterston will make their "opening statements."

As an example, let's take a page from an old fairy tale and say that the defendant is accused of eating an old woman and her granddaughter.

Sam Waterston will begin the trial by explaining this accusation. He may even explain how the defendant kept the old woman and little girl alive in his stomach for days before a noble woodsman could cut them out and pull them, still drenched in bile, from the defendant's steaming gut.

I know, it sounds like a delightful fairy tale. But remember: THIS IS NOT EVIDENCE. This is just Sam Waterston's version of what happened, and no matter how much he spits on you when he's talking, it doesn't make it true.

After Sam Waterston finishes yelling, the defense attorney will have a chance to tell his side of the story. He will probably say something about the defendant being not guilty, and how traumatic it was for him to be cut open with an ax. You can ignore this part.

After this, the trial begins. Sam Waterston must attempt to prove beyond a reasonable doubt that the events unfolded as he claims they did. He may show you evidence. Some of the evidence may be disturbing. He may show you documents or photographs, say, of a half-digested child. He may show you the ax, and he may try to chop you with it. But it's important that you pay attention, even if you are accidentally chopped.

Sam Waterston may also ask witnesses to sit on the white horse and give testimony. Sitting on a white horse magically compels them

JULY 15

1940, LONDON: Former British prime minister Neville Chamberlain begins writing "The Appeaser," his weekly newspaper column for the London *Times,* in which he attempts to resolve readers' personal conflicts and dilemmas, usually by suggesting that one party offer the other party Czechoslovakia in return for promising not to kill millions of Jews. His column is horribly unpopular.

to tell the truth. Also, they will have seen what Waterston can do with an ax, so they will be too scared to lie.

After each prosecution witness speaks, the defense attorney will have a chance to "cross-examine" them. This means he can ask them questions and examine them physically, fondle their hair, feel their clothing and skin, etc. Let's say the grandmother tells about the defendant coming into her house and eating her and then wearing her clothing.

Now, because the defense attorney is a folksy old man, he will try to cozy up to the grandmother, using old-fashioned terms like "aeroplane" and "phosphate" and "vagina." There's no question that Grandma will be charmed by him. There's no question that he is what the old folks call a "smoothie" (a kind of yogurt drink). Maybe she will even elope with him. This will seriously undermine her testimony!

Once Sam Waterston has called all his witnesses and finished making his case, he will put his clothes back on. Now it will be the defense attorney's turn to show you evidence or call witnesses. He may call in an expert witness. An expert witness is someone who was not there to see the crime, and doesn't know anything about the case, but knows better than everyone else.

You should know that the defense attorney might call a mesmerist to the stand to attempt to hypnotize you. Remember: IF YOU FEEL AT ANY TIME THAT YOU ARE BEING HYPNOTIZED, JUST PUT ON YOUR MASK. The mask not only protects you from hypnosis but also prevents you from hearing, seeing, or saying anything, and hides your identity. Since we no longer sequester jurors during long trials, the judge may or may not ask you to wear this mask all the time. If so, a blacksmith will be on hand to weld it shut.

Once both sides have presented their cases, YOUR JOB BEGINS. You as a jury must decide if Sam Waterston has proven BEYOND A REASONABLE DOUBT that the defendant broke that law. Note that I did not say BEYOND *ALL* DOUBT. Whenever humans are involved, there will always be doubt. That is why we have the magical white horse.

No, Sam Waterston merely must make the case such that any reasonable person would agree that the defendant is guilty. You're a reasonable person, aren't you?

While you are making your decision, the jury will go into a room to discuss it. In this room there will be sandwiches and water, and on the walls will be mounted various kinds of swords and other kinds of weapons. The jury's decision must be unanimous, and while deliberations may get heated, we discourage you from actually using the weapons. Certainly don't use the epée against the saber. That would be suicide.

Once the jury reaches a verdict,

JULY 16

1951, NEW YORK: J. D. Salinger publishes *The Catcher in the Rye*. Despite a popular urban legend, if you read it backwards, it does not tell you to kill John Lennon. It is instead about a teenager who is depressed because he can't remember the correct words to a poem by Robert Burns. Naturally, this struck a chord with the American public, who also cannot remember poems, launching the book onto the bestseller lists and making Salinger a rare literary celebrity.

The unending controversy surrounding the novel eventually drove Salinger into seclusion. He ceased publishing new works in 1965 and retreated to rural New Hampshire, where he has since been sighted only occasionally, and then only with the aid of night-vision cameras and infrared tracking devices.

Figure 84: J. D. Salinger

Most of these devices belong to Tim Masters McPherson, the nation's preeminent Salinger hunter. According to McPherson, a thirty-eight-year-old New Hampshire accountant, he actually met Salinger at the Price Chopper grocery store one afternoon in 1998.

"It was strange, because it wasn't a

CONTINUED ON THE NEXT PAGE

JULY 17

1957, NEW YORK CITY: Exactly one year before her death at the age of forty-four, Billie Holiday attempts a comeback with a recording of Disney's "Zip-a-Dee-Doo-Dah." However, the record is soon pulled from the shelves after Ms. Holiday's somber rendition causes several hundred children across America to become catatonically depressed.

JULY 16 CONTINUED

Salinger-spotting day for me. I was just doing groceries," McPherson wrote on the Internet. "I suddenly turned around, and there he was, buying some brown rice. At first, I didn't recognize him without the night vision. His skin was not green, and his eyes had pupils. It was like talking to an actual human being."

According to McPherson, Salinger seemed to have no idea who McPherson was. ("Or perhaps he was just toying with me. That's what Thomas Pynchon used to do before I nailed him in '94.") Either way, Salinger chose this moment in the health-foods aisle to make an astounding revelation: He had been writing.

During his period as a recluse, he had in fact completed dozens of novels—all of them sequels to the *Catcher in the Rye*. They recounted, he said, Holden Caulfield's further adventures as a drunken, poem-forgetting boy who then discovers he has magical powers. He goes to a special private school for magicians, which he finds (predictably) unbearable. Ditching school once again, he finally discovers his true destiny: to do battle with an ancient evil wizard named "Phony."

"At first I thought it was a joke," wrote McPherson. "But I stared at him and looked into the big human pupils of those dark soleful [sic] eyes, and I knew he had no clue, and I wasn't going to be the one to tell him. Not that afternoon. Not at the Price Chopper." Salinger shook McPher-

CONTINUED ON THE NEXT PAGE

you will write it on a slip of paper and give it to the judge.

That's it!

Your jury service is complete. There is no need for you to ever think about any of these people again—not Sam Waterston or his seersuckered friend, not the grandma or the half-digested girl; not the victims of the maniac you may have just acquitted or the thirteen-year-old boy you've just condemned to spend his adolescence in an adult prison where he will brutalized. Those people are all dead to you now, because YOU ARE A GOOD PERSON.

Being a juror is perhaps the greatest privilege of citizenship. It is better than voting. Better than free speech. And naturally, it is much, much better than habeas corpus. For while those rights can be taken away, EVERYONE in the United States is entitled to have their fate decided by an untrained panel of resentful people chosen at random.

However, the system does not work unless we all play our part. EVERY U.S. CITIZEN must serve on a jury. There are no more exemptions anymore just for being famous or black. Also, as of this year, certain animals, such as Seeing-Eye dogs and macaws, are also required to serve. So if you are blind or if you are a macaw, sit back down. YOU'RE NOT GETTING OFF THIS TIME.

However, witches should report to room 1245 for drowning.

That is all.

END QUOTED TEXT!

JULY 18

64 AD, ROME: The Great Fire of Rome erupts in the Circus Maximus. A popular legend has it that Emperor Nero "fiddled while Rome burned." But as the violin would not be invented for another thousand years, it is presumed that this saying actually refers to Nero's habit of masturbating with a lyre.

JULY 16 CONTINUED

son's hand and left the store happily. McPherson followed him home at a discreet distance, but in deference to his privacy, McPherson did and said nothing for almost two weeks. At that point, he claims, he couldn't resist. He sent Salinger a copy of *Harry Potter and the Sorcerer's Stone* "just to see what he would do, I guess. Just to flush him out."

McPherson claims to have then collected forty-five minutes of high-quality video of Salinger standing by a small bonfire in his backyard, feeding page after manuscript page into the flames. "I don't know what he was burning, but I tell you: I sure didn't need the night vision that night. That fire was bright as day."

You can buy McPherson's video online.

JULY 19

2007, THE SKIES ABOVE THE UNITED STATES: I fly home from Los Angeles. I am almost seated next to Loni Anderson.

THE MOLE-MEN:
ARE THEY
THE NEW HOBOES?

JULY 20

1859, LONDON: The Clock Tower at the Palace of Westminster is completed. Though it is commonly known as "Big Ben," certain know-it-alls (like the Internet) will tell you that "Big Ben" actually refers to the bell in the clock. The Internet is wrong. The name is that of the hunchback who originally *rang* the bell. Despite the nickname, he was actually normal size for a hunchback. Now, of course, there aren't many hunchbacks in the bell-ringing business, and the hunch that is worn by the current bell-ringer is purely ceremonial.

JULY 21

1921, HONG KONG: "King Kong Plays Ping-Pong in Hong Kong With His Ding Dong!"[a] This would be King Kong's only visit to Hong Kong, though he would be a table-tennis fan for all of his short, tragic life.

a. Headline courtesy of the *International Herald Tribune*.

THE SEVEN PORTALS TO THE HOLLOW EARTH

As I alluded in my previous work[174] while many are speculated upon, there are only seven known portals to the lands below that are or were once open. THESE ARE THEY:

NUMBER ONE: "SYMMES HOLE ALPHA," THE ARCTIC SEA

John Cleves Symmes is one of those lunatics we sometimes talk about.

There is not much you need to know about him. He was born in 1779 in New Jersey to a prominent family and then quickly went in-

Figure 85: Symmes's Gravestone. Perhaps Unsurprisingly, Not Even the Model Hollow Earth Is Actually Hollow.

sane. He had a family of his own, and a son whom he named Americus, because he was insane. But he largely ignored his family as he instead developed with increasing intensity the strange theories that would be his legacy.

Like many of his time, Symmes was obsessed with polar exploration.

Many fantasies had been spun of what we would find once we reached the poles. Strangely, none of them involved vast, empty expanses of desolate ice. Instead, the

174. Please see page 191 of *The Areas of My Expertise* under the heading "Virginia."

imagination-starved scholars and
poets agreed that we would find either (a) warm, open polar seas that
would connect Europe to Asia; (b) a

JULY 22
1873, ALBANY: Celluloid is used to make
the first "pocket comb." It is later discovered that it works equally well on hair.

vast magnetic mountain drawing all compasses to it; (c) both; or (d)
at the very least, an amazing revolving restaurant.

But most ridiculous of all was the idea dreamed up by John Cleves
Symmes: that at both ends of the earth there opened great holes,
miles and miles across, that led down and into to the Hollow Earth.

It was Symmes's belief that the earth is *hollow*, like an egg, minus
the yolk and the white (technically, albumen), of course; and also
more spherical than egg-shaped; and also huge, with dirt and humans on the outside.

But on the inside! Oh, the inside! According to Symmes, once you
traversed the holes, you would be sailing in a beautiful, upside-down
sea. Eventually you would reach the green shores of an upside-down
land, where you would meet the upside-down people who dwelled in
great cities some eight hundred miles beneath our feet.

Like all utopian visions of the nineteenth century, the people of
the Hollow Earth were stronger and smarter than we, and also nine
feet tall. They were, in short (or tall), a better version of ourselves,
for they were the original humans, and we their mere wretched descendants, made smaller both in stature and in character by millennia of surface dwelling.

According to Symmes, we, despite all the great advances of
nineteenth-century industrialized cities (Cities! Steam-horses! Civil
wars!), were nothing but the awful inbred cousins of the first humans, who still dwelled in the unspoiled, underground promised
land from which we had the misfortune once to spring.

If you are detecting a mythical tone to this story, then you are
smarter than I thought, or else you have purchased the Hodgman

JULY 23
1988, HOLLYWOOD: Billy Bragg performs "The Internationale" on *Solid Gold.*

literary tone detector that I've been spamming you about.[175]

For indeed, Symmes imagined not just a lost paradise, but one doubly lost. After all, for many generations, many humans—not just Americans—imagined an underworld. Whether it was called Hades, Tartarus, the "Pit," or the "Ultra-Pit," the deep places were home to dark creatures and lost souls, while the heavens were reserved for, well, heaven.

In the nineteenth century, as war and science stalked the land in tandem, hope for heaven faded. The true lost souls were the ones still living, hopeless, on earth. It is perhaps not surprising that men like Symmes would reverse the equation and imagine the inner earth not an inferno, but a new inverted paradise, and lit dimly by a weak, red, internal sun.

Symmes first developed his ideas in a circular he printed in 1818 (ironically, the circular itself was perfectly flat and rectangular, though it did contain a secret compartment). In it he begged for funds to begin a polar expedition to find the open holes that he was sure existed—and the path to the wealth and perfection that lay within.

And so it may not come as a surprise that Symmes's ideas gained a certain currency during the nineteenth century and fired the popular imagination.

But here is the surprise: Symmes was not wholly deluded. There is indeed a vast hole in the Arctic Circle that leads down into the earth. But it is largely blocked by the Pietra Negra, the vast, glossy, black, magnetic mountain that draws all compasses to it. And in any case, Symmes would never get to see it. For as you may know,

---

175. Please see page 523 under the heading "The Hodgman Literary Tone Detector: And Why You Should Buy It."

Symmes suffered from Latitude Fever and grew horribly sick any time he ventured farther north than Michigan and farther south than Mexico City. Pathetic.

As for his "Hollow Earth" theory, here Symmes was simply wrong. The earth is not "hollow" in the proper sense. Rather, it is just as

JULY 24
1980, LONDON: Comedian Peter Sellers dies of heart failure. Having lost one of their most bankable stars, United Artists would attempt to carry on the popular *Pink Panther* series of films using Sellers's decaying corpse and attaching it to ropes and pulleys. This effort would later become the inspiration for both the movie *Weekend at Bernie's* as well as the remake of *The Pink Panther* starring Steve Martin as the decaying corpse of Peter Sellers.

you'd expect: full of rock and dirt and lava and hell (although the hell part is actually pretty small and provincial, especially compared to the great cavern-cities of the mole-men).

NUMBER TWO: MONTICELLO, IN VIRGINIA

Yes, I have mentioned the mole-men again. You may recall them from my previous book, and you may ask: Who are the mole-men, and what do they want?[176] Would you be surprised to learn that those were the exact words spoken by THOMAS JEFFERSON?

It is true, as you will learn.

In 1770, a twenty-seven-year-old Thomas Jefferson set out to build a new home for himself amidst the many acres of Virginia farmland he had inherited from his father. It was as he walked and explored the land that he first discovered the mole-manic palace known as Monticello.

Jefferson was understandably startled to discover an Italianate villa of unknown origin rising out of the earth of his ancestral lands. But he was even more surprised by what he found inside.

There, beneath the great dome, and by dim greenish light, he encountered a small group (or "Parlor") of mole-men dining on

---

176. Please see page 541 under the heading "Answers to Your Questions About the Mole-Men."

JULY 25
1990, SOMEWHERE IN THE PACIFIC:
The controversial Yale Feline Studies Lab
quietly reopens with private funding on an
unnamed island.

weevil pie and discussing world affairs.

They had, according to Jefferson's autobiography, pallid, papery skin and long spindly arms terminating in powerful, clawed hands. Their faces were dominated by their fiercely twisted teeth and their enormous eyes that never closed, though a membrane would rise to cover them whenever they were digging or, as in this case, when they were surprised. And they were covered all over with a kind of slimy mucus, which made it difficult for them to keep their powdered wigs on.

But though they were initially startled, the mole-men would soon greet Jefferson kindly.

"They touched my face," wrote Jefferson, "and hissed, as is their custom. You might imagine my fright, and it took some time to remove the mucus. But as we came to speak, I realized that though they dwelled in darkness,[177] they were creatures of the Enlightenment."

Indeed, despite their near-constant hissing and acidic drool, the mole-men were courteous, eloquent, and WELCOMING. They showed him around the mansion, built long ago in the traditional mole-manic style. They showed Jefferson dinosaur bones and two-dollar bills they had brought with them from deep in the earth. And in time they would tutor him in the fine art of writing Declarations of Independence.

And so, here, NEAR A HOLE IN THE GROUND, Jefferson found his first true intellectual comrades.

Though a wealthy gentleman planter, young Jefferson possessed a restless intellect and curiosity about the natural world that was considered somewhat unseemly among his colleagues in the Virginia House of Burgesses. He was constantly trying to separate church

---

177. Technically, they live only in partial darkness, as the mucus itself is luminous.

from state and end primogeniture and combine macaroni and cheese. Plus he was ungodly tall, a redhead, and had a high, reedy voice. And so it was that his peers—staunch men who liked their god and state mixed and their macaroni uncheesed—would from time to time burn Jefferson as a witch. Jefferson tolerated this with equanimity, choosing instead to stare at the flames and wonder how they worked.

JULY 26
1847, LIBERIA: Liberia declares independence from the United States. Established by freed American slaves, the country had been the dream of the American Colonization Society, which believed that the only answer to the slavery problem would be to send all the blacks back to Africa. Cheered by their early success, the Society went on to propose that all of the poor Indians displaced by the Trail of Tears should move to New Indiana, an island in the Black Sea. Those Native Americans who were not dead politely declined.

But these strange Monticello dwellers were scientists and philosophers: mole-men of reason. Like Jefferson, they were Deists. They believed profoundly in a Creator. How could they not? For long ago they had dug deep and found the great Century Toad that had secreted the earth so long ago. But from their repeated attempts to speak to the toad, they knew also of its cruel indifference toward its own creation and those who walked upon the earth—or scuttled deep within it.

"No God, nor King, nor Toad may own us," said one mole-man to Jefferson on one of his many visits. This was Genuine Hissfurther, a mole-manic pamphleteer and, eventually, Jefferson's close friend. As he later wrote, "Each of us carves his own tunnel through hard stone, and each must cast his own light into the darkness, and deal with the bats as best he can."[178]

While there had once been a mole-manic dominion upon the surface of Virginia,[179] it had been long abandoned. Now, however, Hissfurther and his parlor of like-thinking mole-men had returned to create a new nation, based on principles of secular self-government,

---

178. For his part, Hissfurther explained, he ate the bats.

179. They were drawn to the surface after heavy rains.

JULY 27
1931, HAPPY BIRTHDAY, JERRY VAN
DYKE! The former costar of *Coach* is
still considered to be the most successful
(separated) Siamese twin in the history of
entertainment.

natural rights, and low taxes on worm semen. They had come to Monticello to craft their Declaration of Independence, both because of the place's historical significance, and also because the light was better.

"I understand," said Jefferson in his high, reedy, nearly mole-manic voice. "You are saying that it is time to rise up."

And so it was that Jefferson, who until that year had been a wealthy dilettante and proud subject of the British Crown, began his metamorphosis into a revolutionary. Under Hissfurther's fond tutelage, Jefferson began to envision a free nation of independent, educated yeoman farmers living off the giant luminous fungi the mole-men taught him to grow in Monticello's basement.

"The tree of liberty must be refreshed from time to time with the blood of patriots and tyrants," hissed Hissfurther. It is this phrase that Jefferson would later famously repeat, though he never realized that his friend was speaking literally.[180]

NUMBER THREE: SHESHNA'S WELL, BENARES, INDIA

In India, the mole-men were known as the Nagas—the underground snake-men who were quick to anger and difficult to please—and Sheshna's Well was the passageway to their grand underground city called Patala. In other lands they were known by other names: the Sleestaks, the Visitors, Our Reptiloid Masters.

But such legends misrepresented the mole-men. First of all, they are not *lizard*-men. Indeed, they have more in common physically with naked mole-rats than moles proper (although they are not naked; their waistcoats and knickers are woven from the finest giant

---

180. Literally. For further tree-care tips, please see page 565 under the heading "The Best Mas Ever."

earthworm setae). But when you are staring down a bottomless well and all you can hear is hissing, it is an understandable error to make.

Nor have they ever sought to be our masters. Despite the conspiracy theories you may have read, the mole-men have never interbred with the British royal family or the Bush dynasty with the goal of infiltrating the highest reaches of government so as to harvest the blood of our babies to power the spaceliners that will bring them to the next planet they plan to pillage from within. You are thinking of the Belgians.

Rather, for many millennia, the mole-men kept a dark and quiet life, tending their glowshrooms, their bloodbeetle hutches, and the various under-creatures they raised for food, transportation, and companionship. Among their many hideous steeds were the great-

JULY 28
1932, WASHINGTON, DC: President Hoover evicts the encamped "Bonus Army" of disgruntled World War I veterans from their tent city, while at the same time ordering his secret strike force of pneumatic soldiers to find and kill the secretary of the treasury, Hobo Joe Junkpan. It is believed that Bob Dylan's ballad "The Robo-Men and Hobo Joe" is based on this dark chapter of American history. But honestly, who can tell?

Figure 86: The Hated Dirt Puma

JULY 29
1969, NEW HAVEN, CT: The *Apollo 11* moon landing is staged in the moon room of Payne Whitney Gymnasium at Yale University.

worms, the lesser-worms (used in teams to pull a dust chariot), the giant alligator, the pseudo-saur (not a dinosaur at all, but an iguana blown up to monstrous size using a pump), and the so-called dirt puma—a blind, rancid-smelling semi-mammal prized for its speed and many skin diseases.[181]

As in many civilizations, they did not always wear powdered wigs and fine clothing made of worm hair. They, too, had their dark ages of tribal warfare and primitive superstition. They once believed, for example, that the dim, reddish sun that warmed them at the earth's core actually *revolved around them.* Only later did they determine that the sun itself is motionless, tethered to the earth by a strand of hardened saliva terminating at the Century Toad. (Many daring deep-earth explorers, called dirtonauts, died making these discoveries.)

But by SY (surface year) 1300, they had already embraced the scientific method and had developed an early sort of representative government. Under the mole-manic common law, the emperor of their Dominion, called the Hiss-Chief, would not make any decision without first consulting the parliament of burrowing pinworms, mites, and other parasites that the other mole-men had chosen for him.

By SY 1500, having explored the core lands and opened diplomatic relations with hell, the mole-men turned their eyes and fangs upward.

Their first attempt at a surface colony in North America was a failure. Having built Monticello and opened the great marble mines of West Virginia, contact from the surface colonists suddenly ended in SY 1525. A search party found Monticello abandoned and emptied but for one haunting clue carved in the wall: the word "Croatoan."[182]

---

181. Today, of course, they largely travel by monorail.

182. "Croatoan" was a notorious mole-manic serial killer known for eating his victims whole and leaving his signature at the scenes of his terrible crimes. As of this writing, he is still at large.

Then, in 1561, the dirtonauts discovered France. The indigenous
French welcomed the strange visitors warmly and immediately asked
if they could poach a mole-man baby
in butter and eat it.

With this, the dirtonauts knew

JULY 30
1908, SIBERIA: Thousands of acres of
remote forest are mysteriously leveled in
what would come to be known as THE
TUNGUSKA EVENT. Speculation as to
what caused the event has run rampant
ever since: A meteor collision? A mob of
angry lumberjacks? Tree-loathing aliens?
Am I going to be the only person who sees
the obvious and suggests: ALL THREE?

they had met kindred spirits. For
even the mole-men knew how disgusting their own babies were, and
how open-minded one must be to eat one.

Thus began nearly three hundred years of tremendous cross-cul-
tural exchange between the Lands Above and Below—a period
known as "THE GREAT NITROGEN CYCLE." Like the earthworm, the mole-men churned the soil of Western thought, fertilizing
it with new ideas in science, philosophy, art, and politics. They also
made the soil of Europe infinitely richer with their own dung.[183]

They taught architecture to Palladio and learned political science
from Locke. They were the model for Rousseau's "noble savage,"
and that is why Rousseau would later suggest in *Emile* that all children should be abandoned in caves by their parents until they reach
the age of twelve (which is still how it is done in Brookline, Massachusetts).

But Rousseau was a wishful thinker. Just because the mole-men
spat acid and had great yellow teeth and often vomited up rocks and
stones, they were not savage. Indeed, swallowing and regurgitating
stones was considered to be a gentlemanly habit among the mole-
men, akin to the surface habit of taking snuff and by the end of the
eighteenth century, the mole-men were vomiting snuff as well.
Rather, they stood at the vanguard of the political enlightenment.

---

183. Mole-man castings are still the best fertilizer you can buy, if you can find it at the garden
center. It's sometimes sold under the name "night soil" or "Sleestak turds."

JULY 31

1972, WASHINGTON, DC: Sen. Thomas Eagleton, running mate to Democratic nominee George McGovern, resigns from the race when it is revealed that Eagleton had received electroshock treatments. Unfortunately, electroshock treatments were all the rage in the Senate at that time, and as McGovern searched for a new VP candidate, he had difficulty finding any who had not attended the swinging "zap club" parties that were held every other Saturday at various secret locations.

They were first of the major nations to depose their king (though the truth was, the king had been dead for more than a century, and the lice and pinworms were just running things on their own from his rotting corpse). And they also wrote the first Declaration of Independence, forming the Free Republic of the Topsoilers in 1745.

In this, the mole-men would anticipate and inspire the two revolutions that would change the face of the surface world forever. As Voltaire put it so eloquently, "If the mole-men did not exist, we should have to invent them." And then he vomited up some sharp stones. By that time, everyone was doing it.

NUMBER FOUR: PHILADELPHIA, PA, INDEPENDENCE HALL

While Jefferson is largely given credit for writing the Declaration of Independence, contemporary historians note that few of the concepts contained therein were especially new. The opening passage in particular is taken directly from the Mole-Manic Declaration of Independence of the Thirty-fourth Passage, Ninth Level.[184]

But if Jefferson were stealing, he was stealing from the best. For the mole-men were avid and experienced Declarationists. By the time of the Second Continental Congress, what had once been a single monolithic mole-manic empire had declared itself into some 28,000 free republics, many of them consisting only of two or three citizens, and another just of their shadows on the wall.

---

184. "When in the Course of human Events, it becomes necessary for one People to dissolve the Political Bands which have connected them with another, and to assume among them the Powers of the Earth, if you have trouble dissolving the Bands, try dripping some of your acidic saliva upon them. That usually does the Trick."

So we must presume the influence of Genuine Hissfurther, for his and Jefferson's friendship had deepened in the intervening years. They were often seen walking through Philadelphia together, Hissfurther's pet millipedes scrambling beside them. Indeed, Hissfurther had taken up

AUGUST 1
1799, EGYPT: Napoléon's occupying armies remove the nose of the Great Sphinx of Giza, believing it contains the Ark of the Covenant. Transporting the nose to Paris, Napoléon commissioned a thirty-man nose-picking crew to find the Ark. Most of them died or disappeared within the nose, which, it turned out, contained only a giant secret room full of deadly asps.

residence in the dank dirt basement of the same boarding house where Jefferson resided. It would have been easy enough for him to have tunneled over from time to time to Jefferson's rooms to read a draft or lend an elegant phrasing.

But whether Hissfurther was an active collaborator in the drafting of our nation's founding document or merely a passive supporter, his friendship with Jefferson was controversial. John Adams complained bitterly of the influence of the mole-men on the Congress, pointing out that many of them had not even been educated at Harvard.

At first, Benjamin Franklin found Hissfurther and his colleagues to be fascinating company. He even invented sunglasses for them,[185] as well as a primitive sunscreen made of tallow and thick gravy. But when the mole-men saw Franklin's pet wild turkey, they freaked out, standing and screeching at it for about half an hour outside of the Pennsylvania State House, much to Franklin's offense. Then Hissfurther's millipedes ate the poor creature, and that was the end of their friendship.

Franklin thereafter took a much more critical look at Jefferson's draft of the Declaration, suggesting many changes to root out "the burrowings of Jefferson's ant-men" before it was submitted to Congress.

But Franklin had no say over the most profound change to the

185. Please see page 432 under the heading "May 9."

AUGUST 2
2009, TUXEDO, NY: The Annual New York State Renaissance Faire opens today. LOOK FOR ME AT THE BIRDS OF PREY EXHIBIT. I will be wearing my wizard's cap, as usual. . . .

document. Jefferson's original draft, as you likely know from your history books, contained a strong denunciation of slavery. This undoubtedly showed the mole-manic sway upon Jefferson's thinking, as Jefferson himself had long owned many slaves, while the mole-men had emancipated the Troglodytic Men some three centuries before.

But Jefferson's fellow slave owners refused to sign the Declaration until this passage was taken out and lynched. Jefferson, though deeply wounded, assented to the compromise. And at that moment, Hissfurther and his delegation arose silently in protest and left the room, their millipedes clicking along the polished floors behind them.

When Jefferson rushed after them, they were already gone, leaving nothing behind but the hole they had quickly carved with their teeth and spittle. Jefferson wondered if he would ever see Genuine Hissfurther again.

As for the hole, it is there still, though you cannot go down it, because it is a national park, and also the Philadelphians have filled it with pennies.

NUMBER FIVE: NEW YORK CITY, NY, WEST SEVENTY-NINTH STREET

After this, mole-manic contact with the surface world dwindled rapidly. Some blame the mole-man known as Robespierre, who took the mole-manic principles of revolution to frighteningly bloody heights in France, personally presiding over of the guillotining of thousands of his perceived enemies and devouring their heads before the cheering mob.

Others blame Andrew Jackson, who took office condemning the

mole-men as "too fancy-pantsy"[186]
and accusing them of ruining the
White House lawn with their burrows. When Jackson caught one
attempting to pay a visit of state to the White House, he immediately clubbed it to death. The stuffed body of "Skritch" is still on
display in the White House basement, WHICH I EXAMINED ON
A VIP TOUR.

AUGUST 3
1936, BERLIN: Jesse Owens wins a gold
medal in the 100-yard dash at the Berlin
Olympics, humiliating Adolf Hitler, who
barely made it to ninth place.

But by the time Jackson signed the Indian-and-Mole-Man-
Removal Act, most of the mole-men were already gone. They had
the advantage the Indians did not, for they could leave a world that
hated them, and dig themselves another.

By the end of the nineteenth century, most of the mole-manic
embassies had been closed and filled in with dirt. The great networks of tunnels and caverns the mole-men had built under Paris,
London, New York, and Boston were abandoned. Men came with
electric lights and chased the dirt pumas out and filled the tunnels
with trains. And men would ride those trains, and still do, and stare
out into the darkness with puzzlement and yearning—in some ways
still fearing the mole-men; in some ways still wanting them . . . still
waiting for a race of fanged, noble savages to come and tell them
how to think and live.

There have been those who have tried to find them again. In 1904,
Theodore Roosevelt attempted to build what he termed "A Zoomway
to the Netherlands" in Central America, digging largely with his own
teeth.[187] But instead, all he found was the Panama Canal.

More recently, some have speculated that the new Denver International Airport is actually just a cover story for a secret excava-
tion project designed to find the ancient mole-manic city of Agartha.

---

186. In all fairness, their pants, when they wore them, were very fancy. And pantsy.

187. Please see page 318 under the heading "Fast Facts About Teddy Roosevelt."

AUGUST 4

1693, ÉPERNAY, FRANCE: Benedictine monk Dom Perignon invents the process of bottle-fermenting wine, producing for the first time the product we now know as champagne. After tasting the first bottle, he is reported to have cried, "Come quickly, I am tasting the stars." Then he is reputed to have poured the bottle all over his scantily clad girlfriend while cruising the town in a donkey cart.

As evidence, they point out the airport's bizarre remoteness (it is surrounded by miles of empty wasteland patrolled only by scavengers and oxygen pirates), its forty-seven secret sub-basements, and the inexplicable statues of mole-men scattered throughout the terminal. According to urban legend, the developers of the "airport" never found Agartha itself, though they did find the Agartha Interstrata Monorail Station. However, the mole-men had long abandoned it due to its ridiculously inconvenient location and dreadful proximity to Denver.

And what of Monticello, which is visited by thousands of "Jefferson-heads" every year? Surely one or more of them must have stumbled into the strange lands below at one point or another?

Figure 87: For What Possible Reason Would You Put This In Your Airport, Unless YOU WERE SECRETLY DIGGING A TUNNEL TO THE HOLLOW EARTH?

The answer is no, for two reasons. (1) The portal to the hollow earth was hidden discreetly behind a lazy susan that Jefferson had designed for that very purpose, and (2) after the Panama Canal incident, Theodore Roosevelt came and had the whole portal moved to the Museum of Natural History, where it may still be seen today, the lazy susan turning constantly and lazily. But nothing ever comes through.

NUMBER SIX: THE CATACOMBS OF PARIS, FRANCE

But this does not mean that the mole-men cut off *all* contact with the surface world. There is still a mole-manic consulate in Montréal, for example, but it is staffed only by a single Troglodytic Man. If you come there to apply for a visa, he will throw his own feces at you. Many Canadian college students find this to be fun.

And it was in Paris that Jefferson saw them once again. By 1785, Jefferson had agreed to be America's first minister to France. It was a turbulent time in that nation's history. Around Jefferson flowered the beginnings of a mole-manic revolution that he hoped would soon sweep the globe.

And yet Jefferson felt no joy at this time. He was a widower—his beloved Martha had died a few years before. And while he flirted with an actress named Maria Cosway, their romance was stillborn, for she was married. As a new American, Jefferson may no longer have been an aristocrat, but he was still a gentleman, and so he would only have sex with slaves.

As his years in Paris wore on, Jefferson grew despondent, feeling ever more lonely and exiled. At home, the Constitution was being written without him and did not include his proposed "Bill of Rights." (Madison told him it had been lost in the mail.)

And so it is not surprising to learn that Jefferson had begun tak-

---

AUGUST 5

1957, PHILADELPHIA: *American Bandstand* makes its national debut. Each week, Dick Clark would ask teenagers to dance to the latest hits. Then he would ask them to dance faster and faster, as he laughed maniacally and sucked their youthful essence from them. Everyone in America loved this. But then, under pressure from parent groups, the show was canceled in 1989, and Clark began to age.

WERE YOU AWARE OF IT?
"MANILOW'S BANDSTAND"

Many think that Barry Manilow's hit song "Bandstand" was named for *American Bandstand*. Indeed, the reverse is true. While still on local television in Philadelphia, a ten-year-old Manilow performed such a stirring rendition of the song that the program immediately changed its name. Prior to that, it had been called *Weekend in New England*.

IT MADE NO SENSE, BUT THE KIDS LOVED IT!

AUGUST 6
2001, WASHINGTON, DC: President George W. Bush receives a briefing with the ambiguous title "Bin Laden Determined to Strike Within the US, Probably by Flying Planes into Buildings, and Soon, Very, Very Soon." Before reading it, the president asked for a shorter title.

ing long walks alone at night, and that, perhaps unconsciously, his freakishly long legs might point their way downward.

This is how he found himself in the Parisian catacombs one midnight, wandering among its great heaps of bones—a reminder of the fate of aristocrats and commoners, mole-men and non-mole-men alike: the final democracy.

And did he see a light there? Yes: a pale, green luminescence just around the corner stacked with skulls, a light that he remembered now through his Madeira haze of self-pity and sadness.

"Who is there?" he asked, hope warbling his high, reedy voice.

And then a figure turned the corner: a beautiful, mole-manic woman, her skin a coppery color unusual to her race. With her tusks worn down, she might even be taken as human.

"Who is that I see?" asked Jefferson.

History does not record how much Jefferson understood of mole-manic physiology. Did he know then, for example, that their blood is colorless? Or that their lymph is an aphrodisiac? Did he know that the mole-man is born genderless and chooses its sex according to the need of its Parlor? Or that like the oyster, the mole-man may change its gender frequently throughout its life? That for example, Jefferson's once-friend Genuine Hissfurther, having heard via soil-o-gram of Jefferson's recent sorrows, might forget their old quarrels? That Hissfurther might reach out now to comfort the founder's cheek with a newly womanish claw? History does not record the answer. History does not record so many interesting truths.

"My name is Sally Twistfang Termitemound," said the creature. And so they would become lovers. But as it would not do for the future president to have a mole-manic mistress, you probably know her by her "slave name": Hemings.

NUMBER SEVEN: "SYMMES HOLE BETA," ANTARCTICA

And now we come at last to the bottom of the world, to the second of the great polar chasms proposed by John Cleves Symmes. In this case, it is exactly as Symmes imagined it: a hole so vast and gradual in its decline that if you were to walk into it, you would not even notice. For miles upon miles you would walk, and then slowly turn down, until what little sun ever reached that part of the world would disappear completely. It would be replaced by the weak rays of the red Inner Sun that shines at the center of the earth. But I doubt even the most practiced sunologists would be able tell the difference. Soon enough, you would be walking antipodally, in a world previously unknown to humankind, but it would seem to you as bleak and empty and dull as the world you had just left behind. I'm sorry to disappoint you, but the fact is, you'd be completely unaware that anything was different at all. That's how it tends to work with these fabled other-worlds and fantasy lands. And that's how the Century Toad *gets* you.

AUGUST 7
1989, ATHENS: Archeologists discover that Plato's famous allegory of the "Cave" was not just an allegory, but an actual cave where Plato had physically chained his students to rocks. They then were forced to watch his amazing shadow puppets until they either died or mustered the strength to cast off the illusion of their senses and sawed off their own feet to escape. Plato was a very sick man.

AUGUST 8

2000, SOUTH CAROLINA: The sunken Confederate submarine *Hunley* is finally raised from the depths of Charleston Harbor. But much to the dismay of the robot hunters that had so long been seeking it, the Perspiration Drone is not aboard, having (somewhat selfishly) fled to safety aboard the *Hunley*'s single escape pod. What became of it then remains a mystery.

THE HODGMAN LITERARY TONE DETECTOR:
AND WHY YOU SHOULD BUY IT

Hello, Friend—

I normally do not advertise on these pages. For unless you have taken this book out of the library (in which case, you are stealing from me), you have paid for each of these words, and thus should not have to put up with solicitations and come-ons and ads "popping up" all over the place.

In this way, I am different from Benjamin Franklin and his "almanacs," which were full of product placement for his electric bifocals and crummy fireplaces. TACKY.

No, if there is one thing I DO NOT BELIEVE IN, it's ADVERTISING.

SO YOU UNDERSTAND HOW IMPORTANT I THINK THIS PRODUCT IS if I am going to break my own rule and offer you this "popping-up" advertisement for the product known accurately as *THE HODGMAN LITERARY TONE DETECTOR.* The Hodgman Literary Tone Detector is essential tackle for the reading experience.

Obviously, it will help you determine the literary tone of any given piece of writing (if you did not detect the tone of that past sentence, let me tell you: It was "MILD DERISION, BUT MOTIVATED ONLY BY A DESIRE TO HELP YOU BECOME THE BEST READER YOU CAN BE, AND ALSO LEAVENED BY A DESIRE TO SELL HODGMAN LITERARY TONE DETECTORS." Now, read on).

No longer will you be wondering: Is this novel by a noted

AUGUST 9
1849, FRANCE: Physicist Hippolyte Fizeau first records the speed of light in the atmosphere by setting up a lantern on a high and lonely French mountaintop, aiming it at a similar mountaintop several
kilometers away, and then racing the light from one mountain to the other. Not surprisingly, he lost. But
curiously, by the time he reached the other mountain, he discovered that he was a VERY OLD MAN. This
is because he warped the space-time continuum, and he was actually pretty old to begin with.

author dull, or simply boring? Is this a bildungsroman (a novel of growing), a roman à clef (a novel about clefs), or more properly a roboticspouseroman *(The Stepford Wives)*?[188]

Have you ever been reading an op-ed in the newspaper or a cartoon in a magazine or perhaps even this book and wondered to yourself: Is this supposed to be funny? THE HODGMAN LITER-ARY TONE DETECTOR (HLTD) will answer that question for you....

AND THE ANSWER MAY SURPRISE YOU.

What's more, the HLTD is useful in so many other ways.

IT WILL DETECT AUTHORIAL INTENT.

As Roland Barthes once said, "The author is dead." (Barthes is dead now.) But with the HLTD, the author literally[189] comes back to life LIKE A SHAMBLING, TWEED-JACKETED ZOMBIE to explain THE ACTUAL INTENDED MEANING of a piece of literature.

Remember when James Joyce ended *Ulysses* with an endless repetition of the word "yes"? Of course you do. Of course you do. Of course you do. Many modern literary critics suspected this was a typographical error caused by the fact that Joyce was almost completely blind and Irish, thus having forgotten he had already typed the word five hundred times. BUT THOSE PEOPLE ARE WRONG: It actually is meant to represent the orgasm of Leopold Bloom's nonrobotic spouse.[190]

188. *Spoiler alert.*
189. *Not literally.*
190. *Spoiler alert.*

AUGUST 10

1948: *Candid Camera* debuts on television. Previously known as *Candid Microphone* when on radio, and before that *Candid Telegram,* Alan Funt's program revealed the hilarious reactions when normal people were shown that they were constantly being monitored by hidden cameras from birth until death (at the time, this was considered to be an invasion of privacy).

IT WILL HELP YOU PARSE THE MEANING
OF OLDE-FASHIONED WRITINGS.

If you've ever read the THE CONSTITUTION or *MOBY-DICK* or *JAWS,* you will know that people of the past not only spelled differently, they also THOUGHT differently. Modern literary critics may think the intervening years add "layers of meaning" to an archaic text.

THOSE QUACK CRITICS ARE JUST TRYING TO MAKE A BUCK OFF OF YOU.

No, the only way to really understand a book—or for that matter, a national constitution—is to return the brain to the state it would have enjoyed in the year of the original writing.

Not only will the HLTD immediately translate the more obscure terminology of books from the past (a "harpoon," for example, is actually used to inseminate fairies, not impale them), it will automatically adjust your brain to a time when it was perfectly common for men to own slaves and murder their children and blame it on sharks.

REMEMBER HOW WILLIAM EMPSON SAID THERE WERE SEVEN KINDS OF LITERARY AMBIGUITY? Well, you don't have to worry about that anymore: This device will eliminate ALL AMBIGUITY.

FINALLY . . . If you are one of the millions of Americans who already requires a device that inserts electricity into your brain via a thin wire, then you are in luck: THE HLTD IS SUCH A DEVICE.

Like my previous groundbreaking product, the HODGMAN "INNERVOICE" FOR WRITERS, the HLTD is a cumbersome metallic structure that both sits atop *and* surrounds the human head,

AUGUST 11
2007, NEW YORK CITY: Following the success of *Wicked,* author Gregory Maguire publishes *Dick,* which tells the story of *Moby-Dick* from the point of view of the whale.

connecting to the brain via a thin wire inserted through the ear canal.

Available in both chrome and oil-rubbed bronze, it's a handsome head-and-neck enhancement that announces to the world: "I read better than you." Also available: a black satin device-coverlet for fancy occasions.

Some of you may ask, What is this I hear about a *High-Definition* Hodgman Literary Tone Detector (HD-HLTD)?

It is true that Congress has mandated a new *high-definition* standard for all direct-brain connection devices by 2013, and that all current HLTD customers will then need to convert to HD-HLTD at that time, and that this conversion will require extensive surgery.

HOWEVER, that is ABSOLUTELY NO REASON TO WAIT BEFORE PURCHASING this product. Can you really risk not knowing the true tone and intention of everything you read—INCLUDING THIS BOOK—for the next several years?

No. You cannot risk it. I am being absolutely urgent and sincere when I say: YOU NEED THIS PRODUCT NOW. And if you cannot tell that I am being absolutely urgent and sincere, then YOU NEED THIS PRODUCT NOW.

The HLTD is available at all your favorite direct-brain-connection-device retailers including . . .

—Brookstone Brothers

—Radio Shack

—Wire-In-Ear-Device Shack

—The Vermont Country Store

—and the Sky Maul catalogue

AUGUST 12

30 BC, EGYPT: Cleopatra, having been
defeated by Octavian in her attempt to become queen of Rome, commits suicide by
asping herself to death.

700 MOLE-MAN NAMES

Our best estimates of the size of the
mole-man population suggest that,
at its height, the under-empire com-
prised some five million inhabitants, and today perhaps more, but it
is difficult to say, as so few mole-men venture to the surface these
days, except after heavy rains.

In 1790, the first U.S. census provided this polling of a single
mole-man city located below Moundsville in what is now called
"West Virginia." But even this reckoning remains suspect, as the
census taker never returned.

Daniel Chandler, a normal-surface dweller, was last seen burrowing into the Grave Creek Mound with one week's provisions, 250
candles, and a seeing-eye cat named Jeff. Whether he perished somehow in the lands below or chose to stay and live among the mole-
men is unknown. Probably he was betrayed and killed by Jeff. In any
case, all we have is this list of 700 mole-man names, sent back to the
sunlit lands in 1792, tied to the back of an earwig.

Because of the GREAT NITROGEN CYCLE of the seventeenth
and eighteenth centuries (Surface Era), many mole-men took familiar "surface names"—for reasons of diplomacy, fashion, or in some
cases, intermarriage. And many of these names reflect this trend.

Many more mole-men and mole-manic women—and even those
listed here—presumably retain names in the mole-manic native language, a mélange of hisses, grunts, coughs, screeches, and French.
Otherwise, the mole-men named themselves as we originally did—
by our professions, our places of origin, our skills at digging and
tunneling. Some of the most common mole-manic names, for example, were Deepcavern, High-Screechy-Voice, and Groundswallow.

There is currently something of a vogue of mole-man names among affluent parents in places like Park Slope, Brooklyn. It's not uncommon to see private preschool attendance rolls filled with such typical subterranean monikers as "Sniffer," "Hisser," "Horrid-Black-Millipede-Necklace," and "Max."

AUGUST 13

1973, BURBANK: William S. Burroughs makes his sole notorious appearance as a celebrity panelist on *Match Game '73*. He flummoxed his fellow celebrity panelists repeatedly by insisting on "cutting up" their answer cards to create new, random word associations and then convincing host Gene Rayburn to shoot up heroin with him using Gene's long, pointy microphone. Famously, Richard Dawson refused to ever work with William S. Burroughs again.

1. Mr. Alistair Strongclaws, a Declarationist
2. Mr. Desmond Sharp-Nails, a down-digger
3. Mr. Todd Deepcavern, of the Point Pleasant Deepcaverns
4. Mr. Samuel Mossyface, an amanuensis
5. Dr. Eldridge Loamhoard, a barber and mucus scraper
6. Sir Stinson Maggotwrangle, a gentlemole-man of leisure
7. Mr. John Dirtfellow, a beetler
8. Ted-Hannah Thirdgender; and . . .
9. Mary-Robert Thirdgender, the Thirdgender Brother-Sisters
10. Miss "Bronzeface" Millicent Scumly, a frequent surface-traveler
11. Mr. Henry Clay, a compromiser
12. Mr. Twinfang Longtooth, a glowshroomer
13. Mr. Silas Double-Thick-Eye-Membrane, an up-digger
14. Mr. Devlin Smoothwall, a side-scraper
15. Mr. Jonas Rough-Right-Palm-Smooth-Left-Palm, a cornersman
16. Mr. Benjamin Briefgrunts, a down-digger
17. Mr. Nathanael Glowingass, a Declarationist
18. Mr. McHenry Tunnelsup, a Declarationist
19. Mr. Thomas Ashley Innersun, a worm milker
20. Mr. Shambling Herriott Shallowsoil, a large-worm veterinarian
21. Mr. Benonai Extrafingers, an excavationist
22. Mr. Kanawha Marbledwell, a marble miner
23. Miss Annabelle Tunnelsmell, a student of life
24. Miss Millicent Snakefind, a simple hole-wife
25. Mr. Deepdelver McBreakmarble, a worm wooler
26. Captain Rootley Shamblegait, a holer
27. Mr. Morton Silty, a ceiling smoother
28. Mr. Antonio Rootweaver, a rootitect
29. Mr. Purdy Quicksand, a Declarationist
30. Fraggle Blaine, a pamphleteer
31. Mr. Parvis Hanglikebat, a puma skinner
32. Miss Doozer Patience Flexi-Spine, a claw maiden
33. Mr. Mallory Scratchinbleed, a tunnel joiner
34. Doc Minceworm, a fraud
35. Dr. Toothclick Smeagol, a physician
36. Mr. Rhys Wormjockey, a wormer
37. Mr. Eeeeeeeeyusk Screech-Through-Cavern, a hateful hermit

AUGUST 14

1935, WASHINGTON, DC: The Social Security Act passes. Hereafter, every citizen would be assigned a number that would ensure a modest pension in his or her old age and would also determine the order in which every American would be allowed to die. One of the most successful government programs, there are those who feel that it is now facing a major crisis that can only be alleviated by having private investors determine the date of your death.

38. Miss Marian Spelunker-Teaser, a simple hole-wife
39. Mr. Thaddeus Tunneldump, a shallows-man
40. He Who Is Fattened to Feed to the Toad, occupation unknown
41. Mr. Quentin Trollspooked, a lateral digger
42. Miss Claudia Inward Burrowdown, a poetess of some renown
43. Mistress Increase Cavern-Gas, a Declarationist
44. Mr. Stone Philips, a journalist
45. Mr. Cary Granite, a thespian
46. Mr. Stony Curtis, a thespian
47. Miss Angerocklie Jolie, a thespian
48. Mr. Bradrocks Rockpitt, a thespian
49. Mr. Fred Flintstone, a drunk
50. Governor Bradley Quite-Long-Flicker-Tongue, a Parlor gouverneur
51. Virginal Marian Vestigial-Tail-Stump, a virgin
52. Mole-Ratter Pike Peters, a mole-ratter
53. Mr. Eugene Brundlefly, a human baiter
54. Starchy Spud Tuber-Smith, a tubersmith
55. Mr. Nathaniel Gold-Chew, a secret-passagist
56. Horrid-Black-Millipede-Necklace Jeffreys, a simple hole-wife
57. Mr. Phineas Sediment Blacksoil, a disgraced mole-man

58. Double Dig-Arm Mole-Manly, a deep-soiler
59. Miss Minnie Rubble-Cone, a student
60. Pale Bob, a beetle butcher
61. Paler Bob, his creepy associate
62. Mr. Marvis Extra-Albino, a dirt-puma rancher
63. Mr. Timothy Lichen-Breastplate, a ratskin tanner
64. Mr. Morris Deepthings, a Declarationist
65. Mr. Jameson Tunnelswell, a champion tunneler
66. Mr. Harland Tunnelsbest, his rival
67. Mr. Charles William Digges XIV, a surface-dwelling scholar
68. Mrs. Jane Fleshystarrynose, a lair maker
69. Miss Penny Underpass Minerscare, a mere child
70. Mr. Master Palladio Pedosphere, a roundfoot
71. Sir Newton Frostline, unemployed
72. Mr. Noble Megadrill Dew-Worm, a natural philosopher
73. Ms. Joy Bellyscramble, a creature of beauty
74. Sr. Gustavo Wormherder, a worm herder, like his father before him
75. Phineas Decayingplant Matter, a siltman
76. Mr. Stephen Dustpile, a Declarationist
77. Dr. Hieronymous Sandpuppy, pharmacist and creator of "Dr. Sandpuppy's Miraculous Mole Tonic," a popular mole tonic
78. Mr. Humus Carlos Humus, a fertilizer
79. Mrs. Millicent Longcasts, a slimelayer
80. Sire Yonathan Deepdirt, a dirtologist
81. Goodmole-man Cotton Doublehiss, a fangmonger
82. Mr. Allen Wrigglequick, a pamphleteer

83. Mrs. Esther Greaseskin, a wormstress
84. Goody Delilah Doublespawn,
    a toothwoman
85. Mr. William S. Burrows,
    a Declarationist
86. Mr. Drone Unsex, a euosocialist
87. Miss Helena Cough-Cough,
    a student
88. Parson William Rootnodule, a Parson
    of the Toad
89. Captain Skip Slidedown, a dirtonaut
90. Miss Marian Mithril, an heiress
91. Mrs. Patience Gurglescreech,
    a delver
92. Charleston Hunchedover
    Gravesleeper, Esq., an attorney
93. Mr. Stinkdown Tunnelsnuffler, a borer
94. Worshipful Pitkeeper, keeper of
    the pit
95. Miss Lillian Bugcruncher, a school
    maiden
96. Mr. Darnielle Cavergrabber, Jr.,
    ashamed son of the famed villain
    Carl Cavergrabber
97. Mr. Carl Cavergrabber, a thief and
    tunnelwayman; but ironically, not
    actually a caver-grabber
98. Mr. Batfriend Groundswallow,
    a caver-grabber
99. Dr. Mattias Whistlefang, a banker
100. M. Honoré de Lavatube,
    a Declarationist
101. Mr. Francis Carlsbadcavern,
    a guanomonger
102. Mr. Holden Hollowheeze,
    a wallsmith
103. Mrs. Electra Shrunkeneye, a noted
    mystic
104. Sir Arthur Humanfish, a topsoiler
105. Troglobiter Skritchskratch,
    a pseudonym for Dr. Phineas Sunk,
    a pamphleteer
106. Mr. Olmy Olmstash, an olm
    enthusiast
107. Mr. Silas Scratchforward,
    a Declarationist

AUGUST 15

1939, HOLLYWOOD: *The Wizard of Oz* premieres at Grauman's Chinese Theater, with live musical accompaniment by Pink Floyd (not the Pink Floyd you are thinking of, but the original lineup, with Woody Herman on clarinet and "That Infant Sensation," L'il Syd Barrett, on vocals).

---

108. Mrs. Cynthia Caveshrimp, a spawner
109. Mr. Richard Hackbolus, a gemsman
110. Dr. Uriah Heep, a mathematician
    and dirt piler
111. Lord Balthasar Salivate,
    a salivationist
112. M. Docteur Blaise Dustbuster,
    a dustbuster
113. M. Jean Valjean Valdustbuster,
    a fugitive
114. Mr. Thomas Hellnear, an up-digger
115. Mr. Pierre DuPont, a silverstoner
116. Mr. David Mamet, a rock puncher
117. Sir James Echoing Howl,
    a Declarationist
118. Mr. Edmund Tightcorner-Mudhollow,
    a mud philosopher
119. Miss Hillary Aciddrool, a dust bather
120. The Marquis de Lava, a marquis
121. Baron Everhiss Downward, a cave
    merchant
122. Lady Henrietta Mudbreath, a patron
    of the arts
123. Mr. Ignatz Mouse, a half-mouse
124. Herr Johann von Scumpuddle,
    scummer
125. Mr. David Volemole-man,
    a volemonger
126. Mr. Immanuel Facialscars, a "face-
    pusher" (a low-status mole-man
    who digs with his own face)
127. Mr. Hugo Munker, a chipmunk
    hunter
128. Miss Sally Twistfang Termitemound,
    consort to the president
129. Mr. Leandro Soursmell,
    an encyclopedist

AUGUST 16

1977, GRACELAND: Despondent that he never got to travel through time like the president told him he could, Elvis Presley kills himself with prescription medications and a heart attack.

According to a Freedom of Information report, had he lived a few hours more, he would have been visited by two agents from the Federal Timeline Authority (FTA) driving a portable time-van. After years of bureaucratic red tape, the FTA had at last been authorized to activate "AGENT ORION" and send him back in time to keep a rogue agent from preventing the assassination of William McKinley (long story). Ironically, Presley had been wearing his spangled "McKinley" jumpsuit that very afternoon. But it was too late.[a]

a. Or was it? . . .

---

130. Baron Nikolay Dustdevil, a political philosopher and sun-hater
131. Mr. Thomas Wormblood, a scumsucker
132. M. Francois D'Anthill, a philosophe
133. Suckledirt Silverfoot, a dirt pirate
134. Gaspar of the Mound, a vaudevillian termite trainer
135. Lord Manfred Horrideye Slime, a mole-man of means
136. M. Jean-Jacques Grindsfine, a lava-barger
137. M. Benedict de Carpenter Ant, a Declarationist
138. Sir Isaac Quickmud, discoverer of gravity
139. Mr. Genuine Hissfurther, a Declarationist
140. Mr. Moley Mole-Musk, a moleskin trader
141. Devil Anse Doubledirt, a demon hunter
142. Mr. Jonse Bryophyte, a glowshroomer
143. Mr. Judas Slowslime, a gravel sifter
144. Miss Patience Bloodfeeder, a simple hole-wife

145. Mandibular-Jaw Johnny, an ant-man adopted into the care of the mole-men
146. Manidublar-Jaw Ronny, his evil twin brother
147. Dr. Toadseek, a known poisoner
148. Mr. Mortimer Rotmunch, a gentleman dirt farmer and playboy
149. Mr. Manse Cool-Deep-Sludge, a dishonor to the Cool-Deep-Sludge name
150. Mr. Farcavern Nancy, an admired Thirdgender of repute
151. Sssssssssssssssss the Hisser, who went to the surface and became a hobo
152. Mr. Headbobbing Shamblegait, a sideways-digger
153. Permanent Unsex, a failed spawner
154. Mr. Darius Single Nosehole, a deformed tavernkeep
155. Farpatter Sickletooth, a rootmonger
156. Mr. Dominic Pheromonic, a seducer
157. Captain Phineas Deepscrew, a mole-man of the First Dirt Puma Cavalry with an embarrassing name
158. Mr. Maximillian Rootsniff, a beetler
159. Miss Aphra Ashdust, a pheromonist
160. Miss Artemisia Soilchurn, a wormwool carder
161. Miss Anatastacia de Glow-Rot, a lair-mistress
162. Aurelia the Lizardeer, a lizardeer
163. Miss Chloe Deepstealer, a dungmaiden
164. Miss Berenice Double-Forktongue, her half-sister
165. Miss Chloris Jump-Out-and-Shock-You, a startler
166. Miss Cynthia Whogoesthere, a tunnel lass
167. Miss Magnolia Undermagnolia, a mole-woman of two worlds
168. Mr. Martino Doublejoint, a downscraper
169. Mr. Skyler Druyasdust, a hider

170. Miss Ruth Sharpfingers, a teacher of etiquette
171. Mrs. Orinda Rumbletum-Dirtvomit, a refined woman from a bad family
172. Miss Polly Sun-Hate, a deep-dweller
173. Miss Samantha Moon-Indifferent, her cousin
174. Master Judd Sussk, a master spelunker-hunter
175. Brother Jedediah Toadgrind, a heretic
176. Dr. Artemas Eats-his-Young, a devoted father
177. Mr. Asa Mazecave, a labyrinthsmith
178. Mr. Ashley Viscous Spit, a salivationist
179. Mr. Bradford York Puke-Marbles, an educator
180. Mallory of the Underground, a brigand
181. Mr. Clifford Wormclubber, a Declarationist
182. Mr. Constant Hookspine-Hunchover, a double hunchback
183. Mr. Cosmo Muckraker, both a muck-raker and a mu-cracker
184. Miss Sophia Oozefellow, a simple hole-wife
185. Lord Cromwell Wedge-Shaped-Head, a narrow-caverner
186. Mr. Cyrano Sweetmud, an adventurer
187. Mr. Donnell Wormtallow, a chandler
188. Mr. Franciscus Glowbuttocks, a way-lighter
189. Signor Galileo Galilei, an astronomer
190. Mr. Gavin Bloodknuckles, a sloper
191. Mr. Herrick Hideyhole, Esq., an attorney
192. Mr. Hobbes Fecesface, a common pitsmith
193. Mr. Martin Flattenedface, though decscended from face-pushers, actually a very well proportioned mole-man

AUGUST 17

1998, WASHINGTON, DC: President Bill Clinton admits to investigators that he did have "improper relations" with Monica Lewinsky after all, but only if you define "relations" as "oral sex" and "improper" as "awesome."

194. Mrs. Venitia Utterdark, a mud-eeler
195. Miss Veronica Mucus, a seductress
196. Mr. Underhill, who is on a secret mission
197. Mrs. Maria Oozingskin, a callous trimmer
198. Mr. Cotton Pitchblack Spiderfriend, a holesman
199. Pigmentless Maurice Shriveldown, a lout
200. Mr. Morris Quartzfond, a heliocentrist
201. Lord Noah Fungalgrowth, a geocentrist
202. Mr. Titus Gravelscream, an undertaker
203. Dr. Turner Louseridden, a historian
204. Mr. Vandyke Writhingtwist, a novelist
205. Mrs. Beatrice Knifetongue, his wife— together they solve crimes
206. Sir Vincent Chunnel, a visionary digger
207. Mr. Basil Basilisk, a hole blower
208. Mr. Theodore Light-Dodge, a bermer
209. Mr. Crosby Frothspittle, aka the Sub-Mariner, designer of the transatlantic tunnel
210. Dr. Dillon Firedrool, a spawn doctor
211. Mr. Fagan Empty Eyeholes, a seer
212. Mr. Fairfax Stumpyfingers, a scrambler
213. Mr. Fleming Holestench, a Declarationist
214. Mr. Fortescue Smellfinger, a pitmonger
215. Mr. Farrell Culdesac, a sideways-scrambler
216. Mr. Deadend Fletcher, an arrowmaker

AUGUST 18

1969, BETHEL, NY: After THE THREE MOST IMPORTANT DAYS IN THE WORLD, the Woodstock music festival comes to a close. The final act: Sha Na Na, performing their searing neo-doo-wop rendition of "The Star Spangled Banner," at the end of which they set Bowser on fire.

---

217. Mr. Smithland Scared O'Silver, a gold trader
218. Mr. Malcolm Large-Head-Ant, who resembles an ant-man
219. Mr. Sideous Brightslime, a way-lighter
220. Mr. Manfred Ditchhugger, a floor grinder
221. Miss Sarah Sleepinghole, a librarian
222. Mr. Nelson Antfeast, an egg stealer
223. Twistcorner Jones, a detective
224. Miss Charlotte Forktongue, a giant-fly swatter
225. Private Beetle Bailey,[191] a dirtonaut
226. Mr. Brad Bodysegments, still larval
227. Mrs. Honest Trilobite, a living fossil
228. Mr. Horace Tiny Airpocket, a wheezer
229. Mr. Walter Cozy Alcove, a hole decorator
230. Mr. Matthew Algae-Covered, a deep-diver
231. Mr. Lyle Scumskimmer, a scumskimmer
232. Mr. Allen Siltlove, a wormer
233. Amphibious Charlie Howl, a water-breather
234. The Sinister Maxwell Holeplug, a fiend
235. Mr. Myron Antenna-Stumps, an oddity
236. Miss Aquifer Backspines, a great beauty
237. Dirtbag Dan, a dirtbagger

---

191. Probably the inspiration for the famous cartoon soldier. See page 554.

238. Mr. Albert Crayfish Crawfish, a Declaraitionist
239. Mr. Arthropodic Humfrey, a trailsmeller
240. Dr. Phineas Basalt, a golem builder
241. Chiroptera, his animated clay lover
242. Mr. Sharphells Beddingpile, an updigger
243. Dirty Dick Downlow, a vicious underpirate
244. Captain Magnificent Bivalve, a pleasure-borer pilot
245. Fine Fellow Blistercave, a gas sniffer
246. Mr. Mute Campbell Gruntslow, a lanternmaker
247. Mr. Harry Boulderchoke, a speculator in semiprecious and absolutely unprecious stones
248. Sir Sediment Coldblood, a mathematician
249. Dirk Icecurtain, a dirtonaut
250. Mr. H. Rupert Elder, a former surface man
251. Mr. Ralph Hiddenchamber, a maker of secret doors
252. Mr. Dillon Hack-Hack Secretchamber, his chief competition
253. Mr. Phineas Entombed, who has been in a coma for years
254. Mr. Robert Todd Hibernation Hole, a Declarationist
255. Mr. Deepfellow Fissurefinder, a finder of fissures
256. Mr. Flattener Ceilingsmooth, a smoother
257. Mr. Max Grotto, a worm lad
258. Miss Agatha Agartha, a maggot lass
259. Mr. Lance Hellfriend, a disreputable person
260. Miss Kathy Throatpockets, an invalid
261. Mr. Butler Pothole Groundvomit, an apprentice anteater
262. Mr. John Shaft, a private detective and hermaphroditic sex machine
263. Mrs. Baggot Crudknuckles, a widower

264. Mr. Crawlway Twosex, a former
     Thirdgender spawner
265. Mr. Eliot Wormpinch, a firetender
266. Master Sumpy Mitegather, a young
     fungus gardener
267. Lady Yolanda Glowing Cavecoral,
     a socialite
268. Mr. Wellesley Cavecricket, a bug
     bleeder
269. Sir Joseph Detritus, an essayist
270. Mrs. Helena Fecalforage, a nanny
271. Miss Isabel Guanodive, a batkeeper
272. Mr. Cuthbert Decline, a tunnel
     squarer
273. Miss Margery Corprophage,
     a student
274. Miss Gillian Deepcrap, her best
     friend
275. Mr. Owen Daylight, a dreamer
276. Dr. Roland Manyspawn, inventor
     of hole wax
277. Miss Rose Fruitbat, a hole-keeper
278. Miss Charity Hiddenpit, a young
     deformed lady
279. Dickie Driphole, a newsie
280. Mr. Oswyn Fleshy Neck,
     a prosperous fly-fat trader
281. Mr. Wallow Dripstone, a worm rider
282. Mr. Hubrey Glowmuscles, a slimer
283. Parson Edmund Inkblower,
     a Toadist
284. Mr. Preston Edaphobite, a mucus
     spreader
285. Effluvial Mary, a graverobber
286. Sir Hensell Claustrophobe, a tortured
     soul
287. Crazyant, a henchman
288. Polly the Exhumer, a bodysnatcher
289. Mr. Emerson Poisonair, a gas man
290. Mr. Matthew Licklichen, a lichen
     tester
291. Mr. Allen Extramucus, a double-
     slimer
292. Mr. Piers Falsefloor, a Declarationist
293. Mr. Roger Stoopsandsniffs, a smoke
     holer

AUGUST 19
By odd coincidence, this is the birthday not only
of BILL CLINTON and TIPPER GORE, but
also of the actor JONATHAN FRAKES, who
portrayed *both* Clinton and Gore in the 1995
ABC miniseries *The Clintons and the Gores: A
One-Man Show Starring* Star Trek's *Jonathan
Frakes.*

Figure 88: Jonathan Frakes as Tipper Gore.
Note the Cameo from Fellow *Star Trek*
Alum Levar Burton.

294. Miss Julia Bellyscrape, a lady smoke
     holer
295. Mr. Flint Defanged, a switchbacker
296. Flocculant Dave, a pair of eyes in the
     dark, nothing more
297. Mr. Tom Furby, a furby catcher
298. Mr. Deadend, a deadender
299. General Weepsore, a veteran of the
     Hell battles
300. Mr. Errol Foulbreath, a double-digger
301. The Honorable Morton Sulphursmell,
     a judge
302. Miss Delilah Moldcoated, a pit lady
303. Mr. Marcus Mildewed, a tunnel hider
304. Mr. Oxide Rustingskin, a redhead
305. Little Becky Smut-Scavenge,
     an orphan
306. The Piltdown Man
307. Mr. Davey Corpsefinder, a coffin
     scavenger
308. Miss Favorite Filthynails, a simple
     hole-wife

AUGUST 20

1977, SPACE CENTER ONE: The United States launches the *Voyager 2* deep-space probe. On the off chance that it might be found by intelligent alien life, the craft carries with it a golden plate with pictures of a male and female human body, as well as a recording of Jimmy Carter reading *The Joy of Sex* in English, French, and Esperanto.

309. Miss Patience Sootsink-Longclaw, a spawn tender
310. Mr. Gastropodic Tonguefoot, a sentient mollusk
311. Miss Dorothy Sneakup, his keeper
312. Mr. Grover Batblood, a bat leecher
313. Mr. Learned Leechkill, a leech batter
314. Miss Screechina Humid-Closepassage, a cave painter
315. Mr. Dennimore Evercrouch, a short-passagist
316. Dr. Fleshystump Nofoot, a bug healer
317. Mrs. Henrietta Cough-Cough, a hole-keep
318. King Bat-Ears, a self-appointed sovereign of a very small cave
319. Mr. Percival Mudswim, a millipede trainer
320. Doc Pharaoh-Ant, a Renaissance mole-man
321. Mr. Lawrence Dalliapoulos, something of a casanova
322. Mr. Perry Larvamouth, a larva breeder
323. Miss Molly Dungspread, daughter of a dungspreader
324. Mothman, a prophet
325. Mme. Blanche Flycovered, a sticky lass
326. "Pincers" Bill Beetlehead, a mutant
327. Mr. Brill Lavalover, a bug-cake baker, not to be confused with
328. Mr. Brill Larvalover, the second partner in Lavalover and Larvalover Bugcakes

329. Mr. Marius Killvapor, a native Hell dweller
330. Miss Ejecta Longstool, a fertilizer
331. Mrs. Scoria Boredown, a down-driller
332. "Mole-manny" Mole-Manfred Marshfart, a friendly salesman
333. Mr. Jonathan Magma, a mute
334. Sir Magnus Gasblister, the Circumnavigator
335. Miss Deedee Lavaburned, a core-lady
336. Mr. Jasper Tickriddled, a ticker
337. Mr. Gerard Lampreymouth, a sucker
338. Mr. Zachariah Rotleaf, a decaysman
339. Nodig Nocrawl, a pariah
340. Miss Janenessa Fairymound, a tale teller
341. Mr. Jeremy Corpsemunch, a Declarationist
342. Miss Ooona Wormmilker, a maggot maid
343. Mrs. Mariah Digsdown, daughter of a great digger
344. Tartarus Brokentooth, a core hopper
345. Miss Rachelle Holdbreath, a banker
346. Hsukssssssss and his many parasites, an entertainer
347. Miss Damaris Bottomless Pit, a constant faller
348. Mr. Scott Endless-Pool, an entrepreneur
349. Predatory Delia Bloodthirst, a spawnsnatcher
350. Pupal Edith Lies-in-Wait . . .
351. Larval-Stage Edith Lies-in-Wait, and . . .
352. Imago Edith Lies-in-Wait, the only fully formed Lies-in-Wait sister
353. Mr. Judah Ratcatcher, a giant-rat tamer
354. Radon-Sniffer Kit Everfall, a radon detector
355. Mr. Jedediah Winged-Ant, of the mole-manic air force
356. Mr. Elijah Nostrilflap, a sand stormer

357. Mr. Max Sensitive Nosebristles, a dark-sensor
358. Mr. James Graveflower, a fop
359. M. Hiram Skunkeater, a skunker
360. Dr. Lawrence Newtmash, a newt pestler
361. Mr. Malachi Termitestick, a termiter
362. Mr. Obediah Selfsister, a self-twin
363. Krrssssk Huk Huk, the amazing half-man, half mole-man, a freakshow
364. Mr. Stingo Huntmouse, a mouse hater
365. Dr. Sutter Stunvole, a Declarationist
366. Mr. Millard Gophergrab, a practical philosopher
367. Mr. Ralph Rabbitsnatch, a rabbitsnatcher
368. Mr. Richardson Rabbitmassacre, who goes somewhat too far
369. Mr. Octavio Hidesbelow, a founding member of the Bitterroot Society
370. Mr. Jemimah Quickwrithe, a dung shaper
371. Legless Armless Buster Glasslizard, a torso
372. Mr. Dean Muckhollow, a cave tester
373. Mrs. Jonatha Strangedirt, a witch
374. Miss Bridget Boldjump, a pit tester
375. Mr. Cleophus Crydark, a stalactite mender
376. Mr. Saldivar Tendermembranes, a stalagmite mender
377. Old Bessie Funguswise, a glow-shroom surgeon
378. Runty Tom Scrapedown, a runt who was not eaten at birth
379. Miss Flossy Glowhead, whose head is especially luminous
380. Miss Angelica Angelicaroot, a skin shedder
381. Cpt. Dane Frostline, a dirtonaut who is haunted by what he's seen
382. Samebrain Growling and . . .
383. Samebrain Growling, a conjoined twin
384. Dr. Zee, a child prodigy

AUGUST 21
1858, OTTAWA, IL: The first of the famous Lincoln-Douglas debates takes place. Each candidate for the Illinois state legislature was granted an hour to speak, a half-hour rejoinder, and then the chance to respond to funny little daguerreotypes sent in by the voters, including one of a talking snowman who wanted to know if Lincoln thought the blacks were actually human.

---

385. Miss Philippa Skeletonpile, a skull keeper
386. Mrs. Moira Blunttooth Powerjaw, a strong personality
387. Mr. Alistair Heaving Horridcough, a hole scholar
388. Mr. Lancelot Dungbeetle, a bed carver
389. Slimer, a slimer
390. Good Ole' Woolsey Shitsdirt, a hale fellow
391. Ambrose St. Wormcastings, a dung master
392. Sir Jordan Decomposure, a Declarationist
393. Mr. Maximillian Mulchmunch, a traveling manure merchant
394. Mr. Charlie "Keeneyes" Scumcovered, only half blind
395. Regenerated-Arm Ssiss Heech, a former Hell fighter
396. Miss Serenity Lurksfine, a professional mourner
397. "Cerberus" Chester Threeheaded— his "third head" is actually an abscess
398. Miss Heather Leafmold-Rottenpile, daughter of the compost heap
399. Mr. Donnelly Thinskin Visible-Guts, a side scraper
400. Jonny "The Centipede" Smellswell, a dirt farmer who, despite his nickname, only has 98 legs
401. Miss Betsy Paperyhide, a worm talker

AUGUST 22

1647, BLOIS, FRANCE: Denis Papin, the inventor of the pressure cooker, is born. He would then go on to propose (but never build) the steam-driven piston, back when merely PROPOSING a world-changing invention would put you in the history books. What happened when I PROPOSED teleportation? What happened when I PROPOSED artificial space . . . FOR ASTRONAUTS?

NOTHING.

It seems to me a sad, strange world indeed where ACTUAL INVENTIONS and ACTUAL TELEPORTATION trump the flights of pure imagination. But that is the world we live in. Or at least, the world YOU live in.

---

402. Miss Belle Quickmumble Clawbristles, a bead-curtain maker

403. Mr. Zachariah Clitellum Mucus-Ring, a breeder

404. Virgil, your guide to the underworld, a tour guide

405. Mr. Ebenezer Groundapple, a Declarationist

406. Mr. Davis Grubb, a novelist

407. Hunkle Rootgnaw, a hired hand

408. Mrs. Mavis Humanchildstealer,[192] a nabber

409. Declarin' Mudfull Fineground, a Delcarationist, though scorned by fellow Delcarationists for his constant self-promotion and scrawled advertisements on tunnel walls

410. Mr. Milton Deathblossom, a mole-man-eating-plant tender

411. Mr. Scott Pterodactylman, a leather-winger

412. Mr. John Yaya, an industrialist

413. John Smallberries, his partner

414. Mr. Nick Nolte, an actor

---

192. Though politically correct historians will often overlook this fact, let's face it: It happened.

415. Mr. Chiggery Dale Chiggerfond, a chigger hoarder

416. Mr. Martin Sleepsupsidedown, a ceiling lurker

417. Citizen Rotflesh, a revolutionary

418. Citizen Dankmouth, a revolutionary

419. Citizen Oozepus, a revolutionary

420. Mr. Franz Anton Mesmer,[193] the founder of mesmerism, and a glass harmonicist

421. The Magnificent Fangface, a fellow mesmerist

422. Mokey

423. Red

424. Gobo

425. Wembley

426. Boober

---

193. Mesmer, as you know, had lived among the surface dwellers for many years preaching his theories of "animal magnetism." It was Mesmer's contention that as the moon affects the tides, so too did the motion of the planets pull to and fro upon a previously undiscovered liquid within the human body. Mesmer would affect the motion of this "mystery humor" through the body using magnets, staring, and intense, painful hugging. This, he claimed, could cure countless diseases, exorcise demons, and reverse urination. After accidentally causing a young blind woman to cough up a kidney, Mesmer was chased from Vienna and took refuge in Paris, where they are always searching for a new bodily fluid. There his influence and fortune grew as he literally mesmerized the French populace. Finally, he was discredited in 1784 by a commission of scientists including Antoine Lavoisier, Benjamin Franklin, and a young Stephen Hawking, who teamed up to capture Mesmer. Chased throughout Europe, he finally was cornered by the three scientists in the sewers of Vienna. Only by flash-hypnotizing Franklin and his colleagues was Mesmer able to escape. He returned to the Lands Below, ashamed and frankly puzzled. He never understood that humans do not have the secondary circulatory system filled with green magnetic blood the mole-men enjoy.

427. Mr. Elijah Visible Veins, an inner astronomer
428. Mr. John Quincy Wormwool, a politician
429. Mr. Roughfingers and his "Louse"-estra, a traveling musician
430. Ms. Xeni Undergrounddweller, a reporter
431. Master Nicholas Dirty III, a frail young mole-man of only 340 years
432. Young Casey Strongtusk, his protector
433. Mr. Blake Deepchew, a candle snuffer
434. Miss Millie Scalyhide, a hider
435. Dr. Andrew Human-Skin-Mask, a sociopath
436. Mr. Zachary Slightly-Deformed, who is only slightly deformed
437. Mr. Hissy Lizardlike, a reptiloid
438. Mrs. Grubly Fertile-Stool, a fertilizer
439. Mr. Hansel Nobleslime, an upclimber
440. Mr. Ernest Acidweeper, a tunnel burner
441. Miss Jemima Touch-Lava, a lovely lass of the deep core
442. Mr. Merriwether Tunnelswell, who tunnels only fairly
443. Penny Pennylick, a copper eater
444. Mr. Lyman Wooly Eyes, a rare mole-man who actually has eyebrows
445. Miss Amphibia Neverdrowns, of the Sunken
446. Mr. Farley Dopeslime, a dealer in dopeslime
447. Mr. Coughsgood Gravedirt, Jr., a ne'er-do-well
448. Mr. McNabb Sticky-Toe-Pads, an upside-downer
449. Mr. Morris Batmusk, a perfumer
450. Mr. Bennett Hallucinogenic-Skin, a dopeslime supplier
451. Miss Amanda Fathoms, a curious shallow-mistress

AUGUST 23

1992, BURBANK, CA: Nearly a year after his ouster as leader of the Soviet Union, Mikhail Gorbachev begins a stint as the center square on *Hollywood Squares*. But he soon quits after learning that Wayland Flowers and Madame were no longer appearing on the program due to Flowers's death and Madame's hatred of Communism.

Figure 89: "Gorbachev to Block"

452. Miss Angela Horrid-Burning-Touch, eligible for marriage
453. Moab the Drone, a drone
454. Sir Cecil External-Colon, a gentlemole-man with a genetic oddity that everyone can see
455. Mr. Berm Hacksup, a spitter
456. Mr. Lisle Feelsface, a front-digger
457. Old Rotfoot, who is decaying before your very eyes
458. Mr. Thompson Pilesdung, a wealthy merchant
459. Mr. Malthus Newhead, who regenerated his own head, and has never been the same since
460. Mr. Forrest Covered-in-Beetles, who never wants for advice
461. Herr Johann Amberpants, a creator of amber genital coverings
462. Miss Paulina Fleshyneckruffle, an ash maiden
463. Mrs. Ophelia Spawnsyearly, a mother
464. Mr. Mattias Half-Arms, who is unable to regenerate further

AUGUST 24

1853, SARATOGA SPRINGS, NY: Hotel chef George Crum invents the potato chip. At the time, New York state law prohibited the eating of more than just one. But in 1932, Herman Lay decided to change all of that by dusting each chip with a thin coating of opium.

---

465. Mr. Ambergris Posioneggs, a failed Declarationist
466. Mr. Ford Newtsimilar, an apprentice hole starer
467. Missy Sweet-Vocal-Sac, the young bride of . . .
468. Mr. Thunderhuck Croak-Croak, a horrid old mole-man
469. Mrs. Myra Webbedfoot, a treasure hider
470. Mr. Morrison Webbedfingers, her common-law husband
471. Mr. Armskin, a flying mole-man
472. Mr. Methuselah Icefrozen, unspeaking frozen mole-man of the north
473. Mrs. Daphne Pearl-Stool, a rare defecator of pearls; she thinks her shit doesn't stink, and she is absolutley correct
474. Spiracle Hustle-Hide, a dirtonaut-in-training
475. Mrs. Glorious Sunbane, a simple hole-wife
476. Mrs. Hillary Boogery, a gossip
477. Mrs. Dahlia Snotflow, a high-cavern lighter
478. Mr. Richard Underfowl, an under-hen keeper
479. Lord Leslie Canarycatcher, who feeds on miners' canaries
480. Mr. Hart Sharp Downangle, a downer
481. Mr. Pontius Sexdimples, a retired spawner
482. Mr. Myron Grubtongue, a Declarationist
483. Mr. Zebediah Cyst-Covered, a

dirtliner pilot
484. Mr. Hock Ratterscatter, a rat scatterer
485. Mr. Drusus Magnetskull, a living compass
486. Mr. Horton Bugbelch, a debauched former ground soldier, now too fond of bugwine
487. Lady Antonia Oddpolyps, his tolerant wife
488. Mr. Cyril Dreadsbreeze, a self-concealer
489. Mr. Cyrus Rubbedraw, a wall scraper
490. Mr. Nehemiah Bloodwormer, tamer of the Mongolian death worm
491. Mr. Karsty Twotusk, a karstwright
492. Brawny Sinkhole, a maggot wrestler
493. Mrs. Tanya Groundwater, a centipede charmer
494. Hooja the Sly One
495. Jubal the Ugly One
496. Ghak the Hairy One
497. Ghak the Half-Hairy One
498. Ghak the Relatively Smooth One
499. Unspecified Ghak
500. Mr. Ennis Bony-Forehead-Ridges III, a flame tender
501. Mr. Oozing Earhole, at least 1,000 years old, and oozing
502. Mr. Josiah Squints, a far-peerer
503. Mr. Huss Scuttles, a fire transporter
504. Miss Marianna Mudsplatter, a chambermaid
505. Mr. Philip Bloodflea, a rubble picker
506. Miss Talia Snakecharm, a dirtliner attendant
507. Mr. Jeremiah Asspennies—you have all handled his asspennies
508. Mr. Ansel Pouchcheeks, a Declarationist
509. Mrs. Nicola Pokingribs, a cave critic
510. Miss Antonia Tangleteeth, a regurgitator
511. Mr. Flukey Foggy Suckermouth, an air tester

512. Mr. Kenneth Pteroplume, who fashions fine writing instruments from the rudimentary feathers of the undersaurs
513. Mr. Absolution Grimeclaws, a moralist
514. Mr. Farley Furskin, a dandy
515. Mr. Parnassus Fiftymoles, a molemaniac
516. Mr. Wolfgang Molegang, a Declarationist
517. Miss Josefina Bleedlips, a scaler
518. Mr. Ebeneezer Trogfellow, a Troglodytic Man abolitionist
519. Mr. Jacob Bullroar-Throatbellow, a champion sex-croaker, born of two famous sex-croaking families
520. Tiny Timmy Venompiss, a young shroomer
521. Yango of the Outsiders
522. Mr. Bentback Kneecrawl Chinscrape Bloodbelly, a crawler
523. Dr. Hieronymus Deepdark, a Declarationist
524. Father Narrowshoulders, a legendary squeezer
525. Mr. Honoré de Throat-sac, a social observer
526. Mr. Kanewha Bignostrils, a breather
527. Mr. Manderly Single Nosehole, a half-breather
528. Mr. Ditchley Tongueclicker, a deep-tuber finder
529. Mr. Dickinson Strangewheeze, a separatist
530. Mrs. Selma Rotsmell, a rotfinder
531. Mr. Monroe Antipodal, a ceiling-clinger
532. Mr. Alger Hiss, an accused communist
533. Mr. Seward Greasedwell, a hole enlarger
534. Mr. Sidney Crabwalk, a crab walker
535. Mr. Milton Hardgizzard, a grinder
536. Mr. Tobias Sludgemouth, a mud eater

AUGUST 25
1850, ILLINOIS: Allan Pinkerton forms the first American detective agency with the aim of solving crimes through a combination of his probing intellect, almost supernatural powers of deduction, and the bashing in of strikers' faces with pieces of metal. ANOTHER CASE CLOSED!

---

537. Mrs. Jude Twicespawned, a simple hole-wife
538. Miss Priscilla Thirtyfingers, a wall feeler
539. Doc Polydactyl, her mentor
540. Dot Polyarmal, a famous wall feeler
541. Mr. Antelmo Maggotswarm, a maggot caller
542. Miss Octavia Mudpool, a water finder
543. Mr. Oswald Holeophobe, who is largely useless
544. Miss Henrietta Headbumps, who is recognizable in the dark by her many headbumps
545. The Marquis de Giant-Firefly, a hedonist
546. Mr. Lafayette Highhiss, of the Ninth Dirt Puma Cavalry
547. Miss Marjorie Damphands, a lair shaper
548. Mr. Orville Earthpile, who is buried up to his neck
549. Mr. Edwin Seismic-Hands, a quake starter
550. Miss Jemima Backtumors, a bug sheller
551. Miss Ginny Eatsfeces, a rabblerouser
552. Mr. Ruskin Helpbelch, a helpful acid belcher
553. Miss Alicia Eyecrust, a spinster
554. Mr. Melchior Downladder, who only travels in one direction
555. Mr. Felix Teemswithbugs, a Declarationist
556. Mr. Robert Owen Rabbitgrind, a rabbit smasher

AUGUST 26
TODAY IS WOMEN'S EQUALITY DAY, though if I know you, I bet you're just going to get drunk again celebrating the feast day of Saint Adrian of Nicomedia. I hope you're proud of yourself.

557. Mr. John Longhead-Smallbody, a wriggler
558. The Widow Althea Spindlytongue, a matchmaker
559. Mr. Danton Glittermaw, who has gems for teeth
560. Miss Nancy Ninedays[194]
561. Mr. Loomis Lowmoan, a constant distraction
562. Mr. Donnell Drippingpus, a snaker
563. Miss Obdelia Throbbingneck, a hotblood
564. Mr. Irving Fungusface, a living garden
565. Miss Minerva Overbite, a rock chewer
566. Miss Laurel Brightmoss, whose father invented luminous moss
567. Mr. Angelo Open Jaw, who cannot close his jaw
568. Mr. Widemouth Frog, a swallower
569. Half-Developed Efram Strangegills, who still retains his tail and gills
570. Signor Alessandro Chokelava, who trained Palladio
571. Sir Albus Rottingskin, a winged-ant pilot
572. Corrosive Petey Burningpalms, a wall burner
573. Miss Miriam Poisonblisters, alas cannot be touched

---

194. Please see the following section under the heading "Answers to Your Questions About the Mole-Men."

ANSWERS TO YOUR QUESTIONS ABOUT THE MOLE-MEN

But I sense you have further questions regarding our neighbors below our feet. Let me attempt to answer the most common ones.

Who are the mole-men?

They are the race of humanoids who live in the complex warren of tunnels and vast caverns beneath the earth.

What do they want?

It is dangerous to generalize. As with all large, old, complex civilizations, their desires veer between the base biologic need to reproduce and guarantee the safety of their mole-spawn, and higher aspirations. From the beginning, they were subterranean *philosophes*, believing in reason, rejecting superstition, and obsessing over building and refining orderly systems—of science, education, government, and especially tunnels.

Do they look just like moles?

No. As I mentioned earlier in this book, they more closely resemble the naked mole-rat, except without tails, longer teeth, somewhat scalier skin ranging in color from absolutely pallid to ruddy, and of course they stand on two legs. Don't you want to hear more about their higher aspirations?

Do they have fur?

No. Again, they are naked. They are completely hairless except for the sensitive bristles on the ends of their long tongues and fingers and, of course, their powdered wigs.

Do they screech and hiss like rats?

Yes. Obviously. But listen, I just told you that they wear powdered wigs. Doesn't that intrigue you at all?

OK. What do they use to powder their wigs?

Volcanic dust and mashed-up flecks of their own skin. As with most of Europe, mole-men began wearing powdered wigs after the fashion of Queen Elizabeth, who was completely bald but, curiously, not a mole-man.

Wouldn't you say a "mole-woman"?

No. The proper term is "mole-manic woman."

AUGUST 27

1953, CANADA SOMEWHERE: HAPPY BIRTHDAY, ALEX LIFESON! Commonly known as "The Third Member of Rush," he is, in fact, in the band Rush.

574. Dr. Macklin Spinylegs, a message runner
575. Mr. Ambrel Pillbug, who curls up in a ball
576. The Horta
577. Mr. Boone Fleshy Underbelly, a centipede counter
578. Dr. Steve Brule, who makes the rules
579. Miss Alia Bleedingknees, a crawler
580. Old Uncle Hades, supposedly a myth
581. Mr. Hargreaves Gravelvoice, a gravel eater
582. Mr. Timmory Cocooned, still a lively conversationalist, even though he has been caught by a spider
583. Xeno Dig-Dug III, a dig-dugger
584. Mr. Tycho Do, a clown
585. Mr. Jeremy Sunkbottom, a groundsman
586. Miss Hushy Stinkwell, a curious young mole-manic girl
587. Herr Unterdischer-Mann, a German
588. Miss Olive Scabbycheek, a left-tunneler
589. Mr. Herodotus Infected Earhole, a former listener
590. Mr. Harvey Rupert Elder, a former surface-man
591. Mr. Hans Moleman, horribly wrinkled
592. Shane MacGowan, a balladeer who visited the surface frequently until he disappeared
593. Mr. Chugalug Sonarbreath, a directional breather

AUGUST 28

1749, FRANKFURT: HAPPY BIRTH-
DAY, JOHANN WOLFGANG VON
GOETHE! Not only renowned for his contributions to literature and science, he also
marketed the first modern homunculus: a
thirteen-inch-tall little man made of clay,
hair, semen, and "nineteen secret herbs
and spices." (Goethe never revealed the
full recipe, though it is believed to be included in his masterpiece, *Faust*). Having
a homunculus on your shoulder became
a sign of wealth and freethinking in late-
eighteenth-century Germany, but having
more than one was, and is, considered to
be a perversion. I trust you agree.

594. The Hon. Archie Boresup-
Boresdown, who goes both
ways
595. Miss Hortense Few-Pustules,
a mole-manic woman of rare
quality
596. Doctor Morbius Darklove,
a demon hunter
597. Gro-Tesk, The Sub-Human,
a deranged human
598. Sir Manly Shriveled-Head,
a Declarationist
599. "Lead-Like" Dolly Molybdenum,
often confused for a statue
600. Mr. Gregory Glowback,
a tunnel smearer
601. Lady Giovanna Roundmaw,
a patron of the arts
602. Sir Anthony Ten Tentacles,
a mollusk hunter
603. Mr. Sean Manure,
a shiteater
604. Suction-Cupped Jonny, who
was a attacked by a giant
octopus
605. Leather Paws, a champion
digger
606. Mr. Cchuk Hssuk Snslkassk,
who abandoned his surface
names in disgust

Why?

Because mole-men are essentially genderless.

So how does a mole-man have sex?

As the mole-men are greatly dispersed within the earth, with very little contact between the various groupings, they reproduce in a number of different ways. It's very complicated.

Do the mole-men like threesomes?

Yes, sometimes. When a third-gendered mole-man is available. It's really very complicated.

Do some mole-men have a euosocial mating system, where only one member of the group—a "queen," if you will—is allowed to mate with a large number of subservient partners?

Yes.

Do some mole-men lay eggs, like frogs, which are then fertilized by other mole-men and carried around on their backs for weeks or even months?

Yes.

Do some mole-men reproduce hermaphroditically, like the earthworm, passing genetic material secreted from the "male" glands at the front of the body into a ring of slime that then travels down the body until it reaches the corresponding "female" glands?

Yes.

Do some mole-men give birth to underdeveloped live young that must then claw their way in total darkness to a protective pouch near the mole-man's cloaca, where it then lives to the age of seventeen as the parent mole-man travels, sometimes thousands of miles through unlit caverns, until it finds the same subterranean river in which it emerged from its own cloacal sac?

Yes.

I have to say, it does not seem that complicated to me.

Well, I confess you have an admirable knowledge of mole-man reproduction.

Do they like blowjobs?

Yes.

How long does a mole-man live?

Until the amber that surrounds their hearts melts. In some mole-manic

AUGUST 29

2005, THE GULF COAST: Hurricane Katrina drowns an American city while the U.S. government masturbates with a lyre. But I guess they're all doing fine now!

---

607. Mr. Tremont Crawlsalong, a toll collector
608. Miss Jenny Slothodor, a cavern singer
609. Mr. Digory Kirke, a youth
610. Mr. Christopher Half-Crushed, still half useful
611. Mr. Drew Danglemites, a gem swallower
612. Mr. Barry Screwskull, a screwdriver
613. Mr. Dougal Driller, his best friend
614. Mr. Quinn Wetface, an immersionist
615. Miss Quintella Mouthless, a medical oddity
616. Mrs. Daniella Beetlebuncher, a beetle buncher
617. Miss Sadie Sewerstalker, a surface historian
618. Miss Tubera Squirmer, and . . .
619. Mr. Tubero Squirmer, the famed, incestuous Tuber twins
620. Mr. Nikolai Spawncluster, an egglayer
621. Miss Mandible, an elderly detective
622. Miss Salamanda Eyestalk, the living periscope
623. Mrs. Jenna Frogtalker, an acolyte of the Toad
624. Mrs. Malvina Fairworm, a simple hole-wife
625. Miss Grace Has-Lips, has lips
626. Miss Edwina Bristles, has bristles
627. Miss Lisssk Sweetbeetle, a brutalizer

AUGUST 30
1963, WASHINGTON AND MOSCOW:
A direct telephone connection, dubbed
the "hotline," is established between the
White House and the Kremlin. After several prank calls are made on both sides—
one leading to the accidental destruction
of Norway—Nixon decides to conceal the
hotline behind the Oval Office's fake water-
fall. ANOTHER WISE MOVE THAT NIX-
ON NEVER GETS ANY CREDIT FOR.

628. Mr. Jeremy Prickleknees,
a scaler
629. Miss Arthropoda Silk, a silk
defecator
630. The Great Gastropodo, a dire
snail wrangler
631. Miner Quickslugger, a slug
racer
632. Miss Sheila Sharebody,
a lovely parasititic lass
633. Miss Honesty Weblegs, a silk
defecator
634. Mr. Elmer Bringsdark,
a luminous-mucus remover
635. Miss Subterra Daintyclaws,
a dilettante
636. Single-Disgusting-Claw, an
imperfect mole-man, but
good to have next to you
in a hole
637. Mrs. Mildred Surprisingly-
Smoothskinned, a simple hole-
wife
638. Miss Lizzie Onfire, a deep-core
dweller who got too close
639. Mr. Herman Louse, a valet
640. Miss Pumonata No-Gills, an
exile from the Sunken
641. Mr. Clarence "Baleen-Mouth"
Brown, a sifter
642. His Royal Lowness, Fredrick
Gaping Blowhole, the Arch-
Underduke of
Molemansylvania

strains, this makes them long-lived indeed: up to nine hundred years. But then there are the twenty-nine-day mole-men. Since they only live twenty-nine days, they don't even bother to wear clothes, and they are all named Nancy. As you can imagine, the Nancies see things differently from you or me. They live and love fast, mate furiously, and stink of pheromones.

What does a mole-man eat?

Insects, primarily, and dirt, which they filter through their nine gizzards. Occasionally they will feast on a deep-core megatuber. They dislike the giant asparagus tree, as it makes their urine smell funny, and it also makes their urine gigantic.

Do they eat their dead?

Rarely. Those mole-men who dwell near the surface typically unbury their dead by casting them forcefully out of holes onto the earth's surface. They try to do this in remote areas, though occasionally a mole-man corpse is discovered by a surface dweller. But they usually think it's just another dead Chupacabra.

What about the mole-men who live in the deeper parts of the earth?

They return their dead to the Inner Sun.

I've heard a lot about this Inner Sun. What can you tell me about it?

The Lands Below comprise a vast variety of underground terrain, from the narrowest of crawlspaces to glowshroom-lit caves extending for miles, all leading down to a gravity-less center in which hangs the red Inner Sun. Its light and warmth are, as you might imagine, comparatively feeble compared to our own sun, and it is orbited by a shitty moon. Those mole-men who delve this deep live a precarious existence, constantly leaping from rock to floating rock. But they are admired for their tans, and it is their job to accept the dead of others and cast them into the fire.

Are there underwater mole-men?

There are amphibious mole-men, and others adapted to life near and below the great subterranean rivers and deep oceans. They do not all have webbed feet and hands. Most have bones.

AUGUST 31
2006, OSLO: Having been stolen two years earlier, Edvard Munch's *The Scream* is at last recovered. It was not the first time the famous painting, depicting the existential crisis of some kind of alien visiting Oslo, had been stolen. Indeed, it is a frequent target of art thieves due to the fact that, despite what you may think, *The Scream* is actually very quiet—unlike the *Mona Lisa*, which is known as the bane of thieves for its constant, annoying humming.

643. Mrs. Myrtle Hollowsockets, eyeless, but also earless
644. Mr. Oscar Tuskplaque, a chewer
645. Mr. Ernest Tinyscratches, who works very slowly
646. Hydrostatic Charlie, a boneless mole-man and public nuisance
647. Mr. Andrew Breeds-and-Excretes, a mole-man of simple pleasures
648. His daughter, Cloaca
649. Mr. Herbert Supershriek, a Declarationist
650. Mr. Arm-Gnawing Glenn Huisssusss, an autophage
651. Mrs. Eugenia Swollen Inksac, an inker
652. Mr. Morris Charbelly, a core tender
653. Chromatophoric Donnie Eeeeeeeeesk Huk-Huk, shunned
654. Miss Nellie Skinshedder, a skinstress
655. Myron Heeech-sissss Wormscaler, an armor maker
656. Elvira of the Old Ones, who claims to be a god
657. Mr. Aidan Weetail, a mole-man who never lost his vestigial tail
658. Mr. Will Double-Blind, who is extra blind
659. Mr. Angelo Disgusting-Finger, a Declarationist

SEPTEMBER 1

1807, WASHINGTON, DC: Aaron Burr is acquitted of treason. Jefferson's former vice president had already attracted a dark reputation due to his repeated and increasingly elaborate attempts to murder Alexander Hamilton, including, but not limited to: poisoning Hamilton's figs as they grew on the tree, attempting to drop a safe on Hamilton as he walked down the street (twice), and tying Hamilton up and attempting to force-feed him ten-dollar bills. (It turns out Hamilton loved the ten-dollar bills more than the figs.) After finally crossbowing Hamilton in their famed 1804 duel, Burr fled Washington and disappeared into the wilds of the new lands Jefferson had purchased from Napoléon.[a]

Figure 90: Aaron Burr, with Crossbow

Soon, though, whispers came back from the former French territories that Burr, the great enemy, was stirring again. Historians are still not clear what he was plotting. Some say he planned to steal Texas for himself and name himself King Burr, the Hamilton-Slayer. Others say he was planning to drain the Mississippi River and corner the market in muddy, undrinkable **CONTINUED ON THE NEXT PAGE**

a. Please see page 454 under the heading "The Secret Moon Landing."

How do the mole-men move from place to place?

The claws, teeth, and acidic saliva of the mole-man makes him an able tunneler at need, and his glowing lubricating mucus helps him squeeze through tight crevices while also lighting the way. However, as their civilization has grown, they have developed various mass-transit schemes, including omnibus worms, dirtliners, and monorails. And of course, they ride a variety of hideous steeds.

Apart from the hideous steeds you mentioned, specifically the great-worms, the lesser-worms, the giant alligator, the pseudosaur, and the dirt puma, what other hideous steeds do they use?

The Hoary Bats

The Speed Chiggers

The Dark Newts

The Brain Sharks

The Underbears

The Dire Snails

The Quick Slugs

The Subwhales

The Dryground Octopod

The Clydesdales

The Pookas

Is it true the mole-men have 230 words for darkness?

Yes.

Will you list them for me?

All 230?

Yes. That's what you do, isn't it? List a bunch of stupid, meaningless stuff, like hobo names and mole-man names and people who gave birth to animals, and famous safecrackers who were also blind, and thirty-seven prisoners who broke INTO prison, and the eighteen vice presidents who had rubber skin, and the many, many people who have eaten their own bodies in order to survive, and ten recipes for crickets that do not taste like cricket . . .

I didn't make any of those lists, other than the hobo nicknames and the mole-man names, and in both cases, I BEGGED YOU NOT TO READ THEM.

What about Some Insects That Have Been Friends to Man? Or Four Get-Rich-Slow Schemes? Or the Ten Styles of Deadpan? Or Three Words in Esperanto Still in Use Today? Or Several Sexually Suggestive Christmas Songs?

SEPTEMBER 2
1969, DALLAS, TX: The first ATM machine is installed. Standing for "AUTOMATED TELLER MACHINE MACHINE," the first ATM could receive deposits and dispense cash (though only in coins) and was roughly the size of a city block. Despite its name, it was not wholly automated: A single human controller was required to supervise and make manual notations in the customer's bankbook. He would sit in a little dome atop the machine. However, this bank employee was instructed to wear a tinfoil suit and talk like a machine so as not to ruin the futuristic effect.

SEPTEMBER 1 CONTINUED
water. Others claimed he controlled a rudimentary laser satellite and threatened to destroy Monticello should Jefferson not cede him the presidency immediately. Whatever the case, Jefferson put out a warrant for his arrest. A task force of Whiffenpoofs stormed his private volcano and captured Burr as he was attempting to clone himself.

Though solid evidence of treason was murky, Jefferson's personal vehemence toward his former VP made many expect a quick conviction. But the case fell apart when all of the prosecution's star witnesses were found mysteriously dueled to death on this bright, cold September morning. No one knows how Burr did it, but the court was left with no course but to acquit, freeing Burr to live out his life quietly and in shame as a New York attorney and laser satellite consultant.

Later, Aaron Burr's half-formed clone would confess to killing the witnesses against his master, but no one understood what he said, due to his half-formation.

SEPTEMBER 3
1995, THE "WORLD WIDE WEB": The popular auction Web site "eBay" is founded. The first item auctioned: a broken laser pointer.
Soon after, writer and now Fox News personality James Rosen will comment to John Hodgman that eBay is an excellent place to buy original art by the comic-book artist "Neal Adams."
Hodgman's reply: "Ha-ha. eBay. That will never work."
Other schemes that Hodgman has said will never work: Napster, iTunes, MySpace, Blogger, air, food.

660. Miss Millicent Kak!, who insists upon the exclamation mark
661. Mr. Denny Withered-Face, a former face-pusher
662. Marco Deadlyspores, an assassin
663. Mr. Silas Deepspawn Hissycheeks, a Declarationist
664. Mr. Alton Rockfondle, a tunnel-upper
665. Mr. Hieronymous Phlegmquake, a tunnel-downer
666. Tommy Dickfish, an urban legend
667. Miss Alberta Prehensile-Tongue, a flycatcher
668. Miss Carnivora Toothflower, born to be sacrificed to the great toothflower
669. Mr. Porter Suckneck, who climbs on your back and feeds on your blood
670. Miss Centipeda Shroomsniffer, a fungal mistress
671. Mrs. Sabrina Shellback, a dire snail mistress
672. Seeeeeeeeeeeeesnsiesssssss ssk Kak!-Kak!-Smythe, a halfbreed
673. Mr. Mankill Manloathe, a manhunter

OK. You have me there. Please see page 559 under the heading "Some Lists I Confess to Compiling."

You won't get off the hook that easy, Listy McAlamanac. If you tell me the mole-men have 230 words for darkness, I would like to hear ten of them. Otherwise, how do I know you're not lying?

I *am* lying. And to prove it, here are twelve:

1. Ssissisk—"Dark."
2. Husslessisk—"Medium dark."
3. Eskisssssisk—"Extra dark."
4. Eskissssssisk Gold—"The Finest, Darkest Extra-dark in Our Entire Line of Light-Absent Nooks and Crannies."
5. Musskisssisk—"Upper-passage dark," darkness pierced by the occasional spire of hated blue surface-light.
6. Dusskisssisk—"Blind-dark," the extreme dark of deep-core tunnels and caves, where navigation relies entirely on setae-feel and sonar-coughing.
7. Unskdussksssisk—"Fake-blind dark," the kind of dark you experience when you think you are in the deep core, but realize

after a few days that your head has actually just been encased in mud.

8. Truskisk—"Worm-dark," the dark you find when you accidentally walk into the digestive passage of a giant worm. See number 12, below.

9. Prisilisk—Just regular, good-old dark. Nothing special.

10. Enfer-foncé—"Hell-dark," the quality of reddish darkness encountered when approaching the pit.

11. Misskilisk—"Mucus-dark," gentle darkness brightened by mucus-light.

12. Isk—"Final-dark," the warm, inky, eternal darkness that awaits us all at the very end.

That is very poetic. Did the mole-men write poetry?
No. They were not hoboes. They were civilized, humanoid, underground dwellers. CHUDS, if you will. Their most lasting contribution to prose was probably their contribution to the French *encyclopedie*, specifically the sections on magma and the rights of worms.

SEPTEMBER 4
1995, NEW YORK: The same year as the eBay incident, Fox News personality James Rosen sues John Hodgman for revealing to the world that he is obsessed with the comic-book art of Neal Adams. (Fox News's official policy is to favor the work of John Byrne.)

674. Mr. Aloysius Underbear, who only vaguely resembles an underbear
675. Mr. Jiminy Seemsdead, who has been in hibernation for many decades
676. Mr. Philip Declares, a Declarationist
677. Mrs. Selena Urinestench, a pheromoner
678. Cpt. Donner Well-Sealed-Mouth, a dust tolerator
679. Dr. Grant Gaspocket, builder of the first super-dirtliner
680. Miss Gemma Fallingflesh, a professional molter
681. Sir Sneakshaft, once a great strategist
682. Mr. Gerald Walkingstick-Bug-for-a-Hat, a stick-bug dealer
683. Mr. Geoffrey Badwig, is not fooling anyone
684. Mr. Hiram Obviously-False-Beard, see above
685. Mr. Nate Neverclothed, who goes as the Century Toad intended
686. Mrs. Ursula Cryptsleeper, a grave-dweller
687. Mr. Ralph Underthunder, a cavern shaker
688. Mr. Fingold Spawncooker, an eggsitter
689. Mr. Tom Ten Thousand Teeth, only a slight exaggeration
690. Miss Sallie Threehearts, a necessary redundancy

SEPTEMBER 5

1882, NEW YORK CITY: The Knights of Labor hold the first Labor Day parade. Designed to honor the common working man (but without all the socialist/pagan overtones of May Day), the annual parade featured giant balloon representations of a Robber Baron being murdered and the great Snake of Capitalism eating its own tail.

Most famous, of course, was "Joey the Child Laborer." It is still renowned as an incredible feat of balloon engineering, because Joey rained real tears from his moppet eyes, and plus, it is very hard to make a balloon look starving.

In later years, the parade would feature a float depicting the Triangle Shirtwaist Factory fire, including actual burned corpses, posed as though they were waving to the crowd. After this, they decided to tone down the "Labor" part of Labor Day and just focus on selling school supplies.

---

691. Miss Sallie Threehearts, see above
692. Mr. Teddy Mollusky, who merely has very fine bones
693. Mr. Fat Freddy Passagefill, a passage blocker
694. Mr. Calvin Manylisps, a hisser
695. Fortunato the Jester, a mysterious voice behind the wall
696. Master Mason Michael Rattlebreathe, head of the mole-manic Masonic lodge
697. Mr. Moncy Chompdown, who founded a competing lodge that admitted troglodytic men
698. Mr. Marcel Real-Hair, who has hair
699. Miss Canada Softwrinkles, whose father was once ambassador to Canada
700. Mr. Olaf Crushed-to-Death, who is flat

Did they write novels?

There have been in history a great number of "Hollow Earth" novels, largely written by surface dwellers such as Jules Verne, Edgar Rice Burroughs, and Lewis Carroll. Whereas most of these books follow the adventures of the surface man or woman as they travel through the fantastical, upside-down world of the land below (where the upside-down metaphor became absurdly literalized), mole-man literature is obviously the opposite.

Hushy Stinkwell and Her Adventures in the Blazing World, for example, tells of a young mole-manic woman who follows a rabbit up through its hole and into a bright "wonderland" populated by strange creatures. Donning special glasses to protect her eyes,[195] she was astonished, for example, by how *tiny* the bugs, snakes, and lizards were, and how most of them never spoke.

Much of the novel is lost on modern readers, though, as it mainly is an extended, obscure allegory for the now-extinct political upheavals of the Lands Below. It is presumed, for example, that the man who had no mites

---

197. Please see page 432 under the heading "May 9."

was a symbol for the failed Hiss-Chief. While the beetle-pie that Hushy finds labeled "Eat Me" was considered, at the time, to be an uproarious sexual innuendo (it's impossible to explain to a non-mole-man. It has to do with the fact that "beetle" in the mole-manic language is very similar to the word for "cloacal life sac").

SEPTEMBER 6
1901, BUFFALO: The anarchist Leon Czolgosz assassinates President William McKinley at the Pan-American Exposition. As he died, McKinley forgave his assassin. "I should never have visited the Anarchist Tent," he said. "But I hear the Anarchists make the best corn dogs."[a]

a. For further details, please see page 299. And it is true about the corn dogs.

The story ends with the queen of the bright "Blazing World" spilling a great crock of salt upon Hushy, causing her to shrivel up and die. But it is all a dream. When she awakens, Hushy is lying on the glowing moss next to her sister, who is still reposing under an asparagus tree, quietly reading and spawning.

I think I know that story. What does the baby that turns into a pig signify?
This is not an allegory. The mole-men thought babies and pigs were the same creature. This was because they could not tell them apart when they stole them.

Why were the mole-men stealing human babies and pigs?
They wanted to educate them. They felt terrible that human children had to live on the savage surface. But because of their poor eyesight, the mole-men accidentally dressed and raised many pigs to old age, and even elected a few to Parlor leadership. Later, some of these well-dressed pigs escaped back to the surface. Author George Orwell, they say, was pretty angry about totalitarian government, but it was not until he saw a pig dressed up like a mole-manic diplomat that he got the idea for the novel *Animal Farm*.

Did Irving Berlin write a song about the mole-men?
Yes. He wrote a pacifist song called "Stay Down Here Below" in which

SEPTEMBER 7
1936, TASMANIA: The last known thylacine, or "Tasmanian Tiger," dies in captiv-
ity at the Hobart Zoo.
After the success of the Tasmanian Devil,
the Tasmanian government had attempted
to rebrand many of its native species as fe-
rocious and uncontrollable ... hence we get
the Tasmanian Killing Mouse, the Tasmanian Blood Dove, and the Tasmanian Wal-
laby of Infinite Danger. Yet of these, only
the thylacine rivaled its marsupial cousin
in its literal thirst for blood and habit of
traveling by spinning very quickly through
trees. Hunted to extinction, the last known
thylacine was named "Benjamin." OR SO
HE CLAIMED.

a mole-man says to his young spawn
to not dabble in the warlike affairs
above. You can hear Groucho Marx
sing it on *The Dick Cavett Show*.

What about the song "Molemansylvania
6-5000"?

I'm surprised you even know about
that song. It's by Glenn Miller, of
course, but curiously, it's not actually about the city of Molemansylvania itself (Miller had never dug
deeper than 350 feet in his whole life), but the Molemansylvania
Hotel in New York City. A grand hotel in the presumed mole-manic
style, it was formed as a giant mound of earth, and visitors were en-
couraged to dig out their own rooms, or enjoy one of the villas, or
"dirt-gloos." But this was never more than a cultural misapprehen-
sion. Mole-men lived in dirt-gloos only occasionally, and they hardly
ever slept at all.

Figure 91: A "Deluxe King" Suite at the Molemansylvania Hotel

Where else do they appear in popular culture?

The list goes on and on . . .

— Beatrix Potter's "The Tale of Jeremy Sunkbottom"

— Larry in the television program *Three's Company*[196]

— The original *Superman* serial, "Superman and the Mole Men"

— *Beetle Bailey*

— *Tintin and the Mole-men*, yet to be published in English

— And of course, the common carnival game known as Whack-a-Mole-Man

SEPTEMBER 8

1974, WASHINGTON, DC: Gerald Ford pardons Richard Nixon.

Ford's pardon was the first use of the new, state-of-the-art White House pardoning pool. Previously, a presidential pardon was conveyed in the unhygienic shallows of the Potomac River.

But now Ford could wash Nixon of his sins in perfect privacy, in a heated pool with Jacuzzi jets, and using a brand-new brush made from the beard of Rutherford B. Hays (the Grant Beard Brush had long since been stolen).

Where did the mole-men come from?

The first primitive mole-men arrived in what is now Alaska some 25,000 years ago by tunneling through the icepack covering what is now the Bering Strait.

They mistook the ice, tragically, for a new kind of dirt, which they called "dirt clear." Many mole-men still believe that their ancestors formed a colony there beneath and within the ice that was, naturally, lost once the ice passage finally gave in to the Bering Sea. This lost colony of "Molemantis" is a prominent myth in mole-manic culture, especially mole-manic talk radio.

No, no, I mean, Where do they COME FROM? Are mole-men just humans who started living underground?

No. Why would a human dig underground and start eating dirt and insects?

---

196. Please see page 422 under the heading "Wacky Neighbors."

SEPTEMBER 9

1886, BERNE, SWITZERLAND: The Berne Convention is adopted, establishing the force of copyright across international borders.

The Convention was formed at the urging of Victor Hugo in a desperate effort to block the unauthorized musical version of *Les Misérables* then being staged by the immortal vampires Schönberg and Boublil. Hugo failed, of course, and *Les Miz* is now considered a classic among humans and vampires alike.

To escape predators?

Didn't I tell you about the Brain Sharks? The Pookas? The Clydesdales? You think they don't eat people?

Then are we just mole-men who crawled out of the earth?

No. This false idea that man and mole-man share a common heritage goes back to antiquity. Aristotle, for example, believed that the mole-men were spontaneously generated from our own buried feces. But that is nonsense. The truth is very simple: Mole-men evolved as a completely separate species under the earth.

What about the Century Toad?

What about it?

Well, isn't it the traditional belief of the mole-men that they were originally born of the Century Toad, the giant toad that sleeps in the center of the earth, waking for one day every hundred years to feed? And that one day, nine thousand years ago, the Century Toad ate a snake, a rat, and a mole? And those three old enemies fought so hard in his belly over the next hundred years that, by the time he woke up again, the old Century Toad vomited up what was left, and that was the first twenty mole-men? And then the Century Toad, seeing the poor creatures he made wriggling and hissing on the ground before him, gave them the gift of his burning spit and told them to populate the underearth, for it will be their dominion forever and ever?

OK. You know what? I'm not going to get into this with you.

Why are you so closed-minded?

Because that's a fairy tale. Not even the mole-men believe it anymore.

Some do.

Some small Parlors do, yes. But the fossil record is clear. Mole-man evolved from mole-ape. Case closed.

I grant you that's one theory.

It's not a theory! It's science. Even if you completely discount Darwin, the reality is, the mole-men *found* the Century Toad 469 years ago. They have now been observing it for hundreds of years. They have a research station down there for this very purpose. And not once, in all that time, has this giant toad just *puked* out a new life form.

That doesn't mean that it didn't happen exactly one time, nine thousand years ago, after he ate a snake, a rat, and a mole.

I am going to tell you for the last time. The mole-man shares no DNA with the mole. Not one single gene. The mole-man has nothing to do with moles. Nothing.

Why are they called mole-men then?

Because Carl Linnaeus made a mistake in his taxonomy and the name stuck! In their own language, they call themselves ILLISK-SIKKSISIKKSSTHIK, meaning "Blind Slime People of the Dark." That's what we SHOULD call them.

Why is it so hard for you even to consider another possibility? Look at the amazing complexity of mole-manic life. Look at the teeth and claws that are just perfect for digging; the saliva that just happens to burn through rock,

---

SEPTEMBER 10

1776, NEW YORK: Nathan Hale becomes the nation's first spy, sneaking behind enemy lines on Long Island after Manhattan had fallen to the British.

    Espionage was still a nascent art at the time, so even though he was equipped with a number of useful gadgets—a ponytail with a secret compartment; a tricorner hat with razor edges; a horse with a gun in its mouth—it did not occur to Hale to use an alias, and his British accent was terrible. He was caught just twelve days into his mission when he was spotted in a Queens tavern, attempting to lead the crowd in a chorus of "I Regret I Have but One Life to Give for My Country," a favorite drinking song among the Colonial rebels. As he was being hanged, his horse deployed its oil slick—but it was too late.

SEPTEMBER 11

Many important things happened on this day in history. In 1609 Henry Hudson's ship the *Half Moon* landed on an island that would later be known as "Manhattan." His landing marked the 312th anniversary of Scottish patriot William Wallace's victory at Stirling Bridge, while 424 years earlier, Isaac II Angelos of Constantinople killed the emperor's assassin Stephanos Hagiochristophorites, paving the way to his own ascension to the Byzantine throne.

In 1850, Jenny Lind, "The Swedish Nightingale," made her U.S. debut in New York. In 1936, FDR dedicated the Hoover Dam, ushering in a new era of hydroelectric power. In 1973, the forces of military dictator Augusto Pinochet killed Chilean president Salvador Allende in a coup d'état—exactly 432 years after the Chilean capital at Santiago had been destroyed by Michimalonco leading a force of some 20,000 indigenous Chilean warriors.

In 1985, Pete Rose beat Ty Cobb's record for base hits, and in 1990, President George H.W. Bush coined the term "New World Order" in a speech responding to Saddam Hussein's invasion of Kuwait. Then, in 1994, Frank Eugene Corder, a recent widower, got drunk and stole a Cessna 150 from a Maryland airport. Shortly after midnight the next day, he attempted to fly it into the White House, instead crashing on the South Lawn.

Famous people celebrating birthdays today include O. Henry, Ferdinand Marcos, Brian DePalma, Kristy McNichol, Moby, Carl Zeiss, Paul "Bear" Bryant, Mickey Hart, Harry Connick Jr., Eric Slovin, Leo Kottke, Brad Bird, Tom Landry, the Italian naturalist Ulisse Aldrovandi, the American rapper Ludacris, the famed French general Turenne who invaded the Spanish Netherlands in 1667 and, on a tragic note, Dylan Klebold, who in 1999 would kill twelve students and wound twenty-three others at Columbine High School before killing himself.

CONTINUED ON THE NEXT PAGE

and the mucus secretion that just happens *to glow in the dark . . . When you look at the amazing slime ring and the cloacal life sac and all the many beautiful, varied ways that the mole-men have sex . . . are you going to tell me that's all a matter of chance? Of random mutation? Is that really LESS crazy than the idea that life might have been intelligently vomited out by a giant toad that lives at the center of the earth? Or maybe, just maybe, it's a little bit MORE crazy?*

OK. Not only is that a completely false equivalency, but it's also an insult to the very legacy of Enlightenment commitment to reason and science that are the founding principles of mole-manic civilization and, for that matter, our own.

OK, let me ask you this: Where are the mole-apes now?

I'm not having this conversation anymore.

You can't answer because there are no mole-apes, are there? And THERE NEVER WERE.

That's enough. I don't know who you are, or how you got in my book, but you're out of here.

One more question. Please.

OK. Fine.

Do the mole-men like to do it moley-style?

Yes. Very much. All night long.

AN URBAN LEGEND REGARDING THE DECLARATION OF INDEPENDENCE

From the moment it was written, many were convinced that the Declaration of Independence contained within its more opaque passages evidence of deep mole-manic magic, especially in the introduction, when the document encourages the people of the new nation to assume "the powers of the earth."

Indeed, it's long been rumored that if you recite the Declaration three times while looking in a mirror at midnight, the mole-man known as Bloody-Screechy will take you away to the Lands Below and feed you to the toothflower. However, if you have ever tried this at a pajama party, then you know that the worst that ever happens is that Bloody-Screechy shows up for a while and talks about the natural rights of man.

DID YOU THINK I WAS GOING TO TELL YOU ABOUT THE SECRET TREASURE MAP ON THE BACK OF THE DECLARATION OF INDEPENDENCE? HA-HA. THAT IS JUST AN URBAN LEGEND!

SEPTEMBER 12
1940, LASCAUX, FRANCE: Four French teenagers and their dog discover a hidden system of caves with massive primitive drawings of horses, birds, and aurochs, which sound very exciting but are just an extinct kind of giganto-bull.
The mystery of who made the drawings remained unsolved until the teenagers and their dog revealed that the culprits were a bunch of Paleolithic cavemen who were only *dressed up* as a luminous French cave monster. Another case solved by the French teenagers and their dog, whose name, I will never be able to convince you to believe, was "Robot."

SEPTEMBER 11 CONTINUED
In 1962, the Beatles recorded their first single, "Love Me Do."
This day is also the national holiday of Catalonia, honoring Barcelona's fall to the Bourbon crown, and the feast day of Saint Deiniol, the sixth-century Welsh bishop renowned for his incredible physical strength. And in 2001, Alice Trillin, wife and muse to the *New Yorker* writer Calvin Trillin, died of heart failure—a complication of the radiation treatment she had received for lung cancer twenty-five years earlier.
I mean, it just goes on and on and on. I can't believe you forgot about all of this.

1937, NEW YORK: *Law & Order* debuts on NBC radio.

The original cast featured Orson Welles as Det. Monty Cranston, Eddie Anderson as his long-suffering partner Det. Van Jones, Sam Waterston as the highly principled and yelly DA Sam Waterston,[a] and Bruno Kirby as Fu Manchu.

a. Please see page 496 under the heading "What to Expect While Serving as a Juror."

SOME LISTS
I CONFESS TO
COMPILING

SEPTEMBER 14

1341: Dante Alighieri, author of several popular tour guides to the afterlife, dies. Upon finally visiting the actual Inferno he had previously only imagined, he was surprised to learn that Hell does not actually consist of nine concentric circles, but is actually a few relatively cramped caves of no particular shape (plus one furnished waiting room with French people in it).[a] Frankly, it just hasn't been the same since the pope closed Limbo.

a. For more on what lurks below, please see page 505 under the heading "The Seven Portals to the Hollow Earth."

SEPTEMBER 15

1885, ONTARIO de CANADA: Famed circus elephant "Jumbo" is killed by a train. One legend has it that Barnum's great pachyderm gave his own life to save another, pushing a smaller elephant named "Tom Thumb" out of the path of the train and safely onto a group of small children. A lovely story of heroism and children-crushing, to be sure, but is it just another Jumbo-load of Barnum bunkum?

There are just as many who suggest that Jumbo committed suicide . . . that after all those years of zoos and trains, the big, sad beast stood on the tracks, the hot white circle of the locomotive's headlamp growing on his face like an African full moon, and waited to be taken home to the land he just couldn't ever forget. But that's just sentiment: Elephants forget all the time, especially if they drink the way Jumbo did.

Luckily, Jumbo's worldwide celebrity did not end at his death. At some thirteen feet high, his corpse was a much-desired oddity: The skeleton went to the Museum of Natural History, his Volkswagen-sized heart went to Cornell University, and his hide was stuffed and proudly displayed on the campus of Tufts University until 1975, when it was destroyed in a fire (the university had been hit by a train). This is where we get the saying "An elephant always dies twice."

But as for Jumbo's brain, its whereabouts remain a mystery. I certainly don't have it in a jar, and I certainly haven't attached electric probes to it or hold séances around it trying to understand why Jumbo killed himself.

WERE YOU AWARE OF IT?

Jumbo was not named for his size. On the contrary, like his skeleton, heart, and skin, we took the word "Jumbo" right from the elephant himself. Originally a corruption of the Swahili word "*jumbe*," meaning "tragically enslaved beast," "Jumbo" is now a catch-all phrase for anything surprisingly huge, be it a jumbo jet or a jumbo-sized elephant brain jar. JUST AN EXAMPLE! THAT DOESN'T MEAN I HAVE HIS BRAIN IN A JAR.

SOME INSECTS WHO HAVE BEEN FRIEND TO MAN

Insects, worms, and bugs are not ALL bad. Remember:

— The Erie Canal was bored by BEES.

— Little Timmy was pulled from an avalanche by a WAXWORM, who asked for no reward.

— A bad epidemic of SCABIES warned London of the blitz. They were passed from a German spy to his British lover and on and on until they crawled into Winston Churchill himself, where they wrote on his skin: WE SHALL NEVER GIVE UP.

— The MAYFLIES all died before they could carry out their plan to create a giant, sentient mayfly cloud that would chew our faces off and choke our cities in a century of buzzing darkness.

Actually, I guess they don't deserve too much credit for that, since mayflies only live for a single day anyway. BUT YOU GET THE POINT.

FOUR GET-RICH-SLOW SCHEMES[197]

— Knife-dulling

— Door-to-door sales of doors

— Fire-peddling

— Wishin'

SEPTEMBER 16
1968: In a desperate attempt to appear "with it," Nixon appears on the comedy variety program *Laugh-In* and delivers the show's trademark line, "Sock it to me, you fucking cocksucker."

THE TEN ACCEPTED STYLES OF DEADPAN

AMERICAN STYLES

— Great Stone-face Style

— Smiling-Corpse Style

— Pensive-Gorilla Style

— Fully Paralyzed-Gorilla Style

— Worldly Possum Style

— Diffident-Asshole Style

EUROPEAN STYLES

— The E. L. Wisty Procedure

— The Streeb-Greebling Method

— Steady Jowls

— The Nihilism

197.
GET-RICH-SLOW SCHEMES FOR CHILDREN
Because children may be paid so little compared to adults, there is a much wider array of occupations available to them by which they will never profit, including . . . chimney-climbing, well-depth testing, orphan impersonation, schoolyard sleuthing, superhero sidekicking, and schooling.

SEPTEMBER 17

1814, BALTIMORE, MD: Francis Scott Key publishes "The Star Spangled Banner," celebrating the Americans' lack of total defeat in the British attack of Fort McHenry and the nondestruction of its still young flag.

Since you have likely sung this song, you will know that it is a terrible song. To sing it properly, you need a vocal range spanning nine octaves, the ability to sing two tones at once, and the ability to purr.

What's worse, when it was first introduced, there were three additional stanzas, including one that simply called for the singer to screech like an eagle for nineteen minutes. This version of the song is rarely heard this way today—C-Span plays it when it goes off the air.

Still, it became very popular . . . far more popular than the national anthem Benjamin Franklin proposed ("Turkey in the Straw"), and finally became our official national song in 1931. Tragically, Francis Scott Key died just one year earlier. He was demonstrating the song at a local carnival and suffocated on his own phlegm. Most historians agree: He deserved it.

THREE ESPERANTO WORDS IN COMMON USE TODAY

— *Saluton*—"Hello"

— *Soros*—"Destroy-Bush"

— *Esperanto*—"Esperanto"

WERE YOU AWARE OF IT? "VERA AUX FALSA?"

We all know that George Soros is a billionaire philanthropist who hates George Bush. But did you know *why*?

It all has to do with this little-known fact:[198] He doesn't speak funny because he was born in Hungary, but because George is one of the estimated 1,000 people in the world who are NATIVE SPEAKERS OF ESPERANTO.[199]

Originally named Grygory Schwartz, Soros was a Hungarian by birth. But in the home, he was raised speaking Esperanto by his father, Tivadar—an early *studento* of the international made-up language of peace.

But it was not until Grygory was sixteen that Tivadar smuggled his son out of Soviet Budapest and then arranged to have him smuggled to the secret Esperantish Temple in the West. There he would receive his true Esperanto name and, written within it, his destiny: To

198. Literally.

199. The great "Oni Mil."

continue the ancient battle between the Esperantans and the Bushes, the noted American political dynasty who hate Esperanto almost as much as they hate English.

To ever remind him of his cause, Soros was given the first name of his enemy and trained from an early age in the *Vojo de la krokodilo*—"the way of the crocodile."

SEPTEMBER 18
1709, STAFFORDSHIRE (ENGLAND): The great critic and dictioneer Samuel Johnson is born.

Almost immediately, James Boswell began following him around, documenting every last witticism that fell from his infant lips. This was greatly unnerving, especially since Boswell had not yet been born. In his famed dictionary, Johnson thus defines "biographer" as "an embryonic proto-Scotsman who haunts and ever watches." This definition still appears in many dictionaries.

This is the traditional Esperantish martial art, combining elements of French savate, the ancient Greek pankration, and old-fashioned international financial speculation. While it may sound complicated, it actually is a very simple, internally consistent martial art that is based on the philosophy that, with just a little study, anyone can understand being punched in the face.

WERE YOU AWARE YOU COULD HIT SOMEONE WITH A CROCODILE? IT IS SO!

SEVERAL SEXUALLY SUGGESTIVE CHRISTMAS SONGS

Regarding CHRISTMAS SONGS or "CAROLS," everyone has their favorites[200] But, you might worry, so few of these songs are sexually arousing.

You are wrong. It turns out that the happy tunesmiths impris-

---

200. Personally, I could listen to "Good King Wenceslas" over and over again, all year long, because (a) you have to admit it's catchy, and (b) it speaks to me. We all hear our own stories in our favorite songs (that is why Tom Waits sings only in werewolf language—you can pretend it is about anything you want!). So I suppose I feel some kinship with the saintly martyred king of Bohemia, as I too enjoy looking down on feasts from afar, and I also have feet that are supernaturally hot and melt the snow as I walk.

SEPTEMBER 19

1783, PARIS: Joseph-Michel and Jacques-Étienne Montgolfier demonstrate their newly invented hot-air balloon by sending aloft a balloon carrying a rooster, a sheep, and a duck.

This impressive display of animal levitation caused many onlookers to swoon and cry out in fright. Skeptics pointed out that the duck, who could already fly without a balloon, had to be in on it somehow. Plus, the sheep was on fire.

oned down on "Tin Pan Alley" have provided us with a surprising number of sexually provocative holiday-time songs.

There are so many of them . . . from the relatively innocent "I Saw Mommy Kissing Santa Claus" to the wheedling diamond-lust of "Santa Baby" to the transparently pornographic "Santa Claus Got Stuck in My Chimney" and "Grandma Got Run Over by a Reindeer."

Not to mention . . .

— "Rudolph the Red-Nosed Reindeer"

— "Christmas Is Coming (The Goose Is Getting Fat)"

— "It Came Upon a Midnight Clear"

— "The Nutcracker Suite"

— "Greensleeves"

— "The Chipmunk Song"

— "Deck the Halls (With Boughs of Penis)"

How to explain it? Is this some last cultural remnant of the old Saturnalian spirit of eroticism that predates our current holiday?[201] It's difficult to say. But across them all, the message is the same, and I join them in saying: Merry Sexy Christmas to you and yours.

THE BEST MAS EVER

Speaking of Christmas, while I am not personally a religious man or a pornographer, I am nonetheless seduced by the trappings of the season.

---

201. Please see the section below under the heading "The Best Mas Ever."

Even as I write this, I am enjoying my famous eggnog (secret ingredient: alcoholic eggs) and I have lit a merry little Yule log here at my feet, where I am roasting chestnuts to give to the inevitable carolers, Persian magi, and crippled English children who come to my door this time of year.

SEPTEMBER 20
1796, VIRGINIA: At the completion of his second term, George Washington sets down to write his Farewell Address, in which he warns the new nation against entangling itself in foreign alliances and, in a little-quoted portion, wonders whether John Adams might actually be some kind of Massachusetts bridge troll.

I have decked my study with boughs of holly and of course POINSETTA, or some say POINSETTIA, though it is actually pronounced *PAHNSEEYA*. Did you know it is a Mexican plant? It is. Named for the renowned ambassador to Mexico James Poinsett, it was brought to our country in 1828 and quickly became favored over its predecessor, the Christ-o-dendron, which was a very similar plant to the pahnseeya but subject to spontaneous stigmata, and thus was considered overly dramatic for the holiday table.

Some might argue we've ended up with an inferior, less godly plant. But as history shows us, so little of Christmas is actually Christian.

Most scholars now agree, after all, that Jesus could not have been actually born on December 25, pointing out that shepherds did not tend their flocks in winter, and thus could not have seen the star of Bethlehem. And of course, there is no way Christ was a Capricorn.

Rather, that date was probably chosen by Emperor Constantine in the fourth century for its convenient coincidence with any number of existing pagan feast days and winter solstice traditions.

Consider the mistletoe that hangs now above my head. Like holly, it is an evergreen, for centuries prized across Europe for its reminder of springtime in darkest winter. It was the symbol of Frigg, the Norse goddess of love, and it was equally prized by ancient druids as a bane against witchcraft and lightning, which I find especially comforting, as both are out to get me.

SEPTEMBER 21

1897, NEW YORK CITY: *The New York Sun* replies to an eight-year-old reader named "Virginia" who asks if Santa Claus exists.

Sun reporter Francis Church, whose experience covering the bleak and bloody Civil War had driven him to drink, was naturally charged with the task of replying to all of the newspaper's eight-year-old readers. And so he set his trembling, trauma-palsied hand to the task.

"Yes, Virginia," he famously wrote, "Santa Claus *does exist*. He is as real as fairies, as real as your baby brother's baby rattle. In fact, if you break that rattle apart, you will find Santa's finger bones and teeth right in there. Take them to a scientist: He will say the same. Santa is (or was) real . . . as real as VIRGINIA, which is to say, YOU, dear child.

"For who is VIRGINIA? A little girl? Yes, but not forever. Eventually you, like all of us, will die and rot. Eventually your fingers and teeth will rattle in the emptiness of all of time and history, just like Santa Claus. Eventually you too will be nothing but a myth, an idea, a hint of innocence that for decades more will inspire us, give heart to us, move us all to tears, even though YOU ARE DEAD.

"Of course Santa exists, and THANK GOD!* Your little baby brother, who knows nothing yet of merciless war and merciless time, laughs at Santa, just as he takes joy at the sound of Santa's bones! HIS BONES! And soon he will laugh at your bones too! Merry Christmas!

"*PS: God does not exist."

Mistletoe was also the only way the druids could get kissed, insofar as they all wore enormous beards that reeked of sour milk and human sacrifice.

These traditions are now synonymous with Christmastime in America, but it was not always so.

Indeed, for much of our nation's early history Christmas was a somber and austere occasion. Both Oliver Cromwell in England and Gov. William Bradford in the Plymouth Colony forbade any observance or revelry other than a literal Mass for Christ. And so it was for many decades that the sole Christmas decoration in most American homes was a child made to stand silently in the corner to contemplate damnation while holding a burning log.

And it is still the case that many television stations will broadcast a looped recording of a child holding a log for twenty-four hours on Christmas Day as a service to those without children or logs.

Indeed, it was not until the middle of the nineteenth century that the Christmas tree was generally accepted into the American home.

Originally a pagan custom, by the sixteenth century, live trees had become a Christmastime fixture in the German guild hall, typically decorated with small cakes, cheeses, and captured enemies.

For many years, German Christmas trees were dark, or else lit only

SEPTEMBER 22
HAPPY BIRTHDAY, BILBO AND FRO-
DO BAGGINS, confirmed bachelors of the
Shire.

by natural luminous mosses. It was Martin Luther, the great reformer, who suggested draping the dry branches with lighted candles, presumably because he felt the custom was not sufficiently dangerous enough for the thrill-happy Protestants. Usually two or three homes per village were lost this way to flames until candles were replaced by much safer oil lamps and, later, Bunsen burners.

Still, most considered the tree a crude Germanic fancy until 1850, when Prince Albert, the consort to Queen Victoria, brought the Christmas tree to England. Albert, of course, was a Bavarian by birth. Many in England feared his foreign influence upon the Queen and the nation.

This wounded Albert, and the wee hours of Christmas Eve of 1850 found him at Osbourne House, the German castle he had designed on the Isle of Wight, unable to sleep and overcome with despair.

For months he had sought approval from the House of Lords to stage a Great Exhibition that would showcase Britain's industry to the world, but he was met only with ridicule. Despite the children he had given the nation, despite his beautiful morning coats, and for all of Victoria's devotion to him, it seemed he would always be loathed as an OUTSIDER.[202]

Now he faced another drab, treeless English Christmas, and having consumed perhaps one too many alcoholic eggs, the Prince Consort fled the house, wandering desolately under the starless night until he reached the sea, where he peered into the icy, churning waves.

"What use am I to anyone?" he murmured. He fingered the Bavarian life-insurance policy in his pocket. "I am worth more dead

---

202. Cockney rhyming slang for "a German."

SEPTEMBER 23
2007, THE SKIES ABOVE THE UNITED
STATES: I fly to Los Angeles. I am seated
across the aisle from Kurt Russell. Now,
listen: I am a happily married man. But
I am not embarrassed to say that Kurt
Russell is an EXTREMELY HANDSOME
MAN. And apparently he grew his eye
back since he escaped from New York.

than alive. I wish I had never been born."

And at that moment, Albert called for his footman to suicide him on the spot. But before he could, Albert was startled to see ANOTHER figure on the quay toss himself into the abyss. Stirred from melancholy, Albert leapt in after him and saved the strange man from drowning.

As they dried off at a nearby guardhouse, Albert regarded the other figure: a foolish little man in flowing white robes, with a long, sour-smelling beard.

"Are you a druid?" asked Albert.

"Only second-class," corrected the druid. His name was Cathbad. The time of the true druids had long been over, he explained to Albert: conquered and dispersed centuries ago by the Romans and Albert's own Saxons. But there were still a few adepts, like himself, hoping to earn his golden sickle.

It was then that Cathbad reminded Albert that long before there was Christmas, the long nights of December were illuminated by other holidays.

Albert's own Germanic Yule, for example, or the Roman feast of Sol Invictus, both celebrating the return of the sun in the darkest part of the year.

Or consider the ancient pagan Saturnalia, when servants became masters, and for the duration of the orgiastic festival a commoner is raised and loved as a king.

"Remember," said Cathbad, "Christmas is not a birthday, so much as it is a re-birth day. Like the evergreen itself, this holiday is a celebration of endurance, life, and hope in winter's longest night. Which itself is not an un-Christian sentiment," said Cathbad. And then he

winked, whispering, "But wouldn't it
only be enhanced by a little animistic
tree worship?"

SEPTEMBER 24
1977: *The Love Boat* debuts on ABC. It
was originally based on the novel *Super-
train.*

And so at last Albert ceased try-
ing to be an Englishman and embraced his German heritage, pulling
a great silver fir from the frozen earth with his bare hands and drag-
ging it back to Osbourne House, where he festooned it with candles
and household servants.

Paradoxically, Albert would soon by this very act become im-
mensely popular, embraced by those who once shunned him. Images
of Albert and Victoria embracing paganism within the royal home
were circulated in magazines throughout the world and quickly became the picture of Victorian Christmastime that every British—
and later American—home would anxiously aspire to.

And it is still said that every time a bell rings, a second-class
druid gets his golden sickle, and a British heathen witch-king finally
finds the love of his people.

Meanwhile, allow me to share with you some of Prince Albert's
own advice for keeping your tree fresh and healthy throughout the
season.

— Always cut off about 2 inches of the stump before dis-
   playing.
— Always keep the tree well watered.
— Remember that its branches will droop over time, increasing its circumference by roughly a third.
— Remember that it watches you and keeps within its
   dark and sticky pitch the memory of 1,000 winters.
— And despite what you may have heard elsewhere, you
   should not add sugar to the tree's water, or aspirin, or
   any other sort of food—unless it is a little human blood.

SEPTEMBER 25

1513 (SY): Spanish Explorer Vasco da Gama claims to have seen the Pacific Ocean. It turned out that his men were playing a hoax on him though: It was just a blue sheet hung up between some trees.

ALL OF YOUR QUESTIONS ANSWERED, OR AT LEAST FIVE MORE

SEPTEMBER 26

1960, ILLINOIS: John F. Kennedy and Richard Nixon engage in the first televised presidential debate. It is largely agreed that Kennedy won the debate, and then the presidency, the moment he walked over and shaved Nixon. The straight razor, badger-bristle brush, and towel he used are currently on display at the John F. Kennedy Presidential Library—the towel kept eternally hot in JFK's honor.

———————————————

MORE ANSWERS

Herewith, as promised, are answers to more of your questions.

DAVE G. OF NEW YORK ASKS: What is chicken butt? And how much should it cost, per cut?

JH REPLIES: I understand your confusion. So-called chicken butt does not refer to the "butt" at all, but to the shoulder of an adult chicken. It is a cheap, fatty cut of chicken that grows tender and flavorful only when braised very slowly, allowing the tough collagen to gradually transform into moist gelatin (also known as "chicken-gel").

As for your question about price, I presume you are referring to the famous rhyme "Chicken butt! Five cents a cut," an old street-merchant's call immortalized in Gershwin's *Porgy and Bess.* But nowadays, a cut of chicken butt probably goes for $2.99 a cut. More if it's organic.

In any case, do not confuse chicken butt with chicken anus, which still costs just five cents a cut.

MICHAEL H. OF BROOKLYN ASKS: What is the worst job?

JH REPLIES: Obviously the answer is highly subjective. Some people, for example, would have no tolerance for being a mere "Internet celebrity" like Jonathan Coulton.[203] Others would find being a

203. Please see page 442 under the heading "Feral Americans."

chicken-anus cutter to be the worst job. In any case, it's clearly a toss-up between those two. I would say, unless you absolutely cannot cut a chicken anus due to some allergy or earlier traumatic experience, choose that over Internet celebrity. It simply pays better, and the e-mailing is a lot less tedious.

SEPTEMBER 28
TODAY IS CZECH STATEHOOD DAY, commemorating the assassination of "Good King" Wenceslas, Duke of Bohemia. Legend has it that his statue in Prague will come to life whenever the homeland is in peril. This did not happen when Prague was invaded by the Nazis in 1939 or by the Soviets in 1945 and 1968 or by playwrights in 1993 or by college students every year thereafter. Still, the Czechs will occasionally gather around Wenceslas's statue and watch for movement. Sometimes, it is said, you can see his eyes blink. But mostly you just hear his high, squeaky voice calling for an oil can. It's sort of sad, actually.

ADAM R. OF SAN FRANCISCO ASKS: I have a 2000 VW Jetta that still runs fine, but seems to need more repairs than it used to. How do I know when it's time to buy a new car?

JH REPLIES: Here's a funny story. I am married.[204] And my wife's first car was a Volkswagen Jetta, circa 1990 or so. It was a disaster. It was already in terrible shape when she bought it, and she treated it very poorly. I don't think she changed the oil once. After six months it shuddered horribly whenever it hit fifty. When we drove together I would hike my knees up to my chest and sob, I was so scared.

Sometimes when she was driving down the highway with the car shuddering like a seizure, other drivers would pull up beside her and point at the car, screaming. She could not figure out what they were screaming about. She would pull over and take a look at the car and everything would seem to be OK. But when she got back on the road it would happen all over again: pointing, screaming, shouting, pale looks of absolute horror. It was a mystery.

Eventually she decided to try to get rid of it. She left it unlocked

---

204. Wait. It gets better.

SEPTEMBER 29
1829, LONDON: The London Metropolitan Police Force is formed—the famous "bobbies," so named because the first thousand officers were all named Robert. Prior to this, there was no meaningful law enforcement in London. It was a lawless land, where child pickpockets ("pickies") thronged the streets frequently singing about food and rippers ("rippies") who actually advertised their services in the newspaper. Once the "bobbies" arrived with their menacing tall hats and quarterstaffs, ripping was driven largely underground, and the pickpockets became merely orphans.

in New York City for weeks on end—not difficult, because she never had been given the keys to the door. After a few weeks of this, she went out to check on the car. A neighbor called her over.

"Is that your car?" he asked.

"Yes," she said.

"You leave the doors open?" he said.

"Yes," she said. "I never got the keys to the doors. And I want someone to steal it."

"They're not stealing it," he said.

"I know," she said.

"I've been watching your car. The people are not stealing it," he said.

"I know," she said.

"They are having sex in it," he said.

"I see," she said.

The next day she found a used condom in the car. She decided it was time to part with the car.

At first she had the nerve to attempt to sell it. She offered it for two hundred dollars to a writer for *Sesame Street.* "Runs fine!" she said. Yes. To get rid of the car, she lied to a writer for *Sesame Street.*

The *Sesame Street* writer took it to be checked out by her mechanic. That night, there was a message on our answering machine. The *Sesame Street* writer sounded shaken, scared.

"I cannot buy your car," she said on the machine. "When I drove it across the Triborough Bridge, people were pointing and screaming at me." Our best guess is that whenever the car was in motion, some part of it was on fire. Flames from the tailpipe? We never knew for sure.

You may ask why she didn't just have it towed away. The answer is, my wife did not know you could do this. Neither of us did. We were

SEPTEMBER 30

2004, IN THE OCEAN: Japanese researchers take the first photograph of a live giant squid in its native habitat. When they finally discovered the squid via remote submersible, it was eating a live whale. However, as soon as it realized it was being filmed, the squid immediately denied eating the whale, claiming it was merely "hugging it with my beak."

younger then, and not yet experts in everything. Eventually, however, someone clued her in, and she had a company take it away for fifty dollars. Years later, she would find out that the company had reconditioned the fiery sex car and sold it again. For all we know, it's still out there.

But that's not the strange thing. The strange thing is, years later, when the time came for my wife and I to buy a new car, we both agreed, immediately: VOLKSWAGEN.

Brand loyalty is, as every marketer knows, a powerful thing, and not always (or even most of the time) do we choose the known over the unknown because it has been good to us. In life, we return just as frequently to what scars us. And what scars us is Volkswagen.

But I digress. You do not require a morality tale. You want advice. So here is a handy rule of thumb: If you have a 2000 Volkswagen Jetta, the time to buy a new car is 1999.

LINDSEY E. OF UNKNOWN LOCATION WRITES: Morrowind is basically an MMORPG,* minus the MMO part (because I don't have Xbox Live). It's filled with almost 300 Non-Playable Characters, and over 1,000 monsters. You can choose your own paths in the game, meaning, if I wanted to be a Balmora Guard that

---

(I add these only in the case that you may have questions on the subjects listed with asterisks or daggers.
* MMORPG = Massively Multiplayer Online Role-Playing Game

OCTOBER 1

1895, BRUSSELS: The first practical time-travel device, Van Damme's "Electrical Time Chute" will have soon been introduced to the world.

smoked considerably deadly amounts of skooma,[†] and had an unhealthy urge to steal anything that I could see, then by Lord Dagoth I would! My question is this: If I were to steal something (say, a Grandmaster's Mortar & Pestle[‡]), and I was caught doing so, and had to pay $4,500 for it, would it be OK to hide in the outskirts of towns, taking ingredients from any plants I pass to make potions, and then sneak into a town to a potion dealer to sell all of my potions to her, still hiding the Mortar & Pestle and paying back my debt to society via the potions I made from the thing I stole?

JH REPLIES: I don't know the answer to your question. But will you marry me?[205]

KIERA D-V. OF NEW YORK WRITES: I was wondering if one of your areas of expertise was Scrabble?

JH REPLIES: Obviously.

KIERA D-V. OF NEW YORK CONTINUES: In a recent game of Scrabble, I cunningly added the letters "U" and "N" to the word "break" to create the word "Unbreak." This was challenged by my

---

† Skooma = A fictional drug/beverage in the world of Morrowind. It is a narcotic made from refined moon sugar. It is illegal and extremely addictive. A book called *Confessions of a Skooma-Eater* [also sometimes called *Confessions of a Dunmer Skooma-Eater*] provides a stirring argument that can turn skooma addicts away from addiction. [This book is a parody of the real *Confessions of an English Opium-Eater*, which concerns the drug laudanum.] Skooma is valuable and often smuggled, but few shopkeepers are willing to buy it. Due to its illegal nature, some shopkeepers will not do business with the player if they are carrying it or its unrefined substrate, moon sugar.

‡ Grandmaster's Mortar & Pestle = Makes in-game potions. The value of the potion is weighed by your Alchemy skill and Intelligence.)

---

205. Please note that I am already married.

competition, Jackie M. As I am sure you know, this word entered the English language with Toni Braxton's 1996 hit "Un-break My Heart." I firmly believe that its exclusion from

OCTOBER 2

1959, MINSK: Lee Harvey Oswald, living in Russia, receives a mysterious message from Nixon in the future from a man wearing an old-timey cape and a huge belt buckle.

the dictionary is an oversight and should not stop its use in Scrabble. My "friend" obviously disagreed and robbed me of my victory.

BEFORE JH CAN REPLY, JACKIE MACL WRITES: I am sure that by now you are in receipt of an e-mail from a "friend" of mine, Ms. Kiera D-V. On August 28, Ms. D-V was engaged in a game of Scrabble. In an attempt to use up her letters, Kiera argued vehemently that "unbreak" is a word. I am afraid this has caused a rift in our once solid friendship, a rift that perhaps only you can repair (*not* unbreak).

JH REPLIES: I am, in fact, about to tear your friendship apart. For Ms. D-V is undoubtedly wrong. Scrabble is not a game of words per se, but a game of words AS THEY APPEAR IN THE DICTIONARY—specifically, whichever dictionary the players stipulate to at the beginning of the game. (I prefer the SOWPODS dictionary).

Like language itself (or, for that matter, friendship), Scrabble thus is a fluid social contract that is gently negotiated and renegotiated upon each meeting. Since dictionaries themselves are constantly updated, no game is played by precisely the same rules. Indeed, had you been playing with THE TONI BRAXTON DICTIONARY OF THE ENGLISH LANGUAGE THAT TONI BRAXTON MADE UP, then I am confident that your friend's "unbreak" gambit would have won the game. But as that dictionary has been lost to scholars since 1996, I fear your friend instead is a loser. And what's more, she always will be. For even if the *Oxford English Dictionary* were to vote "unbreak" into the lexicon tomorrow, tomorrow's dictionary

OCTOBER 3

1283: Welsh Prince Dafydd ap Gruffydd invents "drawing and quartering" as a means of execution, though King Edward is at first skeptical that the practice—burning the subject's entrails before his very eyes before cutting him into four pieces—might not be sufficiently cruel. So confident was Dafydd that his invention would work, he tested it on himself. And guess what: IT WORKED.

was not the one you used on August 28. And what's more, I have just paid the *OED* a great sum of money to blackball "unbreak" from their pages forever. I do this partly out of spite, of course, but also out of a hope that you both may now get on with your lives and stop bothering me. You're welcome, good Scrabbling, and remember my motto:

"STAY THE FUCK AWAY FROM BOGGLE."

WERE YOU AWARE OF IT?
"BANNED FOR 22 POINTS"

Other than "unbreak," there are several other words that are PERMANENTLY BANNED from the game of Scrabble.

YHWH . . . Player loses all points, cursed as a heretic.

AIEOUY . . . Player loses all points, cursed as a "vowel-dumper."

HAILSATAN . . . Do you dare to try it? THEY SAY THE LAST KID WHO SPELLED THIS WORD WENT INSANE!

KEITH B. OF UNDISCLOSED LOCATION WRITES: I am writing to you to ask how you actually did it.

JH REPLIES: It's quite simple really, and you can do it too.

First, I studied the mistakes others made before me.

The lessons I gleaned from other successful people in my field were obvious: Never work for anyone else; own the product of your own labor; do something that no one else is capable of doing; and DON'T USE SNAKES.

Next, I bided my time. I spent several years working a desk job, learning the business inside and out by watching carefully and keeping my head down. But after hours, when everyone went home, I stayed behind and worked on my machine.

Next, I got together a group of specialists: the best in each of their fields. People who would inspire me and challenge me to do better. As we planned, I kept files on each of them, and when possible, I collected their DNA.

OCTOBER 4–15

Perhaps you have wondered why we traditionally observe these ten days as one very, very long day, during which we are not allowed to bathe or change our clothes or sleep. Well, you may thank Pope Gregory XVIII. On this day in 1582, the pope personally turned the papal clock ahead ten days,[a] abolishing the Julian Calendar[b] and ushering in the Gregorian (or "XVIII-ian") Calendar we still use today. Not only did he realign the civil calendar with the tropical year, he also began the long tradition of messing with millions of ordinary people's brains on pure papal whim.

a. You can still see the giant fob he used for this purpose on display at the Vatican: It is encrusted with jewels and bleeds twice an hour.

b. Please see page 301 under the heading "January 1."

It's not legal for me to say "genetic experimentation," but let's just say within seven years I had assembled a crack team of physically and mentally perfect assistants, NONE OF WHOM HAD ANY GENITALS.

And I continued to perfect my machine.

After that, it was just a matter of blinding the guards with a flash grenade and disabling the electric eyes with electric-eye paste.

Because the Frenchman thought I was dead, I knew they wouldn't be expecting a tunneler. But that's just what they got.

By the time I was inside, I was half dead and completely covered in mud. But that was the plan: The mud defeated the heat sensors, and the half-death defeated the half-life sensors.

In two days, I was able to move again and crawled across the floor.

It took me all morning just to reach the control panel.

That's when I deployed the snakes. Yes, I know: I broke my own rule. Unfortunately, old habits are hard to break.

OCTOBER 5

1492, THE SARGASSO SEA: Hopelessly lost, Christopher Columbus is forced to consult with a sea serpent for directions to Asia. Getting advice from the serpents was always a dodgy proposition for explorers, as the serpents always claimed to know the way but were often just as lost as the sailors. In this case, however, the serpent, named Long Twisty Tom, was simply lying when he told Columbus that China was just around the corner. What Columbus didn't know was that Tom had been feuding with the Arawak Indians for some decades (they had stopped feeding him men), and so, seeking a little payback, he sent them four centuries of European domination. Tom himself lived another two centuries before the Japanese caught him and ate him raw.

But when the guards rappelled down from the ceiling and began horse-tasering me, I still managed a laugh.

Because across town my machine was already doing its thing.

And the truth was, I had already taken the item three days earlier when I just walked in, nice as you please.

Because, you see, the Frenchman was me all along.

And the horse-tasered body that crawled in that night? Well, let's just say: It didn't have any genitals. NONE AT ALL.

Because by then, I was long gone.

And *that's* how I did it. And do you know what? I DO NOT HAVE ANY REGRETS.

HOW AND WHERE TO CONTACT ME, AND SOME CLARIFICATION OF MY CURIOUS NEW LIFESTYLE

As I prepare my next book, I wish to say again that I do hope you will continue to contact me and ask me questions. It is so gratifying to be able to talk to my readers directly with only a three-year time lag. We really must take advantage of it, don't you agree? I will wait three years for your answer.

But before you write, I must tell you that I no longer live in my Upper West Side Observatory.

I shall miss that dear old rambling place, and I won't lie to you: Finding an apartment in New York City with built-in bookshelves; several large, true bedrooms; several more false bedrooms; plus a polo room, a haunted gallery, a dueling pavilion, separate rooms for monkeys and vines, a private speakeasy,

OCTOBER 6
1927, ON THE SILVER SCREEN: The first feature-length "talkie," *The Jazz Singer,* is released, starring Al Jolson and Neil Diamond. Jolson's first line was originally written in the script as "You just heard something," designed to indicate to a frightened audience that the talking had begun. But on set, Jolson ad-libbed the double-negative "You Ain't Heard Nothing Yet." He just had to jazz it up. Ironically, Neil Diamond had no lines at all, because he had not been born.

a grotto for having sex in, and a transparent ceiling is difficult to find— and hard to let go of, even when it's clear you have outgrown it.

And I am sorry to have left the Upper West Side, for that is an exciting, exciting place to live.

Ah, the Upper West Side! The birthplace of jazz, the deathbed of vaudeville . . . with everything in between sleeping in perpetual coma. What will I miss about it most? Grand Central Terminal? The Empire State Building? The Bronx?

Sure, I'll pine for those landmarks. But we always miss most the fleeting moments we can never get back: eggs Benedict fresh off the conveyor belt from the central hollandaise vats of West Ninety-eighth Street . . . the all-night rosé raves at Grant's Tomb . . . the Saturday evening wolfhound races down the Broadway mall . . . and when it all became too much, the long rambles through the dells and hollows of Straus Park, where a man could walk uninterrupted from 106th Street all the way to 107th without once remembering he lived in the wildest neighborhood of New York—the place Damon Runyon called "the Rollicking Upper West, where every night is an endless dice game and you can't help but roll sevens again and again, but then the dice turn into shiny, poisonous beetles that flutter up and sting you in the eyes, and the next thing you see is the golden, lidless eye of Alexander Hamilton sitting in his throne at Columbia University."

OCTOBER 7
1977, HOLLYWOOD: Famous radio and television comedian George Burns begins claiming he is God. He is quietly institutionalized and replaced with John Denver.

Figure 92:
The Isidor and Ida Straus
Mescaline Fountain

Let's just say Runyon spent a few too many afternoons drinking from Straus Park's famous mescaline fountain. And I watched it all through my extralong telescope in the comfort of my observatory, laughing and crying and then falling asleep, alone.

But the Upper West Side is a young man's town. I have a family now and new responsibilities and, with my television career, a newfound need for EXTREMELY EXPENSIVE GOURMET FOOD, AND ALSO PILATES.

And so I moved my family to the quiet countryside of Brooklyn, where we now live in a small Utopian community known as Park Slope.

I am sorry that I did not write about this commune in my previous book, because it really is a very special place. But I was worried that if I told you about it, you might move there. And we do not want YOU.

For here in the shadow of the largest city in the country is a quaint, quiet little village of leafy streets, good schools, and strong neighborly spirit. It's the sort of place where everyone knows one another, and we watch out for our neighbors via a system of silently judging them. In Park Slope everyone is equal, except for the children, who are in charge of everything and are allowed to kill you on sight if you don't entertain them.

It's truly a paradise on earth, but it's also very misunderstood. Perhaps you read the book *Under the Banner of Heaven* by Jon Krakauer? OK, imagine now that the Mormons in that book are Park Slopers, and replace the word "polygamy" with "organic markets," and you will begin to get a sense of just what an evil, irresponsible liar Jon Krakauer is, and why the Park Slope children are going to kill him, should he ever be bold enough to show his face here.

First of all, the Park Slope community is diverse. Despite what you may have heard, you don't need to have gone to an Ivy League school to live here. Many of our members have attended only SMALL LIBERAL ARTS COLLEGES. You can tell because everyone has to wear a blazer that is color coded to his or her school. Not only does this embody the human rainbow that is Park Slope, but it also makes dividing up our money easier.

Now, as you know, the current community was born in 1990, founded by a group of exiles from Manhattan. The founders were pilgrims, much like those who settled our great country. They came to Brooklyn's shores seeking the peace and solitude they required to practice their simple, time-honored arts of gutting brownstones and consuming luxury goods.

From the beginning, the founders wanted to live in peace with the indigenous, less wealthy, more ethnic people of Park Slope. They didn't know that scented candles and small-vineyard white wines from Oregon would give those people smallpox. How could they have?

OCTOBER 8

1945, MASSACHUSETTS: Raytheon patents the first "microwave oven." Originally designed as a safe and efficient way to explode puppies, the microwave would eventually revolutionize home cooking—though consumers initially balked at the high price tag and the lead-lined mask and crotch cover that early models required.

Figure 93: An Old-Fashioned Microwave Mask, Worn with a Safety Cape

OCTOBER 9

1983, NEW YORK CITY: As part of a live television special on CBS, David Copperfield makes the Statue of Liberty disappear and then conjures up a "Statue of Slavery to Magicians." Transmission from New York is then abruptly cut.

The word "genocide" is used very loosely these days, and we think that's the real tragedy here. Many people in our community are writers, so we know how the power of ill-used words can be far, far, FAR more hurtful than smallpox. Let's just say this was a sad chapter in our history, but there's no use looking back. All those people are gone now, and NO ONE CAN BE BLAMED.

What about some other myths you may have heard?

Do we wear secret magic underwear?

THE ANSWER IS YES.

Do we refuse to touch people from outside of our community because they are "unclean"?

NOT AT ALL. SO LONG AS THEY GO THROUGH THE CLEANSING PROCESS, WE ARE PROUD TO EMBRACE OUTSIDERS WITH BOTH OUR HEARTS AND OUR BODIES. OR IF YOU PREFER, YOU CAN SKIP THE CLEANSING, AND WE WILL STILL BE HAPPY TO GREET YOU WHILE WEARING SIMPLE COTTON LEOTARDS AND MASKS THAT PROTECT US FROM CONTAMINATION BY YOUR SINS.

Does the cleansing process involve bathing in baby spit?

YOU HAVE TO UNDERSTAND, IN OUR PHILOSOPHY, THE SPIT OF THE BLESSED CHILDREN IS *TRANSFORMED* INTO THE PUREST SPRINGWATER BEFORE THE CONVERT EVEN SETS FOOT IN THE TANK. AND MOST PEOPLE FIND THE EXPERIENCE OF BEING LOCKED IN

THERE IN TOTAL DARKNESS FOR A DAY QUITE RESTFUL —AND OFTEN SPIRITUALLY MOVING.

OCTOBER 10
1973, WASHINGTON, DC: Vice President Spiro Agnew is forced to resign when it is revealed that he had been traveling through China claiming to be Nixon.

When we go to the park, do we crawl on all fours and allow our dogs to hold the leash and also wear clothes?

THAT ONLY EVER HAPPENS ON SATURDAYS BEFORE 9 A.M., AND IT TEACHES A VALUABLE LESSON TO MAN AND DOG ALIKE.

Do we address one another by the numbers the children give us?

YES, BUT ISN'T THIS SIMPLE COMMON COURTESY? I KNOW REFERRING TO ONE ANOTHER BY NUMBER IS "OLD-FASHIONED," BUT DON'T YOU THINK MODERN SOCIETY WOULD BENEFIT FROM SOME OF THE "OLD-FASHIONED" VALUES THAT MADE OUR COUNTRY GREAT IN THE FIRST PLACE?

I hope that clears up at least some of the myths about this wonderful new society that I have joined. But the main thing I want you to know is that I AM STILL THE SAME EXPERT YOU HAVE ALWAYS KNOWN AND INEXPLICABLY TRUSTED.

While living in Park Slope has been an adjustment, I can say very sincerely that I am very happy here, as is my family, and I would say so even if it weren't mandated by THE CODE.

In the meantime, however, please do not write me any longer at the P.O. Box listed in my previous book. For I am not allowed to go there anymore, except when the Rumspringa comes.

Instead, write to me courtesy of the Internet website that belongs only to me: Hodgman@bookoflists2.com, and I will be sure that one of my many flunkies and assistants pretends to answer you.

AN OUTRODUCTION

THE SECRET OF YOUR IDENTITY AND HOW YOU GOT THAT TERRIBLE SCAR

Thank you for reading with me once more, all the way now to the very end. I hope that you have found all of this information useful, but please save your thanks. It is I who must thank you.

As a FAMOUS MINOR TELEVISION PERSONALITY, I have seen worlds beyond even my own imagining, a strangeness beyond the strangest lie.[206] But it was not until I had returned to your world that the full, humbling implications of what I had seen became clear to me. I realize now that even for a FORMER PROFESSIONAL LITERARY AGENT, FORMER PROFESSIONAL WRITER, CURRENT FAMOUS MINOR TELEVISION PERSONALITY, AND DERANGED MILLIONAIRE, there may still be amazing fake facts and invented world knowledge that I STILL HAVE YET TO DISCOVER.

And so I shall not rest. I shall continue to venture beyond the mere AREAS OF MY EXPERTISE into new, uncharted territories. I shall

---

206. May I remind you that I rode in an elevator with Jerry Stiller?

delve further into the deep caverns and dark places that contain the roots of our history. I shall peer more keenly into the high and bright empty sky of the future and attempt to discern what is on that far horizon.[207]

And at the same time, I will keep my feet firmly on the ground of the present. I shall no longer float above it, but observe and document and report to you, dear reader, for I now know that COMPLETE WORLD KNOWLEDGE WILL NEVER BE COMPLETE.

At least, not until I finish the next book. By then, I think I will more or less have it.

NOW, as for the secret of your identity and how you got that terrible scar, you really didn't think I was going to tell you, did you?

Honestly: HOW DO YOU THINK I AM GOING TO GET YOU BACK FOR THE SEQUEL if I give everything away here? After all, I didn't call it *ALL* KNOWLEDGE THAN YOU REQUIRE.

But here's a hint: YOUR IDENTICAL TWIN IS NOT WHO YOU THINK HE IS.

Think about it.

THAT IS ALL.

OCTOBER 12

1969: A man known only as "Tom" calls a Michigan DJ claiming that Paul McCartney has died. This would spark an ongoing legend among fans that continues to this day. As the story goes, sometime in 1966, Paul McCartney was killed in a car accident and had been secretly replaced by a double. Depending on which story you believe, this "doppel-Paul" was either McCartney's identical twin brother, or Stu Sutcliffe, who had faked his own death years before and was now wearing a boyish rubber mask. Rather than reveal this news to the world, however, the Beatles quite naturally decided to merely hint at the truth through a series of opaque cues in their lyrics, record albums, and shiny, fake military costumes. "Evidence" of the conspiracy of silence includes:

— John Lennon reportedly intones "I buried Paul" in a distorted voice at the end of "Strawberry Fields" (and indeed, he was a trained grave digger).

— Ringo Starr reportedly intones "I danced on his grave" at the end of "Octopus's Garden." (This rumor is false. Ringo actually sounds like that.)

— On the cover of *Sgt. Pepper's Lonely Hearts Club Band,* Paul seems to be wearing a badge bearing the initials OPD, which some claim stands for "officially pronounced dead." (It doesn't. The badge actually says "OPP," meaning "Ontario Provincial Police," or, on the mean streets of Ontario, "Other People's Paul.")

— On the cover of *Magical Mystery Tour,* Paul is dressed as a death-black walrus in order to conceal the fact that HE HAS NO BOTTOM HALF.

---

207. Spaceships full of aliens who want to eat us, probably.

OCTOBER 13

1972, HIGH IN THE ANDES MOUN-
TAINS: The Uruguayans wanted you to
believe they had joined civilization. That
they flew in planes and played rugby and
were capable of reason. Then a plane full
of Uruguayan soccer players crashed in
the Andes Mountains and guess what
happened: They ate one another and, even
worse, wrote a book about it. Savages.

TABLE 30:
EXPERTS CONSULTED DURING THE PREPARATION OF THIS BOOK

Mark	Adams	on the subject of finishing books
Rory	Albanese	and all the boys down at O'Mallahans
Chris	Anderson	not the other Chris Anderson. This one.
Chris	Anderson	see above
Colin	Baker	on the subject of snappy, interdimensional dressing
Joshuah	Bearman	on the subject of snowmen
Emily	Bell	on the subject of interpreting the whims of very very quiet men
Alex	Blumberg	my personal assistant in charge of restaurant reservations
Keith	Bodayla	on the subject of how I did it
Ben	Burtt	the true Mr. Beep Boop
Lawrence	Chance	on the subject of Happy Boy Margarine photography
Doctor	Cocktail	on the subject of mock dalmatian blood
Loren	Coleman	on the subject of cryptids and cryptid photography
Dan	Comstock	of the Los Alamos National Laboratory and Enrico Fermi Photograph Depository
Christine	Connor	future author of the novel TIMEY TIMEY TIME
Elizabeth	Connor	"Prepared to Party"
Tyson	Cornell	the famous tattooed man
Gio	Corsi	on the subject of slot machine photography
Julie	Coulter	on the subject of feral man photography
Jonathan	Coulton	on the subject of how he did it
Scott	Dadich	on the subject of expert photography
Dale	DeGroff	on the subject of actual dalmatian blood
Sydny & John	Didier & Urschel	on the subject of Jack Wild, yeti hunter
Charles	Digges	on the subject of remarkable coincidences

CONTINUED

TABLE 30: *continued*

Kiera	Downes-Vogel	on the subject of unacceptable Scrabble words
John T.	Edge	on the subject of the hospitality industry of Mississippi
A tip o' the hat to Eggers		
Lindsay	Elmore	on the subject of skooma
Mike	Epstein	on the subject of Satan's Laundromat
The staff of Essentials, Northampton		on the subject of American Legion Halls in western Massachusetts
Jason	Evans	on the subject of dead and dying rabbits
Kassie	Evashevski	on the subject of the art of negotiation
Tony	Faulkner	on the subject of hook-handed politicians
Paul	Feig	on the subject of mechanical sharks
John	Flansburgh	on the subect of derangement
Jennifer	Flanz	a national treasure
Julia	Fleischaker	on the subject of North American transportation systems
Katherine	Fletcher	probably a clone
flickr		on the subject of photographs of everything
Mark	Frauenfelder	on the subject of making it yourself
Ricky	Gervais	who would prefer a beak on his face to replacing his legs with tentacles
Elizabeth	Gilbert	on the subject of the afterlife
Ira	Glass	on the subject of becoming a television personality
Josh	Glenn	on the subject of hollow earth theories on the Internet
Good Magazine		a fine magazine (not to be confused with *Just Fine* Magazine)
Dana	Gould	on the subject of ape mask safety

OCTOBER 14

2007, THE SKIES ABOVE THE UNITED STATES: I fly home from Los Angeles. I am not seated next to supermodel Rachel Hunter. Now, listen: I am a happily married man. But I was very, very disappointed not to be seated next to Rachel Hunter. Because in the first-class cabin, there are only nine seats, and in this case only eight of them did not contain Rachel Hunter. These seats unfold into great, wide, leathery beds. And the middle of the night, even from across the cabin, I could see Rachel Hunter reclined and sleeping. Now, before this, I would have been very happy never meeting Rachel Hunter in my life. But in that moment I realized that, had I been seated next to supermodel Rachel Hunter, I could have reclined my seat too. I could have reclined beside her and felt the breath of supermodel Rachel Hunter chastely brushing my cheek as I fell asleep on my way home. You have to admit, that would have been a unique experience. And to miss it on a one-in-eight chance really drove me crazy, and I was consequently unable to sleep at all. But I will say she looked terrific, and to answer your obvious question: no eye patch.

CONTINUED

OCTOBER 15

1532: Machiavelli's *The Prince* is first published, advising rulers of European city-states that "since it is difficult to join them together, it is safer to be feared than to be loved."

To this end, Machiavelli recommended that princes always wear scary masks and sneak up on people. Also, you should kick dogs in the face.[a]

Its immediate notoriety led swiftly to several sequels, including . . .

Figure 94: An Official "Machiavelli Scary Mask" Designed by Machiavelli Himself

TABLE 31: *SEQUELS TO MACHIAVELLI'S* THE PRINCE

The Prince in the Workplace	"The Prince's employees are like an army. He shouldn't fear being hated by them. The best way to accomplish this is to constantly quote *The Prince*. Or *The Art of War*. Either way, they will know you are an ass."
The Prince's Guide to Having Sex with Ladies	"There can be no greater incentive to accept things as they are over things as you wish them to be fully naked before your lady, while wearing a scary mask."
The Prince's Book of Dirty Jokes	"Q: What did the Medici say to the lady he was paying for sex? A: The end justifies the means!"
The Prince and the Pauper	"If you are a prince you have an exact double and, take my advice, DO NOT SWITCH PLACES WITH HIM. No matter how much you may wish to see how 'the other 99.9999 percent of the population lives,' having an identical twin out there is surely a danger to your authority. Have that person killed, or at least disfigured."
In the Kitchen with the Prince	"You cannot cook an owl until you totally dominate it."[b]

a. This is more difficult to do than you might think, especially if you are wearing a scary mask.

b. Please see page 348 under the heading "How to Cook Owls."

TABLE 30: *continued*		
The firm of Guion and Handelman	(formerly the firm of Handelman and Guion)	
Tim and Anna	Harrington	the deadly squires
Kasper	Hauser	on the subject of dog smarts and book dog smarts
Joey Herrick, of Natural Balance Pet Foods		on the subject of Hobo Chili for Dogs
James	Hodgman	the motivational speaker and author of *WORK IS A CIRCLE*

CONTINUED

TABLE 30: *continued*

Jessica	Horvath	on the subject of deadlines
Mayor and Mrs. Mayor Howorth		on the subject of good governance through martinis
Ted Seth	Jacobs	the renowned painter of aliens (or Enrico Fermi)
Xeni	Jardin	on the subject of Internet television, aka "Intellivision"
DJ	Javerbaum	on the subject of mint jelly and fine tequila
Richard	Jeffrey	on the subject of the sixth Doctor
Lisa	Johnson	on the subject of Hawley, MA
C. Alan	Joyce	on the subject of the world and its almanacs
Heidi	Julavits	a believer
Jim and Sue	Kaercher and Kaercher Blake	the first family of Hobo Soup
Ben	Karlin	on the subject of actual television, aka "Actuallivision"
Colette	Katsikas	on the subject of Essentialism
Starlee	Kine	on the subject of self-improvement
Kaki	King	on the subject of the novel *Dune*
Roman	Klementschitz	on the subject of underground mole rat photography
Geoff	Kloske	cardigan and sweater vest champion, 2008
Adam	Koford	on the subject of cats on trains
Stephanie	Lawrence	my personal assistant in charge of talking to Marty Krofft
Lisa	Leingang	on the subject of conchordance
Andrew	Leland	a believer
Kimberlee	Lico	of the Ronald Reagan Library
TC	Lin	on the subjecy of lucha libre mask photography

CONTINUED

OCTOBER 16
1846, BOSTON: William Thomas Green Morton, a dentist, demonstrates the use of ether as the first practical anesthetic to a group of surgeons at Massachusetts General Hospital. The demonstration consisted of gathering the surgeons in a group to observe a patient with a neck tumor. Morton then snuck up behind the surgeons and clapped an ether-soaked rag over their mouths until they were unconscious. When the surgeons woke up, they were submerged in bathtubs full of ice. A note was left for them explaining how their kidneys had been removed MIRACULOUSLY and WITHOUT ANY PAIN, but that they should contact the police if they wanted to live. About half died. The stolen kidneys, meanwhile, were sold to a collector and now may be found at Philadelphia's Mütter Museum of Medical Oddities and Stolen Kidneys.

OCTOBER 17

1993, ARKANSAS: Dogpatch USA, a theme park based on the comic strip *L'il Abner,* closes due to increased competition and a general declining interest in funny hillbillies. Never resold or redeveloped, the abandoned park remains standing, though it is now overgrown and intensely dangerous. The "Kickapoo Joy Juicer"—a tilt-a-whirl designed to emulate a state of constant, funny drunkenness—has fallen off its spindle, and the "Rural Poverty Fun Slide" now terminates in a pool of broken glass. On the other hand, other explorers report that the "Roast-Your-Own-Shmoo" hut is still operational but now SHMOO IS MASTER.

TABLE 30: *continued*

John Linnell	on the subject of millionaireship
Dale Long	on the subject of cylon photography
Justin Long	an actual actor
Rachelle Mandik	who refused to be bullied by the dictionary
Merlin Mann	on the subject of increasing productivity by discussing *Lost*
Brett Martin	on the subject of early *Sesame Street*
Nick McCarthy	on the subject of horror movies
Sean	McDonald	on the subject of patience
Jackie	McLeod	on the subject of acceptable Scrabble words
Mssrs. Moore and Eick		on the subject of *Battlestar Galactica*
Phil	Morrison	on the subject of famous comedy duos
Sue	Naegle	on the subject of Bruce Campbell
Tim	Notari	on the subject of Guy Fawkes mask photograpny
Pauline and Dave	O'Connor and Jargowsky	on the subject of the Magic Castle
Whitney	Pastorek	on the subject of remembering past lives
Emo	Philips	on the subject of Bob Harris
Pino of Pino's Prime Meats		on the subject of pig spleen procurement
Matthew	Poland	on the country of Latkievicz
Neal	Pollack	on the subject of medical marijuana
Sam	Potts	"At last everything, and all of it THE BEST"
William	Poundstone	on the subject of bigger secrets
Todd	Pruzan	on the subject of cryptobibliophilia
Roy and Denise	Pulliam	on the subject of high-speed hermit-crab racing photography
Amy	Radford	on the subject of ponytail portraiture
Adam	Rapoport	on the subject of tuxedos

CONTINUED

TABLE 30: *continued*

OCTOBER 18
1976, COLORADO: Charles Grodin plays his legendary forty-five minute Moog solo with the Electric Light Orchestra at Red Rocks.

David	Rees	on the subject of overhead projection
Sarah	Reid	on the subject of live-action role-playing games
The Rendezvous in Turners Falls		a place that keeps its secrets
Monica Richard, , of Natural Balance Pet Foods		on the subject of Chinese Take-out for Dogs
Lyn	Roberts	and family, on the subject of bonfires
Lyn	Robertson	on the subject of hospitality
John	Roderick	on the habits of the wild Alaskans
Adam	Rogers	on the subject of Volkswagen repair
Adam	Sachs	my personal life coach
Luis Miguel Bugallo	Sanchez	on the subject of Irish setter photography
Gina	Sanfilippo	on the subject of axolotl photography
Audrey	Saunders	on the subject of cocktail glassware
John	Sellers	on the subject of paternal herpetology
Maria	Semple	on how to throw the perfect party
Michael	Sharick	on the subject of oiled ham
Susan	Shilliday	your new host at the Montague Bookmill
Allison	Silverman	on the subject of French men and Italian women
Colleen Pence	Sizelove	on the subject of photographing graves
Robert	Sondgroth	on the subject of Chewbacca photography
Eric	Spitznagel	a believer
David	Standish	author of HOLLOW EARTH, yet surprisingly sane
Jon	Stewart	on the subject of things that will change your life (including television and Nasonex)
Darin	Strauss	on the subject of non-Siamese twins
Brian	Tart	on the subject of extreme patience
The Flight of the Conchords		on the subject of deadpans
The Men and Women of e-hobo.com		status as of this writing: "800 of 700 hoboes illustrated"

CONTINUED

OCTOBER 19

1867: French acrobat Charles Blondin, fresh from his triumph of walking across Niagara Falls on a 1,100-foot tightrope, attempts to cross the Atlantic balanced only on the newly laid transatlantic telegraph cable. Unfortunately, he did not notice it was underwater. After carrying his manager on his back for the first twenty-three miles, he amazed crowds by then stopping on the cable, bringing out a camp stove, and preparing an omelet. Then: drowning.

TABLE 30: *continued*

The Plume, Hammer, and Publick Debate Club	on the relative necessity of fingers and toes
Stepha Thomas	on the subject of airport gargoyle photography
Paul "F" Thomkins	on the subject of canned peanut brittle
Jesse Thorn	America's Radio Sweetheart
Paul Tough	on the subject of contact with alien life

Uncle John	on the subject of "near the bathtub" reading	
JS	VanBuskirk	on the subject of Great Auks, Good Auks, and Just Fine Auks
Dick Van Patten, of Natural Balance Pet Foods	a very fine actor and nice man who truly cares about feeding dogs and fake trivia writers. I am grateful.	
Vendela	Vida	a believer
Sarah	Vowell	on the subject of presidents and puritans
Irving, David, Amy, Silvia	Wallace, Wallechinsky, Wallace, and Wallace	the list experts who are themselves a list
Morgan & Rob	Webb & Reid	on the subject of the Drake Equation
Dave	Weich	on the subject of pronouncing "Weich"
Jimmy	Wikipedia	on the subject of true fake trivia
Sean	Wilsey	on the subject of Massachusetts

IMAGE CREDITS

Fig. 30: Copyright holder unknown; image provided by Kelly Cusack; **Fig. 31:** Tim Notari; **Fig. 32:** Library of Congress, Prints and Photographs Division; **Fig. 33:** Michael Sharick; **Fig. 34:** courtesy Joey Herrick, Dick Van Patten's Natural Balance; **Fig. 35:** Ibid; **Fig. 36:** Library of Congress, Prints and Photographs Division; **Fig. 37:** Library of Congress, Prints and Photographs Division; **Fig. 38:** Copper engraving from the book: *Karl Gottlieb von Windisch, Briefe über den Schachspieler des Hrn. von Kempelen, nebst drei Kupferstichen die diese berühmte Maschine vorstellen,* 1783, public domain; **Fig. 39:** circa 1848, found on Wikipedia; **Fig. 40:** Copyright © BBC, courtesy of the BBC and Colin Baker; **Fig. 41:** Ollie Atkins, The White House; **Fig. 42:** Library of Congress, Prints and Photographs Division; **Fig. 43:** Library of Congress, Prints and Photographs Division; **Fig. 44:** Copyright © Alex Gotfryd/Corbis; **Fig. 45:** Library of Congress, Prints and Photographs Division; **Fig. 46:** Army Signal Corps Collection, the U.S. National Archives; **Fig. 47:** Courtesy of The Ronald Reagan Library; **Fig. 48:** by Mike Epstein, Satan's Laundromat; **Fig. 49:** Ibid; **Fig. 50:** Copyright © Bettman/Corbis; **Fig. 51:** Library of Congress, Prints and Photographs Division; **Fig. 52:** Library of Congress, Prints and Photographs Division; **Fig. 53:** 1864, Francis Bicknell Carpenter (1830–1900) ; **Fig. 54:** Library of Congress, Prints and Photographs Division; **Fig. 55:** Photo taken by John Hodgman, spleen provided by Pino's Prime Meats, Manhattan; **Fig. 56:** Ibid; **Fig. 57:** Ibid; **Fig. 58:** Library of Congress, Prints and Photographs Division; **Fig. 59:** by Gina Sanfilippo, axolotl owner; **Fig. 60:** by John Hodgman; **Fig. 61:** Ibid; **Fig. 62:** Copyright © Bettmann/Corbis; **Fig. 63:** U.S. Army Photo; **Fig. 64:** Library of Congress, Prints and Photographs Division; **Fig. 65:** The National Oceanographic and Atmospheric Administration; **Fig. 66:** Official Dept of Justice Photograph; **Fig. 67:** by Amy Radford, of Seattle; **Fig. 68:** Copyright © Steve Marcus/Las Vegas Sun/Reuters/Corbis; **Fig. 69:** by Gio Corsi, http://www.flickr.com/photos/corsiworld/; **Fig. 70:** by Roy and Denise Pulliam, aka somesmokingmonkeys; **Fig. 71:** Copyright © Bettmann/Corbis; **Fig. 72:** J. G. Keulemans (1842–1912); **Fig. 73:** NASA; **Fig. 74:** courtesy of Dragonfly Innovations; **Fig. 75:** photographer unknown, CC share alike license 1.0; **Fig. 76:** by Luis Miguel Bugallo Sánchez; **Fig. 77:** by Julie Coulter; **Fig. 78:** Copyright © John Springer Collection/Corbis; **Fig. 79:** Copper engraving of Janez Vajkard Valvasor, 1689; **Fig. 80:** Jean Auguste Dominique Ingres, 1806; **Fig. 81:** courtesy of Ted Seth Jacobs and Los Alamos National Laboratory, respectively; **Fig. 82:** Marc Averette, via http://en.wikipedia.org/wiki/Image: Polydactylcat.jpg; **Fig. 83:** by Lawrence Chance; **Fig. 84:** Copyright © Bettmann/Corbis; **Fig. 85:** by Colleen Sizelove; **Fig. 86:** courtesy of Roman Klementschitz; **Fig. 87:** by Stepha Thomas, aka "raygun daisy"; **Fig. 88:** believed to be a U.S. government photograph, author unknown; **Fig. 89:** believed to be a U.S. government photograph, author unknown; **Fig. 90:** courtesy of Lucasfilm, DK publishing; **Fig. 91:** Library of Congress, Prints and Photographs Division; **Fig. 92:** by Kevin C. Fitzpatrick; **Fig. 93:** TC Lin; **Fig. 94:** by "JoJan"

OCTOBER 20

1982, VIRGINIA: Day 476 of the constant rain of dead frogs. By now, no one thinks about it anymore. By now, a rain of dead frogs every day is normal.

Every morning, the people of Richmond sweep them off their porches. They shovel them off their driveways, or just crush them with their cars as they attempt to lead a normal life. The sewers are clogged with their bodies. Many roads have become impassable. Volunteers collect them in trucks every afternoon, and at night burn them in giant bonfires. Some in Richmond look into the glow of the fire and recall when their city was lit by fairies. But most don't even remember. They just stare into the fire.

Meanwhile, in San Diego, a new meteorologist has come to town. No one knows his name. No one knows why he is accompanied by two large, boisterous singing women. All they know is: It's raining men. THAT IS ALL.